Palgrave Socio-Legal Studies

The Palgrave Socio-Legal Studies series is a developing series of monographs and textbooks featuring cutting edge work which, in the best tradition of socio-legal studies, reach out to a wide international audience.

More information about this series at
http://www.palgrave.com/gp/series/14679

Laura Affolter

Asylum Matters

On the Front Line of Administrative Decision-Making

palgrave
macmillan

Laura Affolter
Institute of Social Anthropology
University of Bern
Bern, Switzerland

The open access publication of this book has been published with the support of the Swiss National Science Foundation.

Palgrave Socio-Legal Studies
ISBN 978-3-030-61511-6 ISBN 978-3-030-61512-3 (eBook)
https://doi.org/10.1007/978-3-030-61512-3

This Palgrave Macmillan imprint is published by the registered company Springer Nature Switzerland AG
The registered company address is: Gewerbestrasse 11, 6330 Cham, Switzerland

To my parents, Jacqui and Benno, for always believing in me.
And to my aunt Sandra, for caring so much.

Acknowledgements

This book is a collaborative work. Writing it would not have been possible without the support of so many people: colleagues, friends, family and all the people in the State Secretariat for Migration (SEM) who made this research possible in the first place. I am truly grateful for your trust and for your countless contributions to the making of this book.

I am profoundly grateful to Julia Eckert for being such a great mentor, supervisor and wonderful colleague over the last eight years. Thank you for always taking the time to read and engage deeply with my writing, for coaxing me towards asking the "right" questions with your critical comments, for pointing me in new analytical directions, for bringing my attention to the crucial "little" details whenever I could no longer see the wood for the trees and for pushing me when I needed it most. You are a huge inspiration to me.

Thank you so much to my colleagues and friends at the institute in Bern, Anna-Lena Wolf, Ephraim Poertner, David Loher, Johanna Mugler, Raphaël Rey, Johanna Fuchs, Simon Affolter, Simone Marti, Angela Lindt, Kiri Santer, Sharib Ali, Johannes Balthasar Oertli and Reesha Sharma, for sharing your thoughts with me on so many of my chapter drafts. Your ideas have greatly contributed to this book.

Thank you to Ephraim Poertner and Jonathan Miaz for being so open about your research, for allowing me to draw on parts of it, and for the many insightful discussions. Collaborating with you has been great fun and has helped me think differently about several issues in this book.

I am also grateful to Tobias Kelly whose critical yet encouraging words on my doctoral thesis were enormously helpful for turning the thesis into a book. Thank you too to all the colleagues whose insightful comments on other publications of mine have shaped the ideas in this book: Anna Wyss, Anne Lavanchy, Annika Lindberg, Anthony Good, Christian Lahusen, Christin Achermann, Lisa Marie Borrelli, Marion Fresia and Stephanie Schneider.

This research would not have been possible without the openness of the people at the SEM. Thank you for sharing your experiences with me, for allowing me to accompany you in your work and for letting me observe you carry out your daily tasks. I know that cannot have been easy, and I truly appreciate your trust. I am especially indebted to Stephan Parak, the late Matthias Keusch and Fabienne Glatthard for helping me gain access to the field and for enabling this research endeavour. I also thank the Swiss National Science Foundation for funding this research.

I am very thankful to my friends and family for their endless support and encouragement, especially during the time of writing. Thank you for your pep talks; for the early morning coffee encounters; for forcing me to take breaks; for the tasty food and for distracting me with Ping-Pong. For this I am particularly grateful to Chicho, my parents Benno and Jacqui, Sandra, Robin, Myri, Siân, Fabienne, Anna-Lena and Julie.

Thank you, Fabienne, for your support in so many different ways, for never letting this research project stand in the way of our friendship and for being the best friend one could wish for.

Thank you, Siân, for all the legal expertise you offered, always at such short notice.

Thank you, Mum and Sandra, for all your last minute help.

And thank you, Chicho, for always being here for me and for never letting me give up—not even on the little things.

Finally, I would like to thank all the people involved in giving this book its final tweaks. I owe a debt of gratitude to Sandra Heilberg and Isabella Mighetto for their brilliant language editing. Furthermore, I am very thankful for the helpful guidance I received from the team at Palgrave Macmillan and Springer Nature: David Cowan, Liam Inscoe-Jones, Josie Tylor, Naveen Dass and Shukkanthy Siva.

Praise for *Asylum Matters*

"*Asylum Matters* is a significant contribution to the anthropology and social science of administration and asylum. Based on extensive fieldwork, the arguments are always critical but empathetic, and I can think of few better accounts of what it is to be a front line decision maker. The book explores the conditions of possibility that shape asylum decisions, taking us well beyond arguments about the apparently arbitrary nature of much asylum decision making, to show how such work is structured and made possible through routines, tacit forms of knowledge and shared meanings. In doing so, the book demonstrates that the distinction between rules on the one hand, and discretion on the other hand, is misplaced, as all decisions and judgements are made possible and constrained by wider histories and relationships".

—Prof. Tobias Kelly, *School of Social and Political Science, University of Edinburgh*

"*Asylum Matters* is a rare feat, as it combines rich empirical material with valuable theoretical insights. Its carefully crafted arguments avoid the pitfalls of atomistic implementation research and convincingly present the social life of decision-making as learned and shared practices. Well-written and accessible, Laura Affolter's socio-legal study reinvigorates the study of street-level bureaucracy and should be required reading for scholars interested in public administration and migration research alike".

—Prof. Tobias Eule, *Institute of Public Law, University of Bern & Hamburg Institute for Social Research*

Contents

Abbreviations

APPA	*Asyl- und Wegweisungspraxis* (internal guidelines on the "asylum practice" for specific countries)
AsylA	Asylum Act
CBCA	Criteria-Based Content Analysis
COI	Country of Origin Information
DAWES	Dismissal without entering into the substance of the case
FAC	Federal Administrative Court
FDJP	Federal Department of Justice and Police
fedpol	Federal Office of Police
FNA	Foreign Nationals Act
IOM	International Organisation for Migration
LINGUA	Specialised unit for the analysis of origin
RPC	Reception and Processing Centre
SEM	State Secretariat for Migration
UNHCR	United Nations High Commissioner for Refugees

List of Figures

1

Shaping Administrative Practice: The Institutional Habitus

> For me that is ok. […] I mean, if someone uses a word like that who only started [working here] three months ago, I might ask: 'Hey, what does that mean for you?' But if [the decision] comes from someone whom I consider to be a valuable, serious, good employee, then I'll allow it, because I know, I can imagine what it means for them.[1]

So said Nora. We were talking about words like "plausible", "comprehensible", "logical" and "realistic". I had noticed that terms such as these occurred repeatedly in asylum decisions so I questioned her about them. Nora, not her real name but the name I have given her, is a state official working in the Swiss State Secretariat for Migration (SEM). She is the head of an asylum unit and, as such, one of her responsibilities is checking SEM decision-makers' asylum decisions before they are sent out to the applicants. In order for asylum seekers to be legally recognised as refugees and be granted asylum, their claims must be deemed (predominantly) credible by the decision-makers. It was these practices of assessing asylum seekers' credibility—or, more precisely, that of their claims—that Nora and I were discussing. From my observation of SEM asylum decision-makers at work as well as the analysis of case files, I knew decision-makers often used terms such as "plausible", "comprehensible", "logical" and "realistic" to substantiate their reasoning in credibility assessments. I asked Nora about the different criteria and in her reply quoted

[1] Nora, head of asylum unit, headquarters, interview transcript, my own translation.

L. Affolter, *Asylum Matters*, Palgrave Socio-Legal Studies,
https://doi.org/10.1007/978-3-030-61512-3_1

above, she claims that she "knows" or can at least "imagine what it means" for her experienced employees when they say that an asylum narrative is, for example, "logical" or "realistic". She thereby implies that she shares an understanding of these concepts with her employees as well as an understanding of what credible narratives look or rather feel like. It is this kind of shared implicit knowledge as well as shared understandings of what it means to do one's job well that are at the core of this book. To put it in more general terms, I am interested in how state officials working in administrative organisations—hence, the people who "apply" state policies and laws in their everyday work—come to think, feel, know and act in similar ways.

Studying what shapes and influences state officials' everyday practices is important, I argue, because it helps us understand the relatively stable outcomes of administrative practice that can be observed from the outside. Hence, this book is about the production of regularities in administrative work. Starting from Max Weber's ideal type of bureaucracy, the answer to the question what generates regularities of administrative practice seems simple: it is rule-bound conduct (see Weber 2013 [1978]: 220).[2] However, as Weber's concept of the "ideal type" itself implies, in practice, administrative work functions differently. Caseworkers do more than "merely" follow rules as has been highlighted by much social science literature on administrative organisations (see, for instance, Alpes and Spire 2014: 267; Calavita 2005; Eule et al. 2019; Fuglerud 2004: 29; Heyman 1995, 2004, 2009; Liodden 2016: 68; Lipsky 2010; Maynard-Moody and Musheno 2003). Building on this broad body of literature, I argue that we must therefore also pay attention to other factors—beyond written (legal) rules—that shape administrative caseworkers' everyday practices. Such factors include organisational socialisation, the ideological environments in which administrations and their officials work, professional norms and values, embodied knowledge and routines as well as decisional pragmatism (see also Alpes and Spire 2014; Dahlvik 2018; Eckert 2020; Eule et al. 2019; Fassin and Kobelinsky 2012; Heyman 2004; Johannesson 2017; Jubany 2017; Liodden 2016; Miaz 2017; Mountz 2010; Poertner 2018; Probst 2012). However, at the same time, we should not underestimate the role that rules play in guiding administrative work. Rules are, as Hendrik Wagenaar writes, "simultaneously part of the problem as it

[2]The terms "bureaucracy" and "bureaucrats" carry negative connotations. They are often associated with "red tape" and "officialism" and used as criticism (see Downs 1967: 1; Eckert 2020: 7; Poertner 2017: 12). In this book, I mostly use the terms "administration" and "office". However, when referring to literature which uses the terms "bureaucracy" and "bureaucrats", I employ the same terminology. For the people working in administrations, I use the terms "caseworkers", "decision-makers" and "officials" interchangeably.

presents itself [to caseworkers], and part of the solution. [...] [They] structure the situation [...] [and] suggest what is possible and feasible" (2004: 650). Yet, as Wagenaar then goes on to claim, "for the rule to be able to act as a rule it is important that [caseworkers] have a grasp of what the point is of using that rule in a particular situation" (ibid.). Hence, without caseworkers' understanding of and knowledge about these rules, they are socially meaningless. It is only through officials' mobilisation and interpretation of rules when putting them to use that they "materialise in practice" (Eule et al. 2019: 90; see also Moore 1978; Sarat 2007). Without officials' grasp of the rules, the latter would therefore, in the words of Hendrik Wagenaar, merely be a "dead letter" (2004: 650). This reflects the distinction made by socio-legal scholars between "law in the books and law as practice" (Eule et al. 2019: 90). My main concern in this book is, therefore, how administrative caseworkers come to understand, mobilise, interpret and thereby shape legal rules in the course of their everyday work. I show how these practices of interpreting and "making" law are, on the one hand, shaped and structured by the organisational environment the officials work in and are, on the other hand, also constitutive of the latter.

Empirically, my analysis is based on a specific case study: asylum decision-making in Switzerland. Thus, I study the everyday practices of decision-makers working in the asylum divisions of the SEM, which is the state administration in charge of taking first-instance asylum decisions in Switzerland. Caseworkers at the SEM decide whether asylum claims are credible or not; whether asylum seekers are eligible for asylum or refugee status and—in the case of negative asylum decisions—whether or not applicants should be granted temporary protection. In my ethnography of everyday administrative practices in the SEM, I deal with the following questions: What are dominant patterns of decision-making? How are these patterns generated? How are they reproduced through everyday practice? And, most importantly, how do certain patterns of decision-making become the routine or self-evident ones for decision-makers to follow? I am thereby particularly interested in what Hendrik Wagenaar calls "the taken-for-granted routines: the almost unthinking actions, tacit knowledge, fleeting interactions, practical judgements, self-evident understanding and background knowledge, shared meanings, and personal feelings that constitute the core of administrative work" (Wagenaar 2004: 643).

Studying caseworkers' grasp of legal rules—how they mobilise and interpret them in their everyday work—is crucial because in much socio-legal research as well as in so-called street-level bureaucracy studies, laws and policies are understood as something that must necessarily always be interpreted when being fitted with specific situations or cases (Eule et al. 2019: 101;

Hawkins 1992: 11; Heyman 2004: 493; Poertner 2018: 10–11; Wagenaar 2004: 651). Laws and policies are not simply "applied" or "implemented" by the caseworkers, but rather become "shaped and mediated" (Wedel et al. 2005: 34) and are "(co-)produced" (Poertner 2018: 10) through officials' everyday practices (see von Benda-Beckmann 1991; Brodkin 2011: 253–254; Eckert, Behrens, and Dafinger 2012; Eule 2014; Shore and Wright 2011). Hence, if we want to understand how asylum law and policy work, we must study caseworkers' everyday decision-making practices. Beyond this, studying caseworkers' everyday practices is also crucial for understanding the workings of the state, since it allows us to analyse the "everyday production of stateness" (Eckert, Biner, Donahoe, and Strümpell 2012: 15, see also Beek 2016). The state is thereby comprehended not as a monolithic entity, but rather as something that is produced through the everyday practices of state officials as well as through people's imaginations of the state (Bierschenk and Olivier de Sardan 2014; Eckert, Biner, Donahoe, and Strümpell 2012; Fassin 2015; Gupta 1995; Mountz 2010; Sharma and Gupta 2006).

This idea that we must study "what lower-level officials do in the name of the state" (Gupta 1995: 376) is at the core of numerous in-depth studies of asylum and migration administrations and courts (see, for instance, Alpes and Spire 2014; Calavita 1992; Dahlvik 2018; Eule 2014; Eule et al. 2019; Johannesson 2017; Jubany 2017; Kobelinsky 2015; Liodden 2016; Miaz 2017; Mountz 2010; Poertner 2018; Probst 2012; Scheffer 2001; Tomkinson 2018; see also the edited volumes by Gill and Good 2019 and Lahusen and Schneider 2017). The authors all study asylum and migration case- and decision-making from a bottom-up perspective, describing caseworkers' everyday practices in great detail. Furthermore, several of them share my interest in how everyday administrative practices become structured. They focus on different aspects shaping decision-makers' everyday practices, such as organisational socialisation (Dahlvik 2018; Heyman 2004; Jubany 2017; Miaz 2017; Probst 2012), regulatory constraints (Dahlvik 2018; Miaz 2017), collective knowledge and embodied know-how (Dahlvik 2018; Jubany 2017; Liodden 2016; Poertner 2018), pragmatic considerations (Eule et al. 2019; Poertner 2018), professional role perceptions (Johannesson 2017; Jubany 2017), accountability towards peers, authoritative bodies and the general public (Heyman 2004; Johannesson 2017; Liodden 2016; Miaz 2017; Mountz 2010) as well as the broader political environment in which the organisations are embedded (Alpes and Spire 2014; Dahlvik 2018; Fassin and Kobelinsky 2012; Jubany 2017; Mountz 2010).

My book builds on these studies. I argue that it is important to not only study what decision-makers do, but to also analyse what makes them do what they do, in order not to fall into the reductionist trap of bottom-up approaches to the state that Didier Fassin cautions against. Fassin argues that we should not treat practices of state-making as taking place in a vacuum, since state "agents are confronted with explicit and implicit expectations formulated in discourses, laws and rules while keeping sizable space to manoeuvre in the concrete management of situations and individuals" (2015: 4). If we want to understand how the state and policies work in practice, we must, therefore, pay attention to the regulatory constraints and the ideological environments under and in which these practices take place (ibid.: 6; see also Eckert 2020). My study does this by developing the concept of the institutional habitus, building on practice theory, and particularly the work of Pierre Bourdieu. I understand the institutional habitus as the schemes of thinking, acting, feeling and desiring that arise from caseworkers belonging to and working in the SEM (see Bourdieu 1976; Terdiman 1987: 811).

However, before I describe my conceptualisation of the institutional habitus in detail, I will outline two main discussions to which this book makes a contribution through its focus on the shaping and structuring of everyday practices. The first discussion is concerned with the role of so-called discretionary practices in processes of bureaucratic decision-making. The second relates to the widespread critique of credibility assessments in asylum procedures as being "arbitrary" and based on "subjective beliefs".

The Shaping of Discretion

Discretion is at the centre of much of the literature on street-level bureaucracies and I engage with these discussions for two main reasons. Firstly, I challenge the binary distinction made both explicitly and implicitly in some of the literature between "law", on the one hand, and "discretion", on the other. This critique is, of course, not new (see, for instance, Eule et al. 2019: 86–89; Pratt 1999; Pratt and Sossin 2009). However, like Tobias Eule et al., when presenting my research to both academic and non-academic audiences, I have "time and again encountered striking adherence to the idea of a regime ruled by law" (2019: 83). People are often surprised and even outraged by the fact that decision-makers interpret—rather than just "apply"—rules when putting them to use in specific situations. Therefore, it seems crucial to continue stressing the important role that discretionary practices play in administrative decision-making. Discretion is what makes law work (see Eule et al. 2019: 86, 105). It necessarily forms part of law in practice.

Secondly, I argue against the individualist assumption about discretionary freedom inherent in some of the street-level bureaucracy literature (see also Eckert 2020). This critique, again, is not entirely new; several scholars working on asylum and migration administrations have precisely pointed to the importance of studying how discretionary practices are shaped (see Brodkin 2012: 942; Dahlvik 2018; Hawkins 1992; Liodden 2016). Nevertheless, because much of the focus has been on the divergences of asylum decision-making practices rather than on how regularities in administrative practice are produced, I contend that the structuring of discretion has so far received too little attention.

Since the 1960s, studies of administrations—mostly from the social sciences—have stressed the importance of discretion for making law work (see Eule et al. 2019: 86, 105; Pratt 1999; Pratt and Sossin 2009). Discretion is seen as necessary for adapting the rules of law to individual cases (Pratt and Sossin 2009: 303; see also Lipsky 2010; Maynard-Moody and Musheno 2003). By arguing that discretion is indispensable for making law work, these scholars have, therefore, challenged the negative view on discretion held by classical legal scholars such as Albert Dicey (1982 [1885]). According to Anna Pratt and Lorne Sossin (2009), this "conventional view on discretion" understood discretion as something negative; as something that needed to be curbed as much as possible or even eliminated altogether, for instance through establishing new legal rules or control mechanisms (see also Liodden 2016: 69). Furthermore, these "newer" approaches have also challenged the quasi antagonistic relationship between law and discretion conveyed by the "conventional view", which held that "where the law ends, discretion begins" (Pratt and Sossin 2009: 302).[3] Yet, I argue that depending on how discretion is conceptualised, some authors nevertheless continue to (implicitly) reproduce the binary between law and discretion. Hence, Tobias Eule, for example, by drawing on Michael Lipsky, defines discretion as something which exists in so-called "grey-zones", zones in which decision-makers are "not bound by a rule" (2014: 57; see also Lipsky 2010: 14–15). Thus, even if such practices are seen to make law work, the binary distinction still prevails.

When we talk about "discretion" what do we mean? I can identify three distinct meanings which are mainly ascribed to discretion in social science literature. In the first, discretion seems to equate with room for manoeuvre. It refers both to the leeway which street-level bureaucrats have in dealing with

[3]The latter understanding is nicely exemplified by Ronald Dworkin's famous analogy of the doughnut. "Discretion, like the hole in a doughnut", Dworkin writes, "does not exist except as an area left open by a surrounding belt of restriction" (1977: 31).

cases, and to their obligation to make decisions. Thus, it is up to decision-makers to decide which rules to "apply" in specific situations as well as when to "apply" certain rules and when not to. This view is conveyed by Tobias Eule et al. who write that

> state officials always have room for manoeuvre and are thus confronted with the obligation to take decisions – however different these might be. The mobile police officer can decide whom to stop and search in the streets, which workplace to control and whom to take in for interrogation. The frontline caseworker can decide to detain or not to detain an individual lacking legal residency [...]. The asylum centre staff member or detention officer can decide when and which disciplinary sanction to use against residents or detainees, and when to overlook infractions to the house code. (2019: 82)

In a second use, discretionary practices are understood not only as decision-makers' actions of choosing between different legal rules and deciding when (not) to "apply" them, but also as decision-makers' actions of interpreting legal rules when "applying" them to specific cases or situations (see Eckert 2020: 15–16; Hawkins 1992: 11; Liodden 2016: 69). In a third meaning, caseworkers' actions of "establishing the 'facts' of [...] [a] case" are also referred to as discretionary practices (Liodden 2016: 68; see also Galligan 1990: 35; Hawkins 1992: 35).

These understandings differ from the term's "formal" definition in Swiss law. Thus, the Swiss Civil Code stipulates that "[w]here the law confers discretion on the court or makes reference to an assessment of the circumstances or to good cause, the court must reach its decision in accordance with the principles of justice and equity" (art. 4, Swiss Civil Code).[4] Discretion (*Ermessen*) in Swiss jurisdiction is, therefore, understood as a power given by written legislation and seen to exist only then. Contrarily, in my understanding—which draws on the work of the above-mentioned authors—discretion inevitably forms part of law and decision-making in legal procedures, whether it is explicitly stated as such in the written legal text or not (see also Heyman 2009: 367). Furthermore, I make use of the term discretion regardless of whether decision-makers themselves feel that they have discretion for taking decisions or not.

If we look finally at the etymology, as Tone Liodden shows, discretion "stems from the Latin word 'discretionem' [...] meaning 'the power

[4]Similar definitions of discretion also exist in other civil law jurisdictions (see Eule 2014: 57; Eule et al. 2019: 87; Liodden 2016: 68). In common law systems, discretion seems to be more self-evidently accepted as playing a central part in decision-making.

to make distinctions'" (2016: 75). This goes to the core of what administrative caseworkers do, for, as Don Handelman claims, "[t]here is no bureaucracy without classification, without the invention of categories of inclusion and exclusion" (1995: 280; see also Handelman 2004). This also applies to the SEM where decision-makers' work comes down to assigning asylum claimants to one of four legal categories: refugee with asylum, refugee with temporary admission, non-refugee with temporary admission (mostly on the basis of so-called "humanitarian grounds") and non-refugee without temporary admission.

In contrast to the "conventional view on discretion", the focus in contemporary social science literature is mainly on the discretionary practices themselves rather than on "the restricting belt" governing them (see Liodden 2016: 69). Hence, as Anna Pratt and Lorne Sossin have noticed, social science studies have mainly focused on the "'extra-legal' and 'non-legal' influences" on decision-making (2009: 304). In connection to this, Julia Eckert notes that some "ethnographic bottom-up perspectives on administration, policy or the state suffer from a lack of attention to the impact of formal rules and public ideologies – often due to the attempt to overcome reductionist top-down analyses that do not attend to variation in bureaucratic practice" (2020: 15–16, see also Fassin 2015: 5). This strong emphasis on variation in bureaucratic practice is something that also applies to the literature on asylum and migration administrations. Thus, much research is concerned with divergences between different asylum or migration administrations, different units within these administrations and, particularly, divergences between individual decision-makers (see, for instance, Anker 1991; Eule 2014; Fassin and Kobelinsky 2012; Hamlin 2014; Johannesson 2017; Miaz 2017; Ramji-Nogales et al. 2009; Rehaag 2012; Spirig 2018).

My point is not to argue that such divergences do not exist. Research has clearly shown that they do. Nevertheless, I argue that these divergences should not be overestimated or, more particularly, that we should be careful not to lose sight of the commonalities that exist. To give an example, some individual asylum caseworkers might be more readily inclined to believe asylum seekers' stories than others, generating diverging outcomes. However, my research has shown that even the decision-makers who are more inclined to believe asylum seekers—the so-called "softies" in the SEM—still end up rejecting the majority of asylum applications they deal with on the grounds of non-credibility. Hence, I argue that it is these regularities that we should pay attention to, inquiring into the different factors that generate such patterns.

Focusing on divergences brings the danger of (implicitly) assigning an overly individualistic quality to discretionary practices. This also becomes apparent in the way the term discretion itself is sometimes conceptualised, as shown in the following statement by Tony Evans who writes that "[a]s a topic, discretion is concerned with the extent of freedom a worker can exercise in a specific context and the factors that give rise to this freedom in that context" (2010: 2). Similarly, Tobias Eule, referring to Norbert Cyrus and Dita Vogel (2003) as well as Anna Triandafyllidou (2003), describes discretionary practices as "'deviant' techniques of individual practice" (2014: 57). With this book, I attempt to overcome this "individualist bent" (Eckert 2020: 9–10). My approach—similar to that of Julia Dahlvik (2018) and Tone Liodden (2016)—is, therefore, not only to study what caseworkers' discretionary practices *are*—thus, how caseworkers deal with their room for manoeuvre, interpret legal rules when "applying" them, assemble cases and produce the necessary "facts" for taking decisions—but also to analyse ethnographically the different factors that shape these discretionary practices. As I will show in this book, the concept of the institutional habitus provides a unique way of doing so by drawing attention to the unthinking, routine and self-evident actions and judgements of decision-makers and how they come to adopt such dispositions through institutional socialisation.

Assessing Credibility in Asylum Procedures: A Subjective Matter?

In turning now to assessing credibility, we can see that an individualistic quality is similarly ascribed to asylum decision-makers' practices by many of the critical studies on credibility determination in asylum procedures. Credibility determination plays a crucial role in asylum decision-making, since credibility constitutes a major precondition for being recognised as a refugee and receiving asylum. In Switzerland, the majority of asylum applicants are rejected not because their claims do not fulfil refugee status requirements, but rather because they are not perceived as being credible; a trend that has also been observed in other countries, such as France (Fassin 2013: 47; Probst 2012), Germany (Probst 2012) and the UK (Kelly 2012: 759). Because of the importance of credibility determination for asylum adjudication and the widespread tendency to reject the majority of asylum applications on the basis of non-credibility, credibility determination has attracted much scholarly attention.[5] Scholars engage critically with credibility assessment

[5]Audrey Macklin (1998), for instance, has dealt with credibility assessment (practices) in Canada, Thomas Scheffer (2001, 2003) has done so in Germany, Nienke Doornbos (2005) and Thomas

(practices), highlighting both the difficulty of taking decisions based on credibility, as well as the obstacles and injustices they generate for asylum seekers. Much critique has thereby been directed at the so-called "subjectivity" and "arbitrariness" of decision-makers' credibility assessments as well as at a caseworker's so-called common sense, their understanding of what constitutes normal or abnormal behaviour, and the role this has in credibility determinations (see Einhorn 2009; Goodwin-Gill 1996; Kagan 2003; Macklin 1998; Ramji-Nogales et al. 2009; Thomas 2009).[6] By doing so, the problem of credibility assessment is often (implicitly) attributed to the individual decision-makers and/or to "the law" for leaving a loophole for subjective decision-making in the first place. This, I argue, leads to decision-makers' practices being attributed an individualist quality, which is a view that I critically engage with in this book (see also Eckert 2020). Thus, Michael Kagan, for instance, claims that "subjective assessments are highly personal to the decision-maker, dependent on personal judgement, perceptions and dispositions, and often lacking an articulated logic" (2003: 374). He criticises that these assessments are, therefore, "very difficult to review and are likely to be inconsistent from one decision-maker to another" (ibid.).

There appear to be two main reasons why much of the critique on credibility assessment practices in asylum procedures focuses on their so-called "subjectivity" and "arbitrariness". On the one hand, it has to do with the outcome orientation of many of these critical studies. Hence, many of the analyses are based on written asylum decisions, making it difficult to deduce

Spijkerboer (2000, 2005) in the Netherlands, Walter Kälin (1986), Olivia Le Fort (2013) as well as Alain Maillard and Christophe Tafelmacher (1999) in Switzerland, Anthony Good (2009, 2011), Jane Herlihy et al. (2010), Catriona Jarvis (2003), Olga Jubany (2011, 2017), Tobias Kelly (2011), Isabella Mighetto (2016), James Sweeney (2007) and Robert Thomas (2009) in the UK and Deborah Anker (1991), Bruce Einhorn (2009) and Michael Kagan (2003) in the USA. Furthermore, many authors dealing with asylum decision-making in general and especially asylum interviews also broach the subject of credibility (see, for instance, Blommaert 2001; Bohmer and Shuman 2008; Dahlvik 2018; Fresia et al. 2013; Poertner 2018; Probst 2012; Miaz 2017; Rousseau et al. 2002; Sbriccoli and Jacoviello 2011; Schneider and Wottrich 2017), as do authors dealing with particular problems applicants face when seeking asylum on the basis of sexual orientation (see, for instance, Jansen and Spijkerboer 2011; Johnson 2011; Markard and Adamietz 2011; O'Leary 2008; Spijkerboer 2013). Finally, there have also been evaluative studies on credibility assessment, for instance, the report "*Breaking down the barriers*" written by Heaven Crawley (1999) for the Immigration Law Practitioners' Association (ILPA), the UNHCR evaluation "*Beyond Proof: Credibility Assessment in EU Asylum Systems*" (2013) and the joint report by Amnesty International and Still Human Still Here "*A question of credibility: Why so many initial asylum decisions are overturned on appeal in the UK*" (2013).

[6]Other authors, however, take their analyses in different directions, focusing, for example, on communication problems in asylum interviews and the obstacles asylum seekers face when trying to successfully—meaning credibly—narrate their stories (see, for instance, Doornbos 2005; Good 2009, 2011; Kagan 2003; Kälin 1986) or on the particular standard of proof in asylum procedures and the way uncertainty is turned into legal certainty through the procedure (see Kelly 2011; Scheffer 2001, 2003).

how decision-makers reached their decisions, as from the "outside" the outcomes of decision-making processes often seem very random and much of what plays into decision-making is not actually reflected in the written reasoning.[7] On the other hand, the critique of the "subjectivity" and "arbitrariness" of asylum, and particularly credibility decisions, may also derive from decision-makers' emic views on their own work. Thus, in my research I found that many decision-makers in the SEM themselves attach a "subjective" quality to their credibility determinations. This is expressed in the following statement made by a decision-maker whom I have called Denise[8]:

> The word 'credibility' already indicates that it's subjective. I have to believe something. [...] And precisely because it's subjective it's easier for me if I've seen [the applicant] myself. That doesn't necessary mean that the decision [I take] is then the correct one, but it makes it easier for me, because then, in addition, I have this personal impression.[9]

As Denise's statement hints at, this view that credibility determinations are, to some extent, always "subjective" is linked to the kind of knowledge that guides and enables credibility assessments, an issue I deal with in detail in Chapter 4. I was told by SEM decision-makers that their credibility assessments often started from a "feeling" or "intuition", a finding which is also shared by many other scholars working on asylum decision-making (see, for instance, Fassin and Kobelinsky 2012; Fassin 2013; Johannesson 2017; Jubany 2011, 2017; Kelly 2012; Macklin 1998; Miaz 2017; Thomas 2009). Such intuitive convictions are usually very difficult to articulate; decision-makers—at least the experienced ones—mostly "just know" whether asylum seekers' statements are credible or not (see also Jubany 2017: 121, 183;

---

[7]There appear to be several reasons for this outcome orientation. First, access to asylum administrations in order to observe decision-makers' everyday practices is often very difficult—or even impossible—to achieve. Second, the outcome orientation of these critical studies seems to be linked to the authors' disciplinary backgrounds and their methodological approaches: many of the authors are legal scholars whose discussions are generally based on analyses of written legal documents. Third, many of the authors are mainly interested in what the outcomes of asylum decision-making mean for asylum seekers and what consequences they have for them rather than how these particular outcomes came into being.

[8]All the names I use in this book are pseudonyms. For reasons of anonymity I have randomly assigned "identification features" such as place of work, educational background and gender to my interaction partners as long as it did not lead to any distortions. Furthermore, as it is important that officials (especially those in higher hierarchical positions) do not recognise their co-workers (or employees), it was sometimes necessary for me to create more than one "fictional identity" out of one interaction partner. I have anonymised all the references I make to asylum seekers and other actors in this book (for instance when quoting field notes or documents from case files) in the same way. My interactions with decision-makers were in Swiss German, German and French. The translations of their statements in this book are mine.

[9]Denise, caseworker, headquarters, interview transcript, my own translation.

Liodden 2016: 264–265). Hence, this is the "feeling" or intuitive knowledge that they refer to as being "subjective". My point is not to argue that an asylum narrative, that to one decision-maker "feels" credible, might not "feel" credible to someone else. Yet, an observation I made in the SEM was that the "feelings" that decision-makers referred to as "subjective" often closely resembled each other and were, at the same time, often quite different from mine, the researcher from "outside". This is also what Nora seems to be referring to in her statement (quoted at the beginning of this introduction) that she "knows" or can at least "imagine" what certain assessments mean for her experienced employees. Hence, I argue that it is crucial to study how such forms of "tacit knowledge", to use Michael Polanyi's (1962 [1958], 1966) term, or "practical knowledge" in the words of Andreas Reckwitz (2003), develop, are acquired by decision-makers and are reaffirmed as well as transformed through their everyday practices. In order to do so, I propose the concept of the institutional habitus.

The Institutional Habitus: A Brief Conceptual Introduction

According to Loïc J.D. Wacquant, the main question practice theory deals with is: in the light of the regularities we observe in social life, what generates these patterns "[i]f external structures do not mechanically constrain action"? (1992: 18). It is precisely this question that interests me with regard to administrative work more generally, and asylum determination practices in the SEM more specifically. The answer to this question, according to Pierre Bourdieu, lies in the habitus. Bourdieu defines the habitus as a system of

> durable, transposable dispositions, structured structures predisposed to function as structuring structures, that is, as principles which generate and organize practices and representations that can be objectively adapted to their outcomes without presupposing a conscious aiming at ends or an express mastery of the operations necessary in order to attain them. (1990: 53)

He argues that the habitus

> is what makes it possible to produce an infinite number of practices that are relatively unpredictable [...] but also limited in their diversity. In short, being the product of a particular class of objective regularities, the habitus tends to generate all the 'reasonable', 'common sense' behaviours (and only these) which are possible within the limits of these regularities, and which are likely

to be positively sanctioned because they are objectively adjusted to the logic characteristic of a particular field. (ibid.: 55–56)

For Bourdieu, the dispositions which constitute a habitus are shared by people belonging to the same social class or social collective. Thus, according to him, people from the same social background, who share certain experiences and histories, tend to have a similar habitus. This means that while the habitus operates from within individuals, it is not strictly individual (Wacquant 1992: 18). At the same time, the habitus does not work in a deterministic way (Hitchings 2012: 62). It is creative and inventive and can produce "an infinite number of practices" (Bourdieu 1990: 55). Yet, the practices a habitus generates will necessarily always fall within "the limits of its structures" (Wacquant 1992: 19).

I find the concept of habitus useful for understanding practices of decision-making in the SEM for three main reasons. First, because it allows us to analyse the "shared subjectivity" I encountered during fieldwork. This fits with what Bourdieu writes about the habitus when he states that "[t]o speak of habitus is to assert that the individual, and even the personal, the subjective, is social, collective. Habitus is socialized subjectivity" (Bourdieu and Wacquant 1992: 126). Second, the concept of habitus proves useful because it allows us to comprehend patterns in decision-making which cannot be explained with reference to explicit rules and informal norms. Thus, as Bourdieu writes, the practices the habitus generates are "[o]bjectively 'regulated' and 'regular' without being in any way the product of obedience to rules, they can be collectively orchestrated without being the product of the organizing action of a conductor" (1990: 53). One such pattern that I deal with in this book is the tendency to reject the majority of asylum applications on the basis of non-credibility; a pattern which has been referred to by many authors as the "culture of disbelief" (Anderson et al. 2014; Jubany 2017; Marfleet 2006), "suspicion" (Alpes and Spire 2014; Bohmer and Shuman 2008), "mistrust" (Griffiths 2012; Probst 2012) or "denial" (Souter 2011). The concept of the institutional habitus provides a way of understanding this pattern without reducing it to being the "mere" outcome of political instrumentality (of anti-immigration politics so to speak) or caseworkers' emotional detachment. The third reason for finding the concept of the institutional habitus useful for understanding practices of asylum decision-making is the importance it gives to the issue of belonging. Institutional belonging, both to the office as a whole as well as to individual divisions of the SEM, on the one hand, shapes what decision-makers come to perceive as their duties and what it means to professionally fulfil them, which, in turn, shapes their everyday practices (see also Affolter et al. 2019). On the other hand, institutional belonging is important because the institution becomes a site where experiences come to be shared and are collectively made.

In his work, Bourdieu mostly focuses on belonging in terms of people's social backgrounds and class. However, in "*An Invitation to Reflexive Sociology*" he also refers to bureaucracies as an example of a social collective. He claims that

> social collectives such as bureaucracies have built-in propensities to perpetuate their being, something akin to a memory or a loyalty that is nothing other than the 'sum' of routines and conducts of agents who, relying on their know-how (*métier*), their habitus, engender […] lines of action adapted to the situation such as their habitus inclines them to perceive it, thus tailor made (without being designed as such) to reproduce the structure of which their habitus is the product. (Bourdieu and Wacquant 1992: 139–140)

My conceptualisation of the institutional habitus builds on this understanding of bureaucratic organisations as self-perpetuating social collectives. I argue that, through belonging to and working in such organisations, caseworkers acquire specific dispositions which shape their everyday practices. These dispositions, in turn, are again shaped and reaffirmed by decision-makers' everyday practices.

Instead of focusing on how SEM decision-makers' social backgrounds shape their dispositions to understand, judge and act, I mainly look at how these practices are shaped by decision-makers' belonging to the office and their experiences on the job. This is not to say that caseworkers' background does not have an influence on their everyday practices. The argument I make in this book is rather that their social backgrounds alone are not enough to explain why they do what they do. For this, we must study the professional values, pragmatic beliefs and (unthinking) routines that decision-makers pick up and come to incorporate through their institutional socialisation. Compared to Bourdieu's concept of habitus, my derivation of the concept is, therefore, less durable. I understand the institutional habitus as something that is acquired on the job, and possibly shed after leaving the institution.

Similar concepts have also been used by Didier Fassin as well as Maybritt Jill Alpes and Alexis Spire. The term Didier Fassin uses is that of the "professional habitus". However, he refers only very briefly to it in the introduction to "*At the Heart of the State*", where he argues that officials' "principles of justice [and] or order" as well as "the values of the common good and public service" are the products of officials' professional habitus (2015: 6). For Maybritt Jill Alpes and Alexis Spire, the "bureaucratic habitus" constitutes one of the principle concepts which they introduce in their article "*Dealing with Law in Migration Control*" (2014). Like me—and as Didier Fassin also seems to imply—the authors argue that it is the habitus that "significantly shapes [...] [caseworkers'] interpretations of the legal frameworks" (2014: 263). However, there are two important differences between their usage of the term bureaucratic habitus and my conceptualisation of the institutional habitus. First, for Alpes and Spire, the bureaucratic habitus "encompasses a set of norms shared by other agents involved in migration control" (ibid.). Hence, they understand it as a set of norms that is shared by all agents working in the field of migration control. In this regard, I conceptualise the institutional habitus in a narrower sense, namely as the set of dispositions shared *within* an organisation—or possibly even within different parts of an organisation. However, this does not mean that I dismiss the impact of the broader ideological environment(s) within which asylum decision-making takes place, but rather that I am interested in how certain ideological values become incorporated by caseworkers working inside these particular organisations (see also Dahlvik 2018; Jubany 2017). Second, in my understanding, the institutional habitus is mainly an analytical term that can be used to describe the assemblage of dispositions which shape what caseworkers do, think and feel. Alpes and Spire, in turn, refer to the bureaucratic habitus in order to describe specific dispositions they encountered during their fieldwork in French consulates, namely the "culture of suspicion" (ibid.: 269) as well as—connected to this—caseworkers' "concern to combat fraud and to defend state interests" (ibid.: 267). This is very similar to what I encountered in the SEM (see Chapter 6). However, in my understanding, the institutional habitus is not limited to these dispositions, but also encompasses other—to some extent even contradicting—dispositions. Furthermore, with this book I aim to show that the "concern to combat fraud and to defend state interests" (ibid.) does not only guide and shape caseworkers' actions, but to also show that the very idea that professionally carrying out one's job means combatting fraud and defending the state's interests is continuously reaffirmed and reproduced through everyday practice in these administrations.

Outline of the Book

Chapters 2 and 3 set the scene for the three main analytical chapters of this book. Chapter 2 provides a methodological note on how I went about studying everyday decision-making practices in the SEM. It discusses the challenges I faced during my research and how I dealt with them, as well as the methodological limits of this study. Furthermore, I engage with what it means methodologically, to study everyday practice(s) from a practice theoretical perspective.

Following this, Chapter 3 offers a description of the Swiss asylum procedure. It discusses the history of asylum politics, policies, law and the first-instance asylum administration in Switzerland since the 1950s, and contextualises the developments within broader trends in the Global North. The chapter also introduces readers to the organisational structure of the SEM as it existed until 2019, to how different tasks are organised within the hierarchical organisation of the SEM, to the main elements of asylum law that structure SEM officials' decision-making practices and to the particular standard of proof in refugee status determination.

The three main analytical chapters of this book deal with the "shared practices" of decision-making. They shed light on what these practices are, and describe the processes whereby these practices become shared. Although each in a different way, the three main chapters are concerned with: how decision-makers' discretionary practices are shaped and structured; the role the institutional habitus plays; what constitutes this institutional habitus; how decision-makers develop such an institutional habitus on the job; and finally, how the institutional habitus is reaffirmed through everyday practice.

Chapter 4 traces the processes of how asylum decisions are produced. It analyses how asylum caseworkers attempt to overcome the uncertainties inherent in refugee status—and particularly credibility—determination, and the role different types of knowledge thereby play. Decision-making practice, it argues, is fundamentally a "knowledge-based activity" (Dahlvik 2018: 57). The chapter highlights the important role implicit practical knowledge—or "gut feeling"—as well as the act of credibility determination itself play in generating decisional certainty for categorising asylum seekers into one of four legal categories: refugee with asylum, refugee with temporary admission, non-refugee with temporary admission and non-refugee without temporary admission.

The fifth chapter explores how asylum caseworkers are socialised on the job and acquire an institutional habitus. It shows how decision-makers learn what appropriate and inappropriate behaviours are and acquire the necessary knowledge and skills for carrying out their job. I argue that caseworkers' desire and need to fit into "the office" (or parts of it) and to be considered good and professional decision-makers, as well as the pressure decision-makers experience from their peers, superiors, but also from politics and the media all play an important role in shaping decision-makers' everyday practices.

In Chapter 6, I examine the norms and values which lie at the heart of SEM officials' day-to-day decision-making, showing what it means to be a good and professional decision-maker in the SEM. The chapter brings to light two substantial goals of the asylum administration: that of protecting the abstract noble value of asylum and that of protecting "national interests" through keeping numbers low: both of people applying for asylum and of people being granted the right to reside in Switzerland. The chapter, thereby, shows how the ethics and ethos of the office shape what decision-makers do and how certain practices become normal and self-evident.

Finally, in the conclusion, I bring together the discussions of the different chapters of this book to show how normative, structural and regulatory constraints and the institutional habitus constitute each other; the latter through the practices it generates. By doing so, I show how disbelief becomes normalised in the office. I also discuss what lessons can be taken from the case study of this book, towards a more general understanding of bureaucratic administrations.

References

Affolter, Laura, Jonathan Miaz, and Ephraim Poertner. 2019. "Taking the 'Just' Decision: Caseworkers and Their Communities of Interpretation in the Swiss Asylum Office." In *Asylum Determination in Europe: Ethnographic Perspectives*, edited by Nick Gill, and Anthony Good, 263–284. Cham: Palgrave Macmillan.

Alpes, Maybritt Jill, and Alexis Spire. 2014. "Dealing with Law in Migration Control: The Powers of Street-Level Bureaucrats at French Consulates." *Social & Legal Studies* 23 (2): 261–274. https://journals.sagepub.com/doi/10.1177/0964663913510927.

Amnesty International/Still Human Still Here. 2013. "A Question of Credibility: Why so Many Initial Asylum Decisions Are Overturned on Appeal in the UK." http://www.refworld.org/docid/518120c64.html, last accessed February 3, 2020.

Anderson, Jessica, Jeannine Hollaus, Annelisa Lindsay, and Collin Williamson. 2014. *The Culture of Disbelief: An Ethnographic Approach to Understanding an Under-Theorised Concept in the UK Asylum System*. Working Paper Series No. 102. Oxford: Refugee Studies Centre. https://www.rsc.ox.ac.uk/files/files-1/wp102-culture-of-disbelief-2014.pdf, last accessed February 3, 2020.

Anker, Deborah. 1991. "Determining Asylum Claims in the United States: An Empirical Case Study." http://repository.forcedmigration.org/show_metadata.jsp?pid=fmo:709, last accessed February 3, 2020.

Beek, Jan. 2016. *Producing Stateness: Police Work in Ghana*. Boston: Brill.

von Benda-Beckmann, Franz. 1991. "Pak Dusa's Law: Thoughts on Legal Knowledge and Power." In *Ethnologie im Widerstreit*, edited by Eberhard Berg, Jutta Lauth, and Andreas Wimmer, 215–227. München: Trickster.

Bierschenk, Thomas, and Jean-Pierre Olivier de Sardan. 2014. "Studying the Dynamics of African Bureaucracies: An Introduction to States at Work." In *States at Work: Dynamics of African Bureaucracies*, edited by Thomas Bierschenk, and Jean-Pierre Olivier de Sardan, 1–33. Leiden, Boston: Brill.

Blommaert, Jan. 2001. "Investigating Narrative Inequality: African Asylum Seekers' Stories in Belgium." *Discourse & Society* 12 (4): 413–449. https://doi.org/10.1177/0957926501012004002.

Bohmer, Carol, and Amy Shuman. 2008. *Rejecting Refugees: Political Asylum in the 21st Century*. London: Routledge.

Bourdieu, Pierre. 1976. *Entwurf einer Theorie der Praxis auf der ethnologischen Grundlage der kabylischen Gesellschaft*. Frankfurt am Main: Suhrkamp.

Bourdieu, Pierre. 1990. *The Logic of Practice*. Translated by Richard Nice. Stanford: Stanford University Press.

Bourdieu, Pierre, and Loïc J. D. Wacquant. 1992. "The Purpose of Reflexive Sociology (The Chicago Workshop)." In *An Invitation to Reflexive Sociology*, edited by Pierre Bourdieu, and Loïc J. D. Wacquant, 61–215. Cambridge: Polity Press.

Brodkin, Evelyn Z. 2011. "Policy Work: Street-Level Organizations Under New Managerialism." *Journal of Public Administration Research and Theory* 21 (Supplement 2): 253–277. https://doi.org/10.1093/jopart/muq093.

Brodkin, Evelyn Z. 2012. "Reflections on Street-Level Bureaucracy: Past, Present, and Future." *Public Administration Review* 72 (6): 940–949. https://doi.org/10.1111/j.1540-6210.2012.02657.x.

Calavita, Kitty. 1992. *Inside the State: The Bracero Program, Immigration, and the I.N.S.* New York: Routledge.

Calavita, Kitty. 2005. "Law, Citizenship, and the Construction of (Some) Immigrant 'Others'". *Law & Social Inquiry* 30 (2): 401–420. https://doi.org/10.1111/j.1747-4469.2005.tb01017.x.

Crawley, Heaven. 1999. *Breaking Down the Barriers: A Report on the Conduct of Asylum Interviews at Ports*. London: Immigration Law Practitioners' Association (ILPA).

Cyrus, Norbert, and Dita Vogel. 2003. "Work-Permit Decisions in the German Labour Administration: An Exploration of the Implementation Process." *Journal of Ethnic and Migration Studies* 29 (2): 225–256. https://doi.org/10.1080/1369183032000079602.

Dahlvik, Julia. 2018. *Inside Asylum Bureaucracy: Organizing Refugee Status Determination in Austria.* IMISCOE Research Series. Cham: Springer.

Dicey, Albert V. 1982 (1885). *Introduction to the Study of the Law of the Constitution.* Indianapolis: Liberty Classics.

Doornbos, Nienke. 2005. "On Being Heard in Asylum Cases: Evidentiary Assessment through Asylum Interviews." In *Proof, Evidentiary Assessment and Credibility in Asylum Procedures*, edited by Gregor Noll, 103–122. Leiden: Martinus Nijhoff.

Downs, Anthony. 1967. *Inside Bureaucracy*. Boston: Little, Brown and Company.

Dworkin, Ronald. 1977. *Taking Rights Seriously.* Cambridge: Harvard University Press.

Eckert, Julia. 2020. "The Office: Ethos and Ethics in Migration Bureaucracies." In *The Bureaucratic Production of Difference*, edited by Julia Eckert, 7–26. Bielefeld: transcript.

Eckert, Julia, Andrea Behrends, and Andreas Dafinger. 2012. "Governance—And the State: An Anthropological Approach." *Ethnoscripts* 14 (1): 14–34.

Eckert, Julia, Zerrin Özlem Biner, Brian Donahoe, and Christian Strümpell. 2012. "Introduction: Law's Travels and Transformations." In *Law Against the State: Ethnographic Forays into Law's Transformations*, edited by Julia Eckert, Brian Donahoe, Christian Strümpell, and Zerrin Özlem Biner, 1–22. Cambridge: Cambridge University Press.

Einhorn, Bruce J. 2009. "Consistency, Credibility, and Culture." In *Refugee Roulette: Disparities in Asylum Adjudication and Proposals for Return*, edited by Jaya Ramji-Nogales, Andrew I. Schoenholtz, and Philip G. Schrag, 187–201. New York: New York University Press.

Eule, Tobias G. 2014. *Inside Immigration Law. Migration Management and Policy Application in Germany*. Farnham: Ashgate.

Eule, Tobias G., Lisa Marie Borrelli, Annika Lindberg, and Anna Wyss. 2019. *Migrants Before the Law: Contested Migration Control in Europe*. Cham: Palgrave Macmillan.

Evans, Tony. 2010. *Professional Discretion in Welfare Services*. Farnham: Ashgate.

Fassin, Didier. 2013. "The Precarious Truth of Asylum." *Public Culture* 25 (1): 39–63. https://doi.org/10.1215/08992363-1890459.

Fassin, Didier. 2015. "Introduction: Governing Precarity." In *At the Heart of the State: The Moral World of Institutions*, edited by Didier Fassin, 1–11. London: Pluto Press.

Fassin, Didier, and Carolina Kobelinsky. 2012. "How Asylum Claims Are Adjudicated: The Institution as a Moral Agent." *Revue française de sociologie* 53 (4): 444–472. https://doi.org/10.3917/rfs.534.0657.

Fresia, Marion, David Bozzini, and Alice Sala. 2013. Les *rouages de l'asile en Suisse: Regards ethnographiques sur une procédure administrative.* Etudes du SFM 62. Neuchâtel: SFM.

Fuglerud, Oivind. 2004. "Constructing Exclusion: The Micro-Sociology of an Immigration Department." *Social Anthropology* 12 (1): 25–40. https://doi.org/10.1111/j.1469-8676.2004.tb00088.x.

Galligan, Denis James. 1990. *Discretionary Powers: A Legal Study of Official Discretion.* Oxford: Clarendon Press.

Gill, Nick, and Anthony Good, eds. 2019. *Asylum Determination in Europe. Ethnographic Perspectives*. Cham: Palgrave Macmillan.

Good, Anthony. 2009. "The Taking and Making of Asylum Claims: Credibility Assessment in the British Asylum Courts." http://www.sps.ed.ac.uk/__data/assets/pdf_file/0014/31154/GoodSOAS.pdf, last accessed February 3, 2020.

Good, Anthony. 2011. "Witness Statement and Credibility Assessments in the British Asylum Courts." In *Cultural Expertise and Litigation*, edited by Livia Holden, 94–122. Abingdon, New York: Routledge.

Goodwin-Gill, Guy S. 1996. *The Refugee in International Law.* Second Edition. Oxford: Clarendon Press.

Griffiths, Melanie. 2012. "'Vile Liars and Truth Distorters': Truth, Trust and the Asylum System." *Anthropology Today* 28 (5): 8–12. https://doi.org/10.1111/j.1467-8322.2012.00896.x.

Gupta, Akhil. 1995. "Blurred Boundaries: The Discourse of Corruption, the Culture of Politics, and the Imagined State." *American Ethnologist* 22 (2): 375–402. https://doi.org/10.1525/ae.1995.22.2.02a00090.

Hamlin, Rebecca. 2014. *Let Me Be a Refugee: Administrative Justice and the Politics of Asylum in the United States, Canada, and Australia.* Oxford: Oxford University Press.

Handelman, Don. 1995. "Comments on 'Putting Power in the Anthropology of Bureaucracy: The Immigrations and Naturalization Service at the Mexico-United States Border' by Josiah McC. Heyman." *Current Anthropology* 36 (2): 280–281. https://doi.org/10.1086/204354.

Handelman, Don. 2004. *Nationalism and the Israeli State: Bureaucratic Logic in Public Events.* New York: Berg.

Hawkins, Keith, ed. 1992. *The Uses of Discretion.* Oxford: Clarendon Press.

Herlihy, Jane, Kate Gleeson, and Stuart Turner. 2010. "What Assumptions about Human Behaviours Underlie Asylum Judgements?" *International Journal of Refugee Law* 22 (3): 351–366. https://doi.org/10.1093/ijrl/eeq027.

Heyman, Josiah McC. 1995. "Putting Power in the Anthropology of Bureaucracy: The Immigration and Naturalization Service at the Mexico-United States Border." *Current Anthropology* 36 (2): 261–187. https://doi.org/10.1086/204354.

Heyman, Josiah McC. 2004. "The Anthropology of Power-Wielding Bureaucracies." *Human Organization* 63 (4): 487–500. https://doi.org/10.17730/humo.63.4.m9phulu49a1l2dep.

Heyman, Josiah McC. 2009. "Trust, Privilege, and Discretion in the Governance of US Borderlands with Mexico." *Canadian Journal of Law and Society* 24 (3): 367–390. https://doi.org/10.1017/S0829320100010085.

Hitchings, Russel. 2012. "People Can Talk About Their Practices." *Area* 44 (1): 61–67. https://doi.org/10.1111/j.1475-4762.2011.01060.x.

Jansen, Sabine, and Thomas Spijkerboer. 2011. "Fleeing Homophobia: Asylum Claims Related to Sexual Orientation and Gender Identity in the EU." Coc Nederlands/VU University Amsterdam. https://papers.ssrn.com/sol3/papers.cfm?abstract_id=2097783, last accessed February 3, 2020.

Jarvis, Catriona. 2003. "The Judge as Juror Revisited." *Immigration Law Digest* (Winter): 16–31.

Johannesson, Livia. 2017. *In Courts We Trust: Administrative Justice in Swedish Migration Courts*. Stockholm University. http://www.diva-portal.org/smash/get/diva2:1072557/FULLTEXT01.pdf, last accessed February 3, 2020.

Johnson, Toni A. M. 2011. "On Silence, Sexuality and Skeletons: Reconceptualizing Narrative in Asylum Hearings." *Social & Legal Studies* 20 (1): 57–78. https://doi.org/10.1177/0964663910391205.

Jubany, Olga. 2011. "Constructing Truths in a Culture of Disbelief: Understanding Asylum Screening from Within." *International Sociology* 26 (1): 74–94. https://doi.org/10.1177/0268580910380978.

Jubany, Olga. 2017. *Screening Asylum in a Culture of Disbelief: Truths, Denials and Sceptical Borders*. Cham: Palgrave Macmillan.

Kagan, Michael. 2003. "Is Truth in the Eye of the Beholder? Objective Credibility Assessment in Refugee Status Determination." *Georgetown Immigration Law Journal* 17 (3): 367–415. https://scholars.law.unlv.edu/facpub/633, last accessed February 3, 2020.

Kälin, Walter. 1986. "Troubled Communication: Cross-Cultural Misunderstandings in the Asylum-Hearing." *International Migration Review* 20 (2): 230–241. https://doi.org/10.1177/019791838602000206.

Kelly, Tobias. 2011. "The Legalization of Human Rights and the Protection of Torture Survivors: Asylum, Evidence and Disbelief." In *Are Human Rights for Migrants? Critical Reflections on the Status of Irregular Migrants in Europe and the United States*, edited by Marie-Bénédicte Dembour, and Tobias Kelly, 1–22. New York: Routledge.

Kelly, Tobias. 2012. "Sympathy and Suspicion: Torture, Asylum, and Humanity." *Journal of the Royal Anthropological Institute* 18 (4): 753–768. https://doi.org/10.1111/j.1467-9655.2012.01790.x.

Kobelinsky, Carolina. 2015. "In Search of Truth: How Asylum Applications Are Adjudicated." In *At the Heart of the State: The Moral World of Institutions*, edited by Didier Fassin, 67–92. London: Pluto Press.

Lahusen, Christian, and Stephanie Schneider, eds. 2017. *Asyl verwalten. Zur bürokratischen Bearbeitung eines gesellschaftlichen Problems*. Bielefeld: transcript.

Le Fort, Olivia. 2013. "Des guidelines pour mieux circonscrire la notion de vraisemblance en matière d'asile." *Jusletter* 18: 1–9.

Liodden, Tone Maia. 2016. "The Burdens of Discretion. Managing Uncertainty in the Asylum Bureaucracy." PhD diss. (unpublished), University of Oslo.

Lipsky, Michael. 2010. *Street-Level Bureaucracy, 30th Anniversary Edition: Dilemmas of the Individual in Public Service*. New York: Russell Sage Foundation.

Macklin, Audrey. 1998. "Truth and Consequences: Credibility Determination in the Refugee Context." Conference Paper. Ottawa: International Association of Refugee Law Judges. http://refugeestudies.org/UNHCR/97%20-%20Truth%20and%20Consequences.%20Credibility%20Determination%20in%20Refugee%20Context.%20by%20Audrey%20Macklin.pdf, last accessed February 3, 2020.

Maillard, Alain, and Christophe Tafelmacher. 1999. *"Faux réfugiés"? La politique Suisse de dissauasion d'asile, 1979–1999*. Lausanne: Éditions d'en bas.

Marfleet, Philip. 2006. *Refugees in a Global Era*. Basingstoke: Palgrave.

Markard, Nora, and Laura Adamietz. 2011. "Keep it in the Closet? Flüchtlingsanerkennung wegen Homosexualität auf dem Prüfstand." *Kritische Justiz* 44 (3): 294–302.

Maynard-Moody, Steven, and Michael Musheno. 2003. *Cops, Teachers, Conselors: Stories from the Front Lines of Public Service*. Ann Arbor: University of Michigan Press.

Miaz, Jonathan. 2017. "Politique d'asile et sophistication du droit: Pratiques administratives et défense juridique des migrants en Suisse (1981–2015)." PhD diss. (unpublished), University of Lausanne and University of Strasbourg.

Mighetto, Isabella. 2016. "The Contingency of Credibility: Gender-Related Persecution, Traumatic Memory and Home Office Interviews." *SOAS Law Journal* 3: 1–37.

Moore, Sally Falk. 1978. *Law as Process: An Anthropological Approach*. London, Henley: Routledge & Kegan Paul.

Mountz, Alison. 2010. *Seeking Asylum: Human Smuggling and Bureaucracy at the Border*. Minneapolis: University of Minnesota Press.

O'Leary, Barry. 2008. "'We Cannot Claim Any Particular Knowledge of the Ways of Homosexuals, Still Less of Iranian Homosexuals…': The Particular Problems Facing Those Who Seek Asylum on the Basis of Their Sexual Identity." *Feminist Legal Studies* 16 (1): 87–95. https://doi.org/10.1007/s10691-007-9080-z.

Poertner, Ephraim. 2017. "Governing Asylum through Configurations of Productivity and Deterrence: Effects on the Spatiotemporal Trajectories of Cases in Switzerland." *Geoforum* 78: 12–21. https://doi.org/10.1016/j.geoforum.2016.11.004.

Poertner, Ephraim. 2018. "Re-cording Lives: Governing Asylum in Switzerland and the Need to Resolve." PhD diss. (unpublished), University of Zurich.

Polanyi, Michael. 1962 (1958). *Personal Knowledge: Towards a Post-Critical Philosophy*. London: Routledge.

Polanyi, Michael. 1966. *The Tacit Dimension*. Chicago: University of Chicago Press.

Pratt, Anna C. 1999. "Dunking the Doughnut: Discretionary Power, Law and the Administration of the Canadian Immigration Act." *Social & Legal Studies* 8 (2): 199–226. https://doi.org/10.1177/096466399900800203.

Pratt, Anna, and Lorne Sossin. 2009. "A Brief Introduction of the Puzzle of Discretion." *Canadian Journal of Law and Society* 24 (3): 301–312. https://doi.org/10.1017/S082932010001005X.

Probst, Johanna. 2012. *Instruire la demande d'asile: étude comparative du processus décisionnel au sein de l'administration allemande et française.* Science politique, Université de Strasbourg. https://tel.archives-ouvertes.fr/tel-00985215/document, last accessed February 3, 2020.

Ramji-Nogales, Jaya, Andrew I. Schoenholtz, and Philip G. Schrag, eds. 2009. *Refugee Roulette: Disparities in Asylum Adjudication and Proposals for Reform.* New York: New York University Press.

Reckwitz, Andreas. 2003. "Grundelemente einer Theorie sozialer Praktiken: Eine sozialtheoretische Perspektive." *Zeitschrift für Soziologie* 32 (4): 282–301.

Rehaag, Sean. 2012. "Judicial Review of Refugee Determinations: The Luck of the Draw?" *Queen's Law Journal* 38 (1): 1–58. https://dx.doi.org/10.2139/ssrn.2027517.

Rousseau, Cécile, François Crépeau, Patricia Foxen, and France Houle. 2002. "The Complexity of Determining Refugeehood: A Multidisciplinary Analysis of the Decision-Making Process of the Canadian Immigration and Refugee Board." *Journal of Refugee Studies* 15 (1): 43–70. https://doi.org/10.1093/jrs/15.1.43.

Sarat, Austin. 2007. "Vitality Amidst Fragmentation: On the Emergence of Postrealist Law and Society Scholarship." In *The Blackwell Companion to Law and Society.* Third Edition, edited by Austin Sarat, 1–11. Malden: Blackwell.

Sbriccoli, Tommaso, and Stefano Jacoviello. 2011. "The Case of S: Elaborating the 'Right' Narrative to Fit Normative/Political Expectations in Asylum Procedure in Italy." In *Cultural Expertise and Litigation*, edited by Livia Holden, 172–194. Abingdon, New York: Routledge.

Scheffer, Thomas. 2001. *Asylgewährung: Eine ethnographische Analyse des deutschen Asylverfahrens.* Stuttgart: Lucius & Lucius.

Scheffer, Thomas. 2003. "Kritik der Urteilskraft: Wie die Asylprüfung Unentscheidbares in Entscheidbares überführt." In *Migration steuern und verwalten: Deutschland vom späten 19. Jahrhundert bis zur Gegenwart*, edited by Jochen Oltmer, 423–458. Göttingen: Vandenhoeck & Ruprecht.

Schneider, Stephanie, and Kristina Wottrich. 2017. "'Ohne'ne ordentliche Anhörung kann ich keine ordentliche Entscheidung machen … ': Zur Organisation von Anhörungen in deutschen und schwedischen Asylbehörden." In *Asyl verwalten: Zur bürokratischen Bearbeitung eines gesellschaftlichen Problems*, edited by Christian Lahusen, and Stephanie Schneider, 81–115. Bielefeld: transcript.

Sharma, Aradhana, and Akhil Gupta, eds. 2006. *The Anthropology of the State: A Reader*. Malden: Blackwell.

Shore, Cris, and Susan Wright. 2011. "Conceptualising Policy: Technologies of Governance and the Politics of Visibility." In *Policy Worlds: Anthropology and the Analysis of Contemporary Power*, edited by Cris Shore, Susan Wright, and Davide Però, 1–25. New York: Berghahn Books.

Souter, James. 2011. "A Culture of Disbelief or Denial? Critiquing Refugee Status Determination in the United Kingdom." *Oxford Monitor of Forced Migration* 1 (1): 48–59.

Spijkerboer, Thomas. 2000. *Gender and Refugee Status*. Aldershot: Ashgate.

Spijkerboer, Thomas. 2005. "Stereotyping and Acceleration: Gender, Procedural Acceleration and Marginalised Judicial Review in the Dutch Asylum System." In *Proof, Evidentiary Assessment and Credibility in Asylum Procedures*, edited by Gregor Noll, 67–102. Leiden: Martinus Nijhoff.

Spijkerboer, Thomas, ed. 2013. *Fleeing Homophobia: Sexual Orientation, Gender Identity and Asylum*. Abingdon: Routledge.

Spirig, Judith. 2018. *Like Cases Alike or Asylum Lottery? Judicial Decision Making at the Swiss Administrative Court*. University of Zurich. https://doi.org/10.5167/uzh-157718.

Sweeney, James A. 2007. "The 'Lure' of Facts in Asylum Appeals: Critiquing the Practice of Judges." In *Applying Theory to Policy and Practice: Issues for Critical Reflection*, edited by Steven R. Smith, 19–35. Hampshire: Ashgate.

Swiss Civil Code, of 10 December 1907 (Status as of 1 January 2019). 210.

Terdiman, Richard. 1987. "The Force of Law: Toward a Sociology of the Juridical Field by Pierre Bourdieu: Translator's Introduction." *Hastings Law Journal* 38 (5): 805–853.

Thomas, Robert. 2009. "Refugee Roulette: A UK Perspective." In *Refugee Roulette: Disparities in Asylum Adjudication and Proposals for Return*, edited by Jaya Ramji-Nogales, Andrew I. Schoenholtz, and Philip G. Schrag, 164–186. New York: New York University Press.

Tomkinson, Sule B. 2018. "Who Are You Afraid of and Why? Inside the Black Box of Refugee Tribunals." *Canadian Public Administration* 61 (2): 184–204. https://doi.org/10.1111/capa.12275.

Triandafyllidou, Anna. 2003. "Immigration Policy Implementation in Italy: Organisational Culture, Identity Processes and Labour Market Control." *Journal of Ethnic and Migration Studies* 29 (2): 257–298. https://doi.org/10.1080/1369183032000079611.

United Nations High Commissioner for Refugees. 2013. *Beyond Proof: Credibility Assessment in EU Asylum Systems*. Brussels: UNHCR. http://www.unhcr.org/51a8a08a9.pdf, last accessed February 3, 2020.

Wacquant, Loïc J. D. 1992. "Toward a Social Praxeology: The Structure and Logic of Bourdieu's Sociology." In *An Invitation to Reflexive Sociology*, edited by Pierre Bourdieu, and Loïc J. D. Wacquant, 1–59. Cambridge: Polity Press.

Wagenaar, Hendrik. 2004. "'Knowing' the Rules: Administrative Work as Practice." *Public Administration Review* 64 (6): 643–656. https://doi.org/10.1111/j.1540-6210.2004.00412.x.

Weber, Max. 2013 (1978). *Economy and Society*. Edited by Guenther Roth and Claus Wittich. Berkeley: University of California Press.
Wedel, Janine R., Cris Shore, Gregory Feldman, and Stacey Lathrop. 2005. "Toward an Anthropology of Public Policy." *Annals of the American Academy of Political and Social Science* 600 (1): 30–51. https://doi.org/10.1177/0002716205276734.

2

Studying Everyday Practice(s) in the SEM

My interest in asylum decision-making and particularly in credibility determination began when, as a graduate student in social anthropology, I was an intern in an NGO running a centre for asylum seekers. The centre provided housing, financial support and social care. My job at the centre had no direct involvement with asylum decision-making; nevertheless, the SEM's decisions about the individual asylum seekers were sent to our office. We, the employees working at the centre, would then distribute the written notifications of decisions to the asylum seekers, and would often end up translating decisions for them. When translating those letters, I was repeatedly unsettled by the reasons given for rejecting an asylum application—most of which seemed to be based on the decision-maker finding the claim not credible. This ignited my interest in studying SEM caseworkers' decision-making practices. I wanted to "find out" why so many negative decisions were based on non-credibility and what criteria the decision-makers used to determine whether asylum seekers' claims were credible or not. I wanted to critically engage with these practices.

As social scientists doing qualitative research, we (should) organise our "research in such a way that […] [we] create the conditions for surprise" (Wagenaar 2011: 243). Hendrik Wagenaar, therefore, argues that ethnography or interpretive qualitative research should be thought of as more of "an extended improvisation than [as] a well-thought-out-in-advance […] strategy" (ibid.: 241). Hence, this is precisely how I went about doing fieldwork. As I gained ever new insights into my research topic, new analytical questions emerged and I began to re-think and question my original hypothesis—which had been affirmed by the literature I initially engaged with—namely, that

L. Affolter, *Asylum Matters*, Palgrave Socio-Legal Studies,
https://doi.org/10.1007/978-3-030-61512-3_2

credibility assessments were arbitrary and based on highly subjective views. Rather, what I came to deal with in this book is how administrative caseworkers come to think, feel, know and act in similar ways and how this generates regularities in administrative practice.

My interest in this book lies with the practice of administrative work in a practice theoretical sense. Following Andreas Reckwitz (2002), I understand "practice" as an assemblage of different elements (see also Schatzki 2002: 71). He writes: "A 'practice' (*Praktik*) is a routinized type of behaviour which consists of several elements, interconnected to one other: forms of bodily activities, forms of mental activities, 'things' and their use, a background knowledge in the form of understanding, know-how, states of emotion and motivational knowledge" (2002: 249). Bodily activities, according to Reckwitz, include activities such as writing, reading and talking; the things that decision-makers in the SEM do most (2003: 290). For researchers dealing with administrative work, this means that we must pay attention to all these different elements (or as many as possible) that constitute a practice: the "taken-for-granted routines"; the implicit and explicit knowledge "brought to bear on concrete situations"; officials' interactions with each other and other actors; the "informal banter and gossip with colleagues during coffee breaks"; their emotional struggles, motivations, doubts and insecurities; as well as the circulation of documents and ideas (Wagenaar 2004: 644). Hence, it means paying attention to what decision-makers say they do in the fullest sense. We must listen to what decision-makers think they should do, what they experience when they do it, and also look beyond what officials say, at what they do or do not do.

This chapter outlines the methodological approach I developed to do this. I describe how I struggled to—and eventually succeeded in—gaining research access to the SEM and how I went about studying everyday practices in the office. I thereby pay particular attention to the challenges I faced when doing fieldwork, not only in terms of getting research access but also, and more importantly, to the methodological challenges arising from a practice theoretical approach. I discuss the ways in which I dealt with and attempted to overcome these challenges and the methodological limitations that remain.

Getting into the "Black Box"

Bureaucracies or administrations have frequently been characterised as secretive, opaque entities (Hoag 2011: 82) or as "black boxes" (Eule 2014). Furthermore, according to Weber, "administrative secrecy constitutes a key dimension of bureaucratic power" (2013 [1978]: 922). In many ways this is what I encountered during fieldwork, as gaining access to the institution proved challenging. However, once I was in, I experienced a lot of openness and transparency towards me.

Gaining access to the field required stamina. In total, it took me one year to get full research access, and one and a half years before I was able to properly start fieldwork. I first tried gaining access "the formal way" by applying via a formal request to the head of the asylum directorate. However, after months of waiting, my request was declined, the main reason for this being that others had previously already done this kind of research.[1] With persistence and the help of my supervisor I finally managed to get permission to observe an asylum interview and interview the official. However, after that I was unsure how to continue with my research until, a couple of months later at a national asylum conference, I met one of the officials who had rejected my original research request. I approached him, presented myself to him and asked him to help me "get in", which he did. Thus, in the end it was through him—and in this more informal way—that I eventually gained access to the SEM. With his help and that of a colleague of his, I finally managed to draft a new research proposal that was approved by the directorate and served as a basis for the anonymisation contract I was asked to sign. The contract stipulated that I was only allowed to take anonymised documents out of the office with me, that all kinds of personal data I had would have to be destroyed by a certain date, that I could only sit in on asylum interviews if the asylum seeker gave consent and that I was only allowed to publish my doctoral thesis after it had been checked by the SEM.

Once I had signed this contract and was "truly in", I was surprised by the openness and trust I experienced from officials in different hierarchical positions. I was, for instance, allowed to observe asylum interviews, read and copy case files (as long as I anonymised them), and attend internal team meetings. Once, after a day of analysing and copying random case files, I even appeared to be the last one left in the building at 9 p.m. However, at the same time, I am aware that certain information was deliberately not shared with me. At times, caseworkers confided in me things they (thought they) were not supposed to, but then asked me not to use this information; a request which I, of course, honour.

[1]This is how I came to know Jonathan Miaz. Jonathan Miaz is a political scientist who also did research on decision-making in the SEM. Later I met Ephraim Poertner, a human geographer working on similar issues. Jonathan Miaz did fieldwork in the SEM between 2010 and 2012, Ephraim Poertner was there between 2012 and 2014 and I eventually conducted my fieldwork between 2014 and 2015. The three of us have since worked closely together on several occasions (see Affolter et al. 2019).

Despite there being some aspects of decision-making that were not shared with me, I believe the fact that officials were so open towards me is of importance and is something worth stressing. It shows that the officials—contrary to a common assumption held by many critics of asylum decision-making—feel that most aspects of their everyday work have no need to be hidden. The assumption that caseworkers need to hide their everyday practices stems from a particular view on administrations and on what research on administrations is about. It is based on the premise that caseworkers do not do what they are supposed to do and that research will uncover such "deviant'" behaviour; or that bureaucracies and bureaucrats are "evil" and that they would not want to have this "identity" uncovered. Neither of these views reflects my stance on decision-makers in the SEM. Rather, I believe that what is important is precisely that decision-makers are mostly confident that they are doing the right thing. For them, their practices are normal and legitimate—they are the self-evident thing to do. Therefore, they have nothing to hide. Taking this seriously is important for understanding how the SEM, and bureaucratic administrations in general, work.

That decision-makers were open towards me does not, however, mean that they did not sometimes—especially at the beginning of my research—adopt a defensive position in our conversations. In general, such a defensive position is something SEM officials quite often adopt towards outsiders. As Tobias Eule (2014: 104) has shown for German immigration offices, this defensive position arises from the "constant criticism" officials are confronted with in their work: criticism by politicians, political organisations and the media, for example, of the office's decision-making being either too harsh or too lenient (see also Lentz 2014: 197). Thus, my empirical material must be read within this context. My field encounters were influenced by this defensive position in two main ways. First, most SEM officials with whom I interacted seemed to categorise me accurately as a "leftist". Therefore, especially at the beginning, when my interaction partners and I were still in the process of establishing mutual trust, it was mostly the "harsh part" of decision-making, their disbelief of asylum stories and decisions to send people back home which they tried to defend, because this was the part they assumed I would be the most critical of. After a while, however, and this is the second way in which the defensive stance of decision-makers influenced my field encounters, many officials began to regard my work as not just a potential threat, but they began to see it as an opportunity to convey a different image of the institution and of its decision-making practices to the outside (see also Eule 2014: 107).

"Getting In"... Literally

At the time of my research, asylum decisions were taken by officials working in the five reception and processing centres (RPCs) mostly located close to Switzerland's "physical borders", and in the eight different asylum units at the headquarters in Bern. I eventually ended up doing research at the headquarters—for the most part in two different units there—and in two of the RPCs. This implied getting in and out of four different buildings in a literal sense, which remained a challenging issue throughout the course of my fieldwork. All four buildings were guarded by security officers based in a glass cubicle adjacent to the first entrance door. Every time I wanted to enter, except for in one of the asylum units where I was given a badge, it was obligatory to present my identity card to the security guards, tell them what institution I was from (the university of Bern) and with whom I was meeting that day. They would then call the person to come and pick me up, because without them the inner entrance door was unassailable. In both RPCs, I was usually left standing in the entrance hall, which always seemed to be overcrowded. There were asylum seekers asking guards for permission to leave, asylum seekers coming back from outside and having to inform the guards of their return, asylum seekers asking for appointments with decision-makers, new asylum seekers arriving, having to register or being body searched, for example. It was different at the headquarters. When I arrived I would always be asked to take a seat in the waiting room to the right. I was never the sole occupant. There would usually be social aid representatives and interpreters waiting to be taken to their respective asylum interviews and occasionally there were other "guests" like myself. While the interpreters often sat chatting together, the social aid representatives, whose role it is to observe asylum interviews from a "neutral perspective" and report on them to the Swiss Refugee Council (see Chapter 3), were mostly preparing for upcoming interviews. This meant they would be reading through the different documents from an applicant's case file, particularly the minutes from the first asylum interview, and taking notes. Social aid representatives usually arrive well ahead of the scheduled interview time because it is only upon registering with the security guards that they receive the documents necessary for preparation.

From this waiting room, one could see over into the glass waiting room on the other side of the guard's cubicle, where asylum seekers waited for their interviews. In this other waiting room there was a small playing area where children—in the company of an adult—could play while they waited for their parents to come back from their interviews. Outside the first entrance door at the SEM headquarters there was a sign stating that all asylum seekers had to enter through a separate door on the left and register on the left side of the security guard cubicle. Both on the left and on the right side there were inner doors passing the guards' cubicle that could only be opened with security badges. On the first day of training for new SEM employees which I was allowed to participate in, we were told that the purpose of having two separate outer entrance doors and two inner doors was in case of "an applicant becoming aggressive" the doors could be locked separately, thus, trapping the person in between the left outer and inner door. For this reason, SEM employees were advised to always use the doors on the right in order to not get accidentally trapped between two locked doors with an applicant.[2]

From a methodological standpoint, not being able to enter the buildings on my own had both advantages and disadvantages. While it sometimes made me feel like a burden for the decision-makers—having to drag them out of their offices to come and pick me up downstairs—and limited my ability to move around freely between the different buildings, it also meant that I always had to be in the company of someone, which for anthropological research is, of course, very useful.

Doing Fieldwork

"You don't do fieldwork, fieldwork does you", Bob Simpson's supervisor once counselled him after he complained about being "manipulated by [a] principal informant" (2006: 125). This nicely shows that we do not just choose our interaction partners, sites and moments during fieldwork, but that they also choose us (see Sökefeld 2006: 24). Martin Sökefeld, therefore, speaks of fieldwork as a "social interaction". He writes that, as ethnographers, we often have to surrender control over the research situation to our interaction partners and that only by ceding control to them can we sometimes gain access to yet unknown spheres of social life (ibid.). I will now not only show how I went about doing fieldwork, but also "how fieldwork did me".

I conducted fieldwork in the SEM between 2014 and 2015 (with some exploratory parts in 2013). Where I carried out my research was more or less decided for me. The person who initially helped me gain research access to the SEM—who was at the time in charge of the office's quality management—asked around amongst the heads of the different asylum units at the headquarters and the RPCs who would be willing to have me. Four heads agreed to this and I was put in contact with them to plan my individual

[2] Training instructor, A-modules, field notes, my own translation.

field-stays. It was agreed that the individual stays would be relatively short so as not to unduly burden the officials, who worked under a great deal of time pressure. The units at the headquarters each allowed me to stay for two consecutive weeks. I could only go to the two RPCs for one or two days at a time, but they allowed me to do so on five different occasions. In addition to this, I visited other divisions and asylum units of the SEM to sit in on asylum interviews, carry out interviews with SEM officials, analyse case files and take part in the three-week training course for new employees. Furthermore, I met with caseworkers every so often for lunch or a drink outside work.

Following People Around

During my time in the different asylum units, I accompanied officials in their daily work, observing what they were doing, asking them about what they were doing, listening to their explanations and occasionally also actively joining in their activities (see also McDonald 2005; Mugler 2019: 54; Müller 2017). I now describe the various aspects of the SEM officials' job that I was able to observe in more detail.

Asylum interviews constitute an important part of officials' work. By following caseworkers around, I was able to sit in on eighteen asylum interviews: six initial short asylum interviews and twelve longer second (or third) interviews (see Chapter 3). Usually, a day or two before the interview, the official in charge would give me the case file so that I could read it and make copies of it before the interview. Often, we would then also discuss the 'case' together which could mean different things.[3] Some decision-makers, for instance, told me what decision they thought they would end up taking before the interview, and why, while others explained to me how they had prepared for the interview or planned to do so. In the case of "old stagers", this was often merely that they had looked through the case file, read through the minutes of the first asylum interview and made a couple of notes. However, some of them—as well as many of the newer employees—showed me elaborate lists of questions they had prepared, and in some cases even chronological diagrams they had made with all the information they already had on a 'case'. On four occasions, I was also able to sit down and prepare the interviews together with the caseworker. Together we went through the different documents in the case file, listing possible questions, which I was also sometimes asked to contribute to, or at least to comment on.

[3]'Cases' is an emic term. Of course, what SEM decision-makers really deal with are not cases but people whose lives are greatly affected by their practices and decisions.

On the day of the interview itself, I would usually accompany the decision-makers to pick up the asylum applicants, interpreters and social aid representatives from their respective waiting rooms. Mostly we would then all walk back to the caseworkers' office in silence, but sometimes some of the actors engaged in friendly conversation with one another. In the decision-maker's office, we would then all take our assigned places. I was always assigned a place away from the square table around which the asylum seeker, the SEM official, the interpreter and the social aid representative sat. Usually, I was placed behind the minute-taker's desk which allowed me to see onto the computer screen and to observe what was written down during the interview. During the actual interview my role was strictly limited to that of observer. However, of course, this does not mean that my presence did not influence the others. I sat there, listened, observed and took notes. I soon gave up trying to write down everything that was said during the interviews because the conversations were usually too fast for me to get everything down on paper and because I always got a copy of the minutes at the end anyway. Instead, I made notes of my other observations. These included things that were said but not written down by the minute-taker—on their own account or because they were instructed not to do so by the decision-makers—different actors' demeanour, displayed emotions (as I interpreted them), the setting of the room, material being used and passed around as well as my own impressions and sentiments. I never said anything in these interview situations except for the few times I was asked to present myself at the beginning of the interview in order to ask for the applicant's consent to my being there. Normally, however, the decision-makers did this for me, either presenting me as someone from the university who was there to observe them work or as someone who was training for the job. In two of the initial short interviews I sat in on, in which there are no minute-takers, as the minutes are written by the caseworkers themselves, I was asked to write the minutes. The caseworker carrying out the interview sat next to me, at times instructing me on what to write.

During breaks in asylum interviews, I usually waited for the decision-maker to come back from taking the other participants to their respective waiting rooms and in the meantime chatted with the minute-takers who often shared their views on the particular 'case' with me or on the decision-maker carrying out the interview. When the caseworkers came back, I normally asked them about their first impressions and how they planned on proceeding.

Asylum interviews—especially those lasting a whole day—are exhausting, even for me, as someone who did not have an active role. Therefore, the decision-makers and I rarely engaged in long conversations after the interview had finished. Normally, the caseworkers printed out the minutes for me and we would arrange to meet a day or two later to discuss the 'case'. Sometimes, by then the decision-makers had already started writing the decision and they showed me the arguments they had developed so far. But mostly they just told me what they thought their decision was going to be—and why they were going to take that particular decision—as well as how they planned on proceeding. I was also repeatedly asked to give them feedback on how they had carried out their asylum interviews because the caseworkers thought I might have some interesting insights from also having observed some of their co-workers do interviews. Because most decisions had not been finalised by the time I left the units, I was allowed to write down the number of the 'cases' and contact the secretaries of the different units on a regular basis to ask if the decisions had been sent out, and then pick up copies of the final decisions when they had been.[4]

It should be noted that the asylum interviews I attended during fieldwork were not completely random. In the first instance, it depended on whether the caseworkers would allow me to sit in (they did not allow me to in only two cases). Furthermore, I was not permitted to attend any *GespeVer* (gender-based persecution) interviews, which are mainly 'cases' in which the claimants have experienced sexual violence or were persecuted on the grounds of their sexual orientation. As a woman I would only have been permitted to attend interviews with female applicants, and there were only a few during my stay. Furthermore, the heads of the asylum units feared that my presence could make the situation even more unbearable for the applicants—these interviews tend to be particularly intimate—so I was excluded from them and I never pushed to be allowed to sit in.

In addition to sitting in on asylum interviews, accompanying officials in their daily work involved sitting in their offices and observing them carry out different tasks: writing decisions; writing letters to applicants; reading reports about different "countries of origin"; writing answers to interpellations which had been passed down the institution's hierarchy and had ended up on their desks; dealing with family reunification requests as well as giving advice to co-workers or asking for advice from them. In these situations, the officials mostly treated me as a novice, explaining what they were doing step by step. They also often printed out the documents they were working on for me so that I could follow better. The same also happened on the days in which I followed the heads of asylum units around. On those days, I was

[4]I was also able to trace decisions that were appealed at the Federal Administrative Court, where I was given permission to study the case files under supervision and make notes of them.

able to observe superiors assign new asylum 'cases' to their employees as well as check the latter's decisions before sending them out to asylum seekers. Furthermore, many people kept stopping by or phoning the heads' offices to discuss various issues, which allowed me to observe interesting interactions. Twice I was also able to sit in and observe so-called "consultation meetings" between a superior and a caseworker in which they discussed specific 'cases' and how the caseworkers should proceed with them. Decision-makers can ask for such meetings if they feel that they need help with a particular 'case'. Furthermore, one superior let me observe him prepare his staff appraisals and to also sit in on one of the appraisal interviews. Lastly, two heads took me to meetings with them: one to an internal meeting of the asylum unit he was in charge of, and one to a division meeting attended by the heads of different asylum units.

During my field-stays, I was usually assigned an office; a place where I could write down my notes and anonymise all the documents I had received. While I never spent much time in my office, having one nevertheless proved helpful for fieldwork. Firstly, because in the SEM, hallways are busy places and caseworkers tend to leave their office doors open. Thus, by just sitting in "my office" I was able to overhear several interesting conversations: caseworkers telling their colleagues about an asylum interview they had just done or were in the middle of doing, caseworkers asking their co-workers for help with a decision or caseworkers jointly looking for arguments to prove the non-credibility of a claim, for instance. The one time I shared an office with three decision-makers, this coming and going was even more easily observable. Furthermore, after a while, decision-makers would just come to my office to talk to me and to tell me about 'cases' they were working on.

Finally, taking the morning coffee break together was common practice in the asylum units. These breaks turned out to be particularly fruitful moments of fieldwork. Sometimes, the conversations during breaks were completely unrelated to work and so I learnt quite a bit about the decision-makers' private lives. Often, however, they would discuss specific 'cases' or aspects of their work—particularly if they were unhappy with them—allowing me to learn a lot about the office.

Method Triangulation

In addition to following people around, observing them and talking to them in and about their everyday work, I conducted interviews with twenty-seven caseworkers from nine different asylum units. Thus, in addition to caseworkers from the units in which I did fieldwork, I also interviewed officials I met during the induction training; officials I was put in touch with by other decision-makers; that I met by chance during one of my field-stays; or that I already knew from before my research. I was able to interview two of the new employees that I met on two occasions. The first, when they had only been working at the SEM for a couple of weeks or months, and the second time after they had been working there for a little over a year. I usually prepared some questions before the interviews and developed preferences for a couple of questions I found worked well in most situations. But, mostly, I proceeded in a very open way in order to see what my interaction partners considered to be important topics (see Wagenaar 2011: 253). I asked officials about observations I had made, asking for explanations and clarifications as well as their reflections on them. Without much probing from my side, decision-makers often started telling me specific "stories" or describing particular 'cases' which then repeatedly led them to search for and show me the specific case file, if it was still in their possession. Such narratives, according to Steven Maynard-Moody and Michael Musheno, are very useful for gaining an understanding of the "normative reasoning and context" that shape administrative work. Thus, they write that

> [w]hen examining moral responsibility, especially when it is deeply embedded in the normative structures of institutions and policy regimes, we cannot expect people, whether frontline staff or upper-level managers, to articulate their actual decision norms. Narratives, on the other hand, provide rich evidence of the normative reasoning and context that shape judgements and actions. Through narratives, storytellers reveal more than they consciously know. (2012: 21)

My interviews, which I recorded either in writing or via audio and later transcribed, include "stories", biographical accounts, normative reflections and abstract descriptions of everyday practice. I often, rather subconsciously at the time, pushed for detailed descriptions of officials' work, asking over and over again why and how they did certain things, which frequently led decision-makers to tell me that there were certain aspects of their work that simply could not be explained: these were things they just did or knew, without being able to put them into words. In hindsight, these questions have proven helpful for discerning decision-makers' implicit knowledge—the things they just know and do without being able to discursively explain why and how—and the taken-for-granted, self-evident aspects of their everyday work.

Another important method I made use of was document analysis. As mentioned above, in my interactions with SEM officials, I was often given copies of the documents they were working on or working with, such as training materials, so-called country of origin reports, internal guidelines on how to deal with applications by people from specific countries, news reports or drafts of asylum decisions, for example. Furthermore, I was able to photocopy and analyse the content of seventy-two case files. Thirteen of these files came from 'cases' I had come into contact with during my fieldwork and in which I had sat in on the corresponding asylum interviews. The remaining fifty-nine case files were from when I was granted access to nearly all the files of 'cases' that had been decided upon by decision-makers from all of the SEM's asylum units on two randomly set dates. Hence, in many of these 'cases' I do not know the decision-makers personally, nor was I present when these 'cases' were dealt with in practice. Nevertheless, they allowed me to get a good overview of the different types of asylum decisions that are made, the different kind of enquiries undertaken by the decision-makers (see Chapter 3) and the different kinds of documents that exist in the SEM.

This "method triangulation" (Hammersley and Atkinson 2007: 184) was crucial for my research for two connected reasons. First, because the data generated through these different methods shed light on decision-making practices from different angles, allowing me to, for example, analytically approach both discursive and non-discursive aspects of everyday practice in the SEM (see also Dahlvik 2018: 19). Second, the different insights I gained from each of these methodological approaches provided me with new ideas, for instance, on what issues to inquire into, what moments to pay special attention to during my observations, what documents to look for, or what questions to ask my interaction partners. In this regard, I gained particularly fruitful insights during the three weeks I was able to participate in the induction training for new SEM employees (see Chapter 5).

The Researcher as a Learner

When "studying an unfamiliar setting" we are, at least at the beginning, always novices (Hammersely and Atkinson 2007: 80). However, as Martyn Hammersley and Paul Atkinson argue, there is an essential difference between what they call "lay novices" and ethnographers, in that "the latter attempts to maintain a self-conscious awareness of what is learned, how it has been learned, and the social transactions that inform the production of such knowledge" (2007: 80). This is precisely what I attempted to do while participating in the trainings for new asylum decision-makers in the SEM.

Being a learner or a novice is, of course, a role we as ethnographers occupy beyond such specific learning situations. In general, it is a helpful role because we often want the people we are working with to teach us about their "everyday worlds" (see Le Compte et al. 1999: 21–22). However, at the same time, it is also important to maintain a balance between ignorance and expertise (see also Hammersley and Atkinson 1995: 103). This appears to be particularly important when studying organisations and "professional worlds" where, as Johanna Mugler argues, researchers must "acquire a considerable amount of expert knowledge" in order "to be taken seriously" by the people we are working with (2019: 65). The training sessions in the SEM constituted an important setting for me in order to acquire this necessary expertise. But they were also unique learning situations in other ways.

What made the training sessions special and, to some extent, also quite challenging was that I was not the only learner there. Except for the trainers, everybody else present was also learning. With regard to my relationship with the other participants this meant that I could not really "be taught" by them, which seemed to make it more difficult to establish a rapport with them. In comparison with the rest of my field-stays, I experienced less openness towards me and less interest in my research endeavours. Some even seemed a bit suspicious of me, but most of them were simply very busy learning new tasks, getting to know their co-workers, and growing used to their new daily routines. The best moments for engaging in conversation with the trainees were, therefore, when we had to work together in groups and try to apply the aspect of law we had just learnt about to specific 'cases'. In those moments I "truly" became a participant like the others and often refrained from taking field notes.

It was also in these moments that I gained the most valuable insights into decision-makers' learning processes: into what they found easy, difficult, surprising or disturbing, for example; into the knowledge and experience they brought with them to the job; into how the different training materials were used and referred to during "practical exercises"; into the questions the trainees posed to their trainers; and the aspects of the job—or rather of the practical exercises we did—that they seemed to struggle with most. But not only was I able to observe how others were learning, I also tried to self-reflexively take notes of my own experiences during the training sessions. The following entry from my fieldwork diary illustrates this:

> I feel just like yesterday. I'm shocked by what these exercises trigger in me. It's really exiting to finally be able to apply the law and to see in each 'case' whether I managed to get it 'right' or 'wrong'. The more complex a 'case', the

more interesting it becomes. Looking around me, I don't think I'm the only one that feels that way.[5]

It was, amongst other things, observations like these that got me interested in how certain practices become "normalised" for decision-makers, helping me shape my analytical research questions. Furthermore, the training materials I received and the notes I took during those three weeks helped me a great deal to get an idea of the regulatory constraints and conditions of asylum decision-making, the different steps of the formal proceedings as well as of the documents and artefacts available for and used in decision-making. They also allowed me to better understand what it was that people were doing during my subsequent field-stays, and to be able to ask more specific questions.

My Interaction Partners in the SEM

Fitting with practice theory, the personalities of the officials I interacted with do not figure prominently in my work. I marginally deal with their educational backgrounds and their motivations for doing the job in Chapter 5. But other than that, for my analysis with its focus on situated practice and on institutional socialisation and learning processes, what is mainly relevant is decision-makers' "position" within the organisation and their professional experience. What was important for my research was, therefore, to include both experienced caseworkers and those who were still quite new to the job, as well as people holding different hierarchical positions, in my sample of interaction partners in the SEM. In the end, nine of my thirty-one interaction partners were "old stagers", meaning that they had worked at the SEM for fifteen years or more. Seventeen of my interaction partners had only been working at the SEM for three years or less at the time I met them. These seventeen all considered themselves to be "quite new to the job" and still had temporary working contracts. In contrast, only five of my interaction partners had been working at the SEM between four and fourteen years and, with the exception of one, all held higher hierarchical positions. This fits with the assessment of several of my interaction partners (all of them "new" employees) that after roughly five years on the job, it was either time to leave, or to move up the hierarchy. In addition to these four officials, three of the "old stagers" I interacted with also held higher hierarchical positions.

As can be seen, the percentage of "new" employees with fixed-term contracts in my sample was quite high, for which there seem to be several

[5] Field notes, my own translation.

reasons. Firstly, it has to do with the fact that in general, at the time of my fieldwork, there were many "new" caseworkers in the SEM. The SEM's asylum directorate had significantly grown in the years previous to my fieldwork and many new decision-makers had been employed in an attempt to reduce the number of pending cases (see Chapter 3). Secondly, it was often easier for me to approach and establish rapport with new employees. On the one hand, this was related to new employees mostly being the same age as me and having a similar educational background (see Chapter 5). On the other hand, they tended to be more physically present in the office. They normally came to the coffee breaks in the morning (whereas quite a few "old stagers" did not) and spent the working days in their offices (whereas quite a few "old" employees were allowed to sometimes work from home or had special tasks which at times took them away from the office). Thirdly, in many asylum units where I did my fieldwork, the superiors decided with whom I would be spending time. I do not know if the superiors always approached specific employees or just asked around who would be willing to "have me". However, I think there are again two probable reasons why I was more often sent to new employees than to their experienced co-workers. On the one hand, I know that two of the "old stagers" that had been approached by the superiors told them that they did not want me to accompany them in their work. Of course, it is also possible that some of the new employees refused my company, and that I am simply not aware of this. Nevertheless, based on my observations, I assume that for new employees it was more important to get the approval of their superiors (who had agreed to receive me and now needed a place for me to be every day) and, therefore, did not want to deny their superiors' request. This might also relate to the fact that new employees hold fixed-term contracts and, thus, getting into (or remaining in) their superiors' good books is crucial for them. On the other hand, it could also be that the superiors directly approached more new employees who, not having been on the job very long, were often less behind with their work than their "older", more experienced colleagues who had accumulated much bigger workloads. Thus, they had more time for me.

Thinking Through and with Practice Theory: Methodological Limits and Challenges

In this final part of the chapter, I address the methodological challenges and limits of grasping everyday practices through ethnography. As stated above, I find a practice theoretical understanding of practice useful because, as Russel

Hitchings writes "[t]his area of scholarship has had some of the most to say about the relatively habitual ways in which we all pass through much of our lives" (2012: 61). I argue that this also applies to many of the things administrative caseworkers do. It should be noted here that it was through my "data", through the observations I made in the SEM, that I arrived at practice theory—which seemed the most useful for analysing my empirical material—and not the other way around. I therefore "use" theory in the way proposed by Hendrik Wagenaar who, drawing on Barney Glaser and Anselm Strauss (1967) writes that "[t]heory is not a final statement about some social phenomena or activity but a 'strategy for handling data' [...]: provisional, open-ended, but always restrained by what the world tells us" (Wagenaar 2011: 260).

Following Andreas Reckwitz's suggestion, decision-makers' "bodily activities", such as writing, reading and talking to each other, their implicit practical knowledge and everyday routines, are at the centre of my analysis. Furthermore, I am interested in how decision-makers' "professional subjectivities" are shaped by their surroundings: the regulatory constraints posed by the organisation, the type of bureaucratic decision-making work they do as well as the laws and policies they must "apply" within the ideological environments they work. I inquire into how decision-makers come to think, act and know things in similar ways, but also how they develop similar understandings of what is moral, ethical and desirable. For this purpose, I draw on Pierre Bourdieu's concept of the habitus, as outlined in the introduction (see Bourdieu 1976). Similar to Bourdieu, Andreas Reckwitz argues that the "conventionalized 'mental' activities of understanding, knowing how and desiring are necessary elements and qualities of a practice in which the single individual participates, not of the individual" (2002: 250). Thus, individuals—in my case SEM officials—become "carriers" of certain practices (ibid.). However, this does not mean that the (institutional) habitus works in a deterministic way or that, as Russel Hitchings claims, "individuals always bow automatically to the dictates of the practice" (2012: 62). Practice also allows for and requires improvisation (see Bourdieu 1990; Shove and Pantzar 2007).

Not everything we do is verbalisable. Rather, some things we do, like cooking or skiing for example, are partially non-linguistic (see Bloch 1991: 189; Martens 2012). This has led some authors to argue that "talk" is not enough to understand practices and that we need to also make use of other qualitative (or even quantitative) methods to be able to more fully comprehend practices (see Browne 2016; Halkier and Jensen 2011; Martens 2012). I agree with these authors that not everything can be expressed through "talk" and that—depending on the research questions we pose (see Shove 2017)—method triangulation may indeed make sense to approach practices from different angles. Nevertheless, following Russel Hitchings (2012), I argue that we also should not underestimate the things that can be verbalised and what we can learn from talking to our interaction partners. As human beings, we are able to reflect on the things we do and to some extent also the things that make us do what we do. We are often even used to doing so. Talking to people during fieldwork, also but not exclusively through doing interviews with them, can, therefore, be useful for learning about such reflections. Furthermore, in retrospective, our interaction partners are usually also capable of telling us about how certain things went, what they did and how they felt in those moments. And conversations can also tell us a lot about norms, rules and principles (see Browne 2016) which, as I will show in this book, are crucial for understanding asylum decision-making.

SEM officials reflect a lot upon the work they do. They have their own theories about what they do, why they do it and what a critical analysis of their work should be about. I learnt a great deal from those theories. Nevertheless, I believe that as anthropologists it is equally important to maintain a critical distance from these theories and interpretations and to not just unquestioningly make them our own. On the contrary, it might sometimes be more fruitful for us as researchers to look at those aspects of what we are studying that our interaction partners have no theories about; the things that are just normal and self-evident to them. However, when doing fieldwork, we also become inured to such normalities. Consequently, Cris Shore and Susan Wright claim that it is important to "maintain sufficient critical distance to be able to keep asking fundamental questions about how [our interaction partners] conceptualise their worlds and what this means for theoretical debates" (2011: 15). In my case, doing fieldwork so "close to home" helped maintain this critical distance because I never completely left my academic surroundings and also during fieldwork, I kept discussing my findings with colleagues. Furthermore, the collaborative work I did with Jonathan Miaz and Ephraim Poertner, the other two researchers working on decision-making in the SEM, also proved to be useful in this regard in that it helped me uncover some of my "blind spots". At the same time, I am sure that other blind spots remain.

References

Affolter, Laura, Jonathan Miaz, and Ephraim Poertner. 2019. "Taking the 'Just' Decision: Caseworkers and Their Communities of Interpretation in the Swiss Asylum Office." In *Asylum Determination in Europe: Ethnographic Perspectives*, edited by Nick Gill and Anthony Good, 263–284. Cham: Palgrave Macmillan.

Bloch, Maurice. 1991. "Language, Anthropology and Cognitive Science." *Man* (New Series) 26 (2): 183–198. https://www.jstor.org/stable/pdf/2803828.pdf, last accessed March 13, 2020.

Bourdieu, Pierre. 1976. *Entwurf einer Theorie der Praxis auf der ethnologischen Grundlage der kabylischen Gesellschaft*. Frankfurt am Main: Suhrkamp.

Bourdieu, Pierre. 1990. *The Logic of Practice*. Translated by Richard Nice. Stanford: Stanford University Press.

Browne, Alison L. 2016. "What Do Mixed Methods Make? Practice Theory, Qualitative and Quantiative Data." Blog Practice Theory Methodologies, April 12. https://practicetheorymethodologies.wordpress.com/2016/04/12/alison-l-browne-what-do-mixed-methods-make-practice-theory-qualitative-and-quantitative-data/, last accessed March 16, 2020.

Dahlvik, Julia. 2018. *Inside Asylum Bureaucracy: Organizing Refugee Status Determination in Austria*. IMISCOE Research Series. Cham: Springer.

Eule, Tobias G. 2014. *Inside Immigration Law: Migration Management and Policy Application in Germany*. Farnham: Ashgate.

Glaser, Barney G., and Anselm L. Strauss. 1967. *The Discovery of Grounded Theory: Strategies for Qualitative Research*. New York: Aldine Publishing Company.

Halkier, Bente, and Iben Jensen. 2011. "Methodological Challenges in Using Practice Theory in Consumption Research: Examples from a Study on Handling Nutritional Contestations of Food Consumption." *Journal of Consumer Culture* 11 (1): 101–123. https://doi.org/10.1177%2F1469540510391365.

Hammersley, Martyn, and Paul Atkinson. 1995. *Ethnography: Principles in Practice*. 2nd ed. London and New York: Routledge.

Hammersley, Martyn, and Paul Atkinson. 2007. *Ethnography: Principles in Practice*. 3rd ed. Abingdon: Routledge.

Hitchings, Russel. 2012. "People Can Talk about Their Practices." *Area* 44 (1): 61–67. https://doi.org/10.1111/j.1475-4762.2011.01060.x.

Hoag, Colin. 2011. "Assembling Partial Perspectives: Thoughts on the Anthropology of Bureaucracy." *PoLAR: Political and Legal Anthropology Review* 34 (1): 81–94. https://doi.org/10.1111/j.1555-2934.2011.01140.x.

Le Compte, Margaret D., Jean J. Schensul, Margaret R. Weeks, and Marrill Singer. 1999. *Researcher Roles and Research Partnerships: 6 Ethnographer's Toolkit*. Walnut Creek: AltaMira Press.

Lentz, Carola. 2014. "'I Take an Oath to the State, Not the Government': Career Trajectories and Professional Ethics of Ghanaian Public Servants." In *States at Work: Dynamics of African Bureaucracies*, edited by Thomas Bierschenk and Jean-Pierre Olivier de Sardan, 175–204. Leiden and Boston: Brill.

Martens, Lydia. 2012. "Practice 'in Talk' and Talk 'as Practice': Dish Washing and the Reach of Language. *Sociological Research Online* 17 (3): 103–113. https://doi.org/10.5153%2Fsro.2681.

Maynard-Moody, Steven, and Michael Musheno. 2012. "Social Equities and Inequalities in Practice: Street-Level Workers as Agents and Pragmatists." *Public Administration Review* 72 (s1): 16–23. https://doi.org/10.1111/j.1540-6210.2012.02633.x.

McDonald, Seonaidh. 2005. "Studying Actions in Context: A Qualitative Shadowing Method for Organizational Research." *Qualitative Research* 5 (4): 455–473. https://doi.org/10.1177/1468794105056923.

Mugler, Johanna. 2019. *Measuring Justice: Quantitative Accountability and the National Prosecuting Authority in South Africa.* Cambridge and New York: Cambridge University Press.

Müller, Anna-Lisa. 2017. "Does Architecture Talk Back? Researching Architecture's Agency." Blog Practice Theory Methodologies, November 24. https://practicetheorymethodologies.wordpress.com/2017/11/24/anna-lisa-mueller-does-architecture-talk-back-researching-architectures-agency/#more-878, last accessed March 16, 2020.

Reckwitz, Andreas. 2002. "Toward a Theory of Social Practices." *European Journal of Social Theory* 5 (2): 243–263. https://doi.org/10.1177%2F13684310222225432.

Reckwitz, Andreas. 2003. "Grundelemente einer Theorie sozialer Praktiken: Eine sozialtheoretische Perspektive." *Zeitschrift für Soziologie* 32 (4): 282–301.

Schatzki, Theodore R. 2002. *The Site of the Social: A Philosophical Account of the Constitution of Social Life and Change.* University Park, PA: Pennsylvania State University Press.

Shore, Cris, and Susan Wright. 2011. "Conceptualising Policy: Technologies of Governance and the Politics of Visibility." In *Policy Worlds: Anthropology and the Analysis of Contemporary Power*, edited by Cris Shore, Susan Wright, and Davide Però, 1–25. New York: Berghahn Books.

Shove, Elizabeth. 2017. "Practice Theory Methodologies Do Not Exist." Blog Practice Theory Methodologies, February 15. https://practicetheorymethodologies.wordpress.com/2017/02/15/elizabeth-shove-practice-theory-methodologies-do-not-exist/, last accessed March 17, 2020.

Shove, Elizabeth, and Mika Pantzar. 2007. "Recruitment and Reproduction: The Careers and Carriers of Digital Photography and Floorball." *Human Affairs* 17 (2): 154–167. https://doi.org/10.2478/v10023-007-0014-9.

Simpson, Bob. 2006. "'You Don't Do Fieldwork, Fieldwork Does You': Between Subjectivation and Objectivation in Anthropological Fieldwork." In *The SAGE Handbook of Fieldwork*, edited by Dick Hobbs, and Richard Wright, 125–137. London: Sage.

Sökefeld, Martin. 2006. "Interaktionspartner im Vergleich: Ali Hassan und Mohammad Abbas in Gilgit." *Ethnoscripts* 8 (2): 7–29. https://doi.org/10.5282/ubm/epub.13152.

Wagenaar, Hendrik. 2004. "'Knowing' the Rules: Administrative Work as Practice." *Public Administration Review* 64 (6): 643–656. https://doi.org/10.1111/j.1540-6210.2004.00412.x.

Wagenaar, Hendrik. 2011. *Meaning in Action: Interpretation and Dialogue in Policy Analysis*. Armonk: M.E. Sharpe.
Weber, Max. 2013 (1978). *Economy and Society*. Edited by Guenther Roth and Claus Wittich. Berkeley: University of California Press.

3

Asylum Decision-Making in Switzerland

This chapter sets the scene for the three main analytical chapters of this book by providing a brief outline of how the Swiss asylum procedure works. It introduces readers to the main elements of (Swiss) asylum law that structure SEM officials' decision-making practices and the organisation they work in. Thereby, the chapter, on the one hand, aims to bring out the particularities of the Swiss case. On the other hand, it highlights the many similarities that exist between asylum determination proceedings in Switzerland and those in other countries of the Global North, particularly in Western Europe. Given these similarities, I argue that while empirically, my research focuses on first-instance asylum decision-making in Switzerland, my analysis, nevertheless, provides insights beyond this specific case study, allowing us to gain a better understanding of asylum decision-making processes more generally.

There are five parts to this chapter. The first part discusses the main developments in Swiss asylum politics since the 1950s and contextualises them within broader global trends. One such trend and, at the same time, consequence of the changing politics, are the numerous adaptations made to asylum law and, connected to this, the proliferation of decision-making categories, which I discuss separately in the second part of this chapter. The third part shows how in the light of global trends in asylum politics, and parallel to the many changes made to Swiss asylum law, a growing—and increasingly specialised—asylum administration emerged: the SEM we know today. What this administration does and how it is organised—or, rather, how it was organised at the time of my fieldwork between 2014 and 2015—is the topic of the fourth part of this chapter. Finally, in the fifth and last part, I discuss

L. Affolter, *Asylum Matters*, Palgrave Socio-Legal Studies,
https://doi.org/10.1007/978-3-030-61512-3_3

the legal categorisations decision-making in the SEM ultimately comes down to and outline the relevant articles from Swiss asylum law which constitute the basis for these categorisations.

Asylum Politics in Switzerland and Beyond

Despite its title, giving a full overview of asylum politics in Switzerland (or globally) is not the aim of this section. That would go beyond the scope of this chapter. What I aim to do instead is to situate developments in asylum politics and decision-making practices in Switzerland since the 1950s within broader trends described in the Global North.

According to Ephraim Poertner,

> two contrasting regimes for the government of refugees exist today: collective protection regimes for people who escape wars and persecution across national borders and are commonly hosted in camps in neighbouring countries – these are typical for the global South; and individual protection regimes concerned with people seeking admission common in wealthy states of the global North. (2018: 5; see also Fassin and Kobelinsky 2012: 448)

I find this distinction useful for two reasons, first, because it reminds us of an important fact, namely that the vast majority of people seek protection in countries of the Global South. Comparatively very few people apply for asylum in Switzerland or Europe in general. Second, different terminologies are used for the people seeking protection in these regimes. As Poertner, building on Didier Fassin (2016a: 66–67), argues, in collective protection regimes "people are collectively regarded as 'refugees' because they fled their countries of origin or residence" (Poertner 2018: 5). In contrast, in individual protection regimes, people are considered as "individual 'asylum seekers' whose 'well-founded fear of persecution' has to be examined in a laborious administrative procedure before they may become 'refugees' legally" (ibid.; see also Jubany 2017: 45). Hence, the terms "refugees" and "asylum seekers" carry different, specific political meanings (see also Zetter 2007: 180). Rather than merely reflecting a difference in status, the two terms represent "a fundamental difference of recognition", as Fassin argues (2016b). Because the focus of this book is on decision-makers' perspectives, I employ the emic terminologies decision-makers themselves use to refer to the people they are dealing with. Thus, I use the terms "asylum seekers", "applicants" and "claimants", also because they fittingly describe people's positions in the legal proceedings at work in countries of the Global North. However, I do not wish to imply that I do not consider these people to be refugees in the broader sense of the term described above. To the contrary, they are all people who have fled their country of origin or of residence and are in need of protection.

As is common in the Global North, the Swiss asylum system is based on the administrative assessment of individual asylum claims. Figure 3.1, which I have taken from Ephraim Poertner's thesis "*Re-cording Lives: Governing Asylum in Switzerland and the Need to Resolve*" (2018), illustrates the number of such individual asylum applications filed in Switzerland each year between 1968 and 2017.

We can see that in the 1980s and 1990s, there was an increase of people seeking asylum in Switzerland. Simultaneously, as the red line indicates, there is a sharp decline in the number of people receiving asylum. Before the 1980s—or, more specifically, between the 1950s and 1980s—asylum was generally granted. This was mostly related to the fact that people applying for asylum had fled communist states (see D'Amato 2008: 178; Däpp 1984; Efionayi-Mäder 2003: 3–4; Haug 1984; Parini and Gianni 2005: 196–201; Piguet 2006: 87–95, 2009: 70–77). Furthermore, in addition to Switzerland's anti-communist stance in the Cold War period; the booming economy at the time (and consequently Switzerland's need for extra labour power) was also a decisive factor for this "welcome reception". Moreover, according to Heinz Däpp, there was also a strong desire at that time, for Switzerland to compensate for its restrictive refugee policy during the Second World War (1984: 212). This so-called "open arms policy" (Piguet 2006: 91) towards people fleeing communist countries continued throughout the 1980s. However,

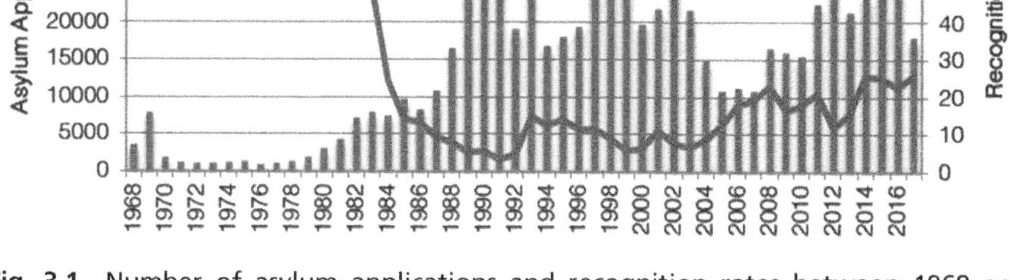

Fig. 3.1 Number of asylum applications and recognition rates between 1968 and 2017 (*Source* Poertner 2018: 5)

while this was happening, Swiss asylum policies were becoming more restrictive towards other refugees. This meant that, in 1973, following Pinochet's coup d'état, when the UNHCR urged countries to receive Chilean refugees, Switzerland reneged on its "open arms policy", because these were now the "wrong" refugees: these were leftists and communists (Meiner 2007: 119; see also D'Amato 2008: 178; Piguet 2009: 77). In the end, the Swiss government, after much pressure from leftist organisations and churches, granted protection to 255 Chilean refugees. Yet, this was a first step towards a more restrictive asylum and refugee policy which has continued ever since. In their analyses of asylum politics in Switzerland, Heinz Däpp (1984), Werner Haug (1984) and Etienne Piguet (2006) identify two main reasons for asylum policies becoming stricter at that time. Firstly, the refugees that started to arrive in the 1980s, no longer neatly fitted into the East/West divide. Secondly, the economic crisis following the 1973 oil crises led to increased unemployment and a ban on labour immigration which restricted possibilities (other than asylum) for gaining residency in Switzerland. In addition, in his detailed analysis, Jonathan Miaz (2017: 79–83) shows how the discourse on *Überfremdung* (foreign domination or infiltration) became increasingly dominant in Swiss politics in the 1970s and eventually merged with the discourse on asylum.

Very similar developments to those of Switzerland are also described for France by Didier Fassin (2016b) and Carolina Kobelinsky (2015), and for the UK and Europe in general by Olga Jubany (2017: 44–46). These authors describe an increase in the number of people applying for asylum in the 1980s with a simultaneous sharp decline in the recognition rate. In order to explain these changes, they identify the same reasons described above in the case of Switzerland: less need for labour power following the economic crisis in the 1970s and refugees no longer fitting clearly into the East/West divide. In their work, Didier Fassin and Carolina Kobelinsky thereby challenge the common interpretation that the rise of asylum applications following the closure of borders for immigration in the mid-1970s is a sign of "immigrants attempt[ing] to pass themselves off as refugees" (Fassin and Kobelinsky 2012: 449). Rather, Carolina Kobelinsky argues (in the context of France), that this interpretation

> ignores two important explanatory factors: the lifting of temporal and spatial restrictions of the Geneva Convention, and the fact that until the formal interruption of labour immigration in 1974 it was easier to obtain a work permit than refugee status. As a result, many potential applicants for refugee status under the Convention did not claim for asylum, as they already had legal residence in France. (2015: 72; see also Fassin and Kobelinsky 2012: 449)

Given that the historical accounts on asylum politics in Switzerland discussed above also describe a strong need for labour power in the 1950s and 1960s, as well as the introduction of an immigration labour ban following the economic crisis in the 1970s, it seems plausible that Kobelinsky's argument also applies to the Swiss context, at least to some extent. Switzerland ratified the 1951 Convention relating to the Status of Refugees (often referred to as the Geneva Convention) in 1955 and later also the 1967 Protocol which removed the temporal and geographical restrictions of the original Convention by extending the definition of refugeehood to encompass people fleeing from outside Europe and also due to events taking place after 1951.

Today, in the Global North, the "fight against abuse", as it is often referred to, is high on the political agenda, accompanied by a widespread discourse on so-called "false" or "bogus refugees" (see Däpp 1984: 216–219; Fassin 2007; Zimmermann 2011). Asylum seekers and migrants in general are often portrayed as a "problem" in today's political discourse and media. They are seen as a "threat" to states' economy, culture and identity (see Dahlvik 2018: 9; Gill and Good 2019: 5–6; Miaz 2017: 11–12). Furthermore, they are increasingly depicted as a "threat" to the safety of countries and their citizens, which serves to justify heightened securitisation measures such as the externalisation of border controls and the restriction of access to refugee determination procedures (see Boswell 2007: 589; Dahlvik 2018: 9; Huysmans 2000; Jubany 2017; Miaz 2017: 13–14; Stünzi 2010). Asylum determination procedures in the Global North today are, therefore, structured around a "politics of deterrence" (Poertner 2017; see also Hamlin 2014; Poertner 2018: 282–287), with no country wanting to be more generous in granting asylum and subsidiary protection than others in order not to create a so-called "pull-effect" (see Fuglerud 2004: 33; Jubany 2017: 62; Liodden 2016: 219; Miaz 2017: 15, 343; Poertner 2017: 17, 283). Indeed, in the initial training sessions for new SEM decision-makers in which I took part, on the very first day, those present were told by a trainer: "You are going to hear this often from now on: We are always afraid of the 'pull-effect'".[1]

In Switzerland, this politics of deterrence is linked to the discourse on *Überfremdung* (foreign domination or infiltration), which as Jonathan Miaz's careful analysis of asylum politics in Switzerland shows, has a long tradition in Swiss German-speaking right-wing politics. For example, the *Nationale Aktion gegen die Überfremdung von Volk und Nation* (the national action against foreign infiltration of the nation and homeland) was founded in Switzerland in 1961. The party subsequently launched several initiatives

[1]Training instructor, A-modules, field notes, my own translation.

against *Überfremdung*, aimed at laying down fixed quotas for the percentage of foreigners in Switzerland. In the 1950s and 1960s, this discourse of *Überfremdung* was mainly aimed at so-called "guest workers" from Italy and Spain, who were perceived as a threat to national identity. In contrast, asylum seekers were, at that time, perceived as victims. However, in the 1970s and 1980s different right-wing parties started transferring the discourse of *Überfremdung* onto the issue of asylum, increasingly portraying asylum seekers as a threat for Switzerland (Miaz 2017: 79–83). While the discourse of *Überfremdung* itself has not really transferred out of right-wing politics, the "fight against abuse", which is very much linked to this discourse, has since then been adopted and put on the political agenda by several "mainstream" political parties too (ibid.: 87–90). It has been the drive behind, and a legitimation for, many of the changes made to Swiss asylum law over the past forty years.

Changing Law and the Proliferation of Legal Categories

Since its introduction in 1981, the Swiss Asylum Act has been adapted more times than any other Swiss law ever has in such a short time period (Maillard and Tafelmacher 1999: 103; Piguet 2009: 84).[2] Such frequent legislative changes to asylum and migration law are not specific to Switzerland and have been described for other European countries too (see Boswell 2003; Eule 2014: 43; Eule et al. 2019: 41–42). What is, however, specific about the Swiss case is that several of the changes to Swiss asylum law were made as the result of political referenda (see Miaz 2017: 16). In addition to the "fight against abuse" and the idea of deterrence, Jonathan Miaz identifies the will to accelerate asylum procedures as a further *leitmotiv* behind the many adaptations of the Swiss Asylum Act (2017: 2). To go into all these changes in detail would go beyond the scope of this chapter, but a detailed analysis can be found in Miaz's doctoral thesis "*Politique d'asile et sophistication du droit*" (2017). In short, the general tendencies of these changes include the introduction of new reasons for rejecting asylum claims, the introduction of new evidentiary requirements as well as restrictions to the possibilities of claiming asylum in the first place and the creation of particular obstacles for appealing asylum decisions (Miaz 2017: 2). The following table shows some of these changes which best illustrate these major trends (Fig. 3.2).

[2]Substantial changes were made to the Asylum Act in 1983, 1984, 1986, 1990, 1992, 1994/1995, 1996, 1998, 1999, 2003, 2005/2006, 2008, 2012, 2014, 2015 and 2016 (see Miaz 2017: 95–96; Piguet 2006: 106; Schweizerische Flüchtlingshilfe SFH 2009: 31–38).

1984	- The asylum procedure is shortened. - In so-called "evidently unfounded cases" the procedure can be shortened by not conducting a second longer interview. - It is no longer possible to appeal asylum decisions at the Federal Tribunal.
1986	- Rejected asylum seekers can be detained up to 30 days pending deportation. - The cantons are allowed to issue a three-month working ban for asylum seekers.
1990	- Applications by people from so-called "safe countries" now lead to a "dismissal without entering into the substance of the case" (DAWES-decision.) - The Asylum Appeals Commission (*Asylrekurskommission*), an independent appeal board (which later becomes the Federal Administrative Court) is created. - The cantons are allowed to stretch the working ban for asylum seekers to six months.
1999	- If applicants do not hand in any identity papers (or render credible why they cannot), this leads to a DAWES-decision (see above).
2006	- If applicants do not hand in any identity papers within the first 48 hours of applying for asylum (or render credible why they cannot), this leads to a DAWES-decision. - The deadline for appealing DAWES-decisions is lowered from 30 to five days. - All rejected asylum seekers are no longer entitled to social welfare. They now only receive emergency aid according to article 12 of the Federal Constitution of the Swiss Confederation, which states that "Persons in need and unable to provide for themselves have the right to assistance and care, and to the financial means required for a decent standard of living".
2008	- The Schengen Agreement and Dublin Regulation comes into effect.
2012	- People who "have refused to perform military service or have deserted" and claim for asylum on these grounds are excluded from refugee status as well as people "who claim grounds based on their conduct following their departure that are neither an expression nor a continuation of a conviction already held in their native country or country of origin" (Art. 3, paragraphs 3 and 4, AsylA).

Fig. 3.2 Changes to asylum legislation between 1984 and 2012 (*Source* My own summary). The information I use here comes from Miaz (2017: 92–97) and from the SRF News website (https://www.srf.ch/news/schweiz/abstimmungen/abstimmung-vom-9-6-2013/asylgesetz/chronologie-asylrecht-sukzessive-verschaerft, last accessed 29.01.2020). The dates I refer to in the table are from when the decision to make the changes was taken (mostly by parliament or by political referendum). However, some of those changes only came into effect a year or more later

A consequence of the changes made to asylum law has been the proliferation of legal categories or labels of protection, a trend which has been described for the Global North in general (see Poertner 2018: 5; Zetter 2007). The graph below, which was created by Jonathan Miaz, nicely illustrates this for Switzerland.

The dark blue bars indicate the percentage of asylum claims being granted, while the orange bars show the proportion of rejected asylum claims. The red and green bars—the latter are only barely visible—show the percentage of so-called DAWES decisions. DAWES stands for "dismissal without entering into the substance of the case". The red bars are DAWES decisions without temporary admission, the nearly invisible green bars are DAWES decisions with temporary admission. Rejected asylum claims with temporary admission are marked in light blue. The yellow bars show the percentage of Dublin decisions. While before 1986 there were only two possible outcomes of decision-making: people were either granted asylum or their claims were rejected, we can since then observe a multiplication of legal categories. In 1986, the legal status of temporary admission was created. This came at a time of rising numbers of rejected asylum seekers who could nevertheless not be deported either under international law or for humanitarian and technical reasons (Sille 2016: 22–24). The emergence of this category fits with what Didier Fassin has called the "humanitarianization of asylum", a kind of "substitution of a right to asylum by an obligation in terms of charity" (2005: 387; see also Fassin 2012). In one of the training courses for new decision-makers that I attended, this understanding was taught to the novices in very explicit terms: "Temporary protection is not a right, but a service [*Dienstleistung*] we provide", the instructor announced.[3] Today in countries of the Global North, such forms of subsidiary protection are granted more frequently than asylum. In the Swiss case, subsidiary protection is further divided into subcategories, as I will discuss later on in this chapter. Figure 3.3 shows the emergence of DAWES decisions in 1990, when this category was newly introduced. We can see how in 1999, when the lack of identity papers was added as a reason for rejecting asylum claims without going into the substance of the case, the number of DAWES decisions significantly increased. After most reasons for taking such decisions were abolished in 2014, in turn, there is a sharp decline. In 2009, we can see the new category of "Dublin decisions" emerging after the Schengen Agreement and Dublin regulation came into effect in Switzerland in December 2008. This agreement, amongst other things, "regulates which member state is responsible for processing an application for

[3]Training instructor, A-modules, field notes, my own translation.

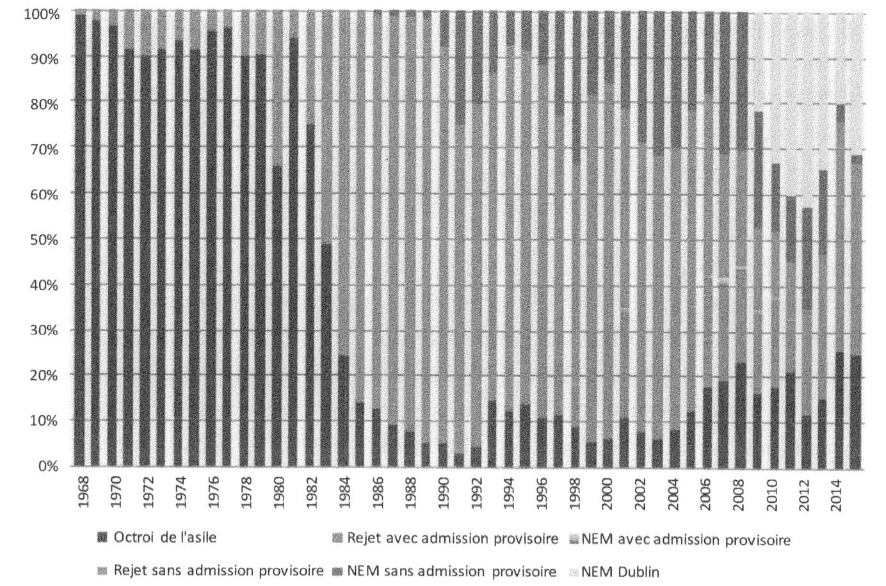

Fig. 3.3 The proliferation of legal categories and first instance asylum decisions between 1968 and 2015 (*Source* Miaz 2017: 168)

asylum": normally the first country in the so-called "Schengen/Dublin" area an applicant enters, or is registered by.[4]

This proliferation of legal categories, together with the increased complexity in asylum law and the growing numbers of asylum applications (especially in the early and late 1990s due to the wars in the Balkan region), has led to the emergence of an increasingly specialised office called the SEM, as I will go on to discuss.

The SEM: A Specialised Asylum Administration Emerges

> You know, thirty years ago this office was a mere section of the Federal Office of Police, the fedpol, just a section. And then when I started [working here] it was the Office of the Delegate for Refugees (*Amt des Delegierten für das Flüchtlingswesen*). That was more like a task force. The idea was to deal with

[4]https://www.refugeecouncil.ch/asylum-law/legal-basis/schengendublin-and-switzerland.html, last accessed 03.02.2020, see also: https://www.sem.admin.ch/sem/en/home/asyl/dublin.html, last accessed 03.02.2020.

> the asylum business and to just get it over and done with. And then [...] later it was merged with the Federal Office for Foreigners and became the Federal Office of Migration and now we're a State Secretariat. Do you see? In thirty years we have gone from being a single section to being a State Secretariat. That explains a lot of things.[5]

In this quote, SEM caseworker Peter accurately summarises the development of the office in charge of dealing with asylum applications since 1981. He shows how since 1981 the office has gone from being a small section within the Federal Office of Police (fedpol) to a State Secretariat, making its director one of the six State Secretaries in Switzerland. The first office in charge of taking asylum decisions was set up in 1981 when the first Swiss Asylum Act came into effect. At that time, the office was a mere section within the Federal Office of Police (fedpol). Being part of the fedpol, the office formed part of the Federal Department of Justice and Police (FDJP), as the SEM still does today. The FDJP is one of seven government departments in Switzerland, each of which is led by one of the seven Federal Councillors which constitute the country's executive. In 1985, the Federal Councillor then in charge of the FDJP founded a new office, the Office of the Delegate for Refugees, with the clear aim of dealing with "the refugee problem" (Kopp 1987). The idea was that this office would exist for a maximum of ten years and that by then "the problem" would be "solved" (Miaz 2017: 98). Apart from taking asylum decisions, it was the office's duty to coordinate the work of the federal government with the cantons and different NGOs working with refugees. It was also in charge of cooperating with international actors and preparing the Swiss state for possible future "problems" (Kopp 1987). By 1990, it was clear that a more long-term "solution" was needed and the Federal Office for Refugees was set up. While the Federal Office for Refugees still formed part of the FDJP, it was no longer a part of the fedpol itself. Fifteen years later, in 2005, the then responsible Federal Councillor, in an attempt to substantially reduce administrative costs, merged the Federal Office for Refugees with the Federal Office of Immigration, Integration and Emigration, which together became the Federal Office of Migration. With this merger, the Councillor's main aim was to steer Switzerland's migration politics in a more "holistic and consequent" way.[6] As can be seen in a media communiqué presented by the FDJP at the time, the merger was meant to solve the "problems that exist nowadays in the 'fields of asylum and foreigners'

[5]Peter, caseworker, headquarters, interview transcript, my own translation.

[6]https://www.sem.admin.ch/sem/de/home/aktuell/news/2004/ref_2004-06-07.html, last accessed 30.01.2020.

(*Asyl- und Ausländerbereich*) [...] in a more effective and economic way".[7] Furthermore, the communiqué states that the aim of the consolidation of the two offices was to be better able to "combat abuse", which clearly reflects the global trends described above. The merger exemplifies how asylum has increasingly become a "vector of immigration", as Carolina Kobelinsky has argued (2015: 87). Finally, on 1st January 2015, in the midst of my fieldwork, the Federal Office of Migration became a State Secretariat in order to "take account of the growing importance of the SEM's work and its expanding range of tasks".[8] A further reason for this "upgrading" was to strengthen the office director's position in international negotiations and place him on the same level as the representatives from other countries so he would better be able to represent Switzerland's interests.[9] Before the Federal Office of Migration (FOM) became the State Secretariat for Migration in 2015, there were only four State Secretaries: one responsible for foreign affairs, one for international finance issues, one for economy and one for education and research.[10] It seems noteworthy that this change came at a time when Switzerland began negotiating the issue of free movement of people (*Personenfreizügigkeit*) with the EU following the acceptance of the referendum "against mass immigration" (*Masseneinwanderungsinitiative*) by a majority of the electorate in 2014.

The institutional changes I have described so far are those which led to name changes of the first-instance asylum administration in Switzerland. In addition, there have also been several other structural reforms. For instance, in September 2013, all the asylum units at the SEM headquarters in Bern were newly put together. While before, decision-makers had worked in so-called regional teams, meaning that each unit specialised in dealing with applications from asylum seekers from specific regions, from September 2013 onwards all of the newly constituted teams were requested to deal with 'cases' from everywhere. When I started doing fieldwork in the SEM in early 2014, some of the teams had because of that only quite recently started working together. A rather substantial restructuration, furthermore, occurred in March

---

[7] https://www.sem.admin.ch/sem/de/home/aktuell/news/2004/ref_2004-06-07.html, last accessed 30.01.2020.

[8] https://www.sem.admin.ch/sem/en/home/ueberuns/sem.html, last accessed 30.01.2020.

[9] https://www.ejpd.admin.ch/ejpd/de/home/aktuell/news/2014/2014-09-191.html, last accessed 31.01.2020.

[10] In 2018, the Directorate for European Affairs was created and its director became the sixth State Secretary.

2019, thus well after I had completed my fieldwork.[11] While this last reform has led to significant changes in the administration's organisational structure and some procedural aspects have slightly changed, the core of SEM decision-makers' work has not: decision-makers still conduct asylum interviews and assess asylum seekers' eligibility to refugee status as well as their credibility, which is what this book is mainly about. The procedural and structural organisations I describe in this book reflect matters as they stood at the time of my research in 2014 and 2015. However, before turning to these descriptions, I would like to briefly highlight some of the major changes introduced by the 2019 reform.

The main aim of the 2019 reform was to accelerate the procedure for which three principal reasons were given: first, to get rejected asylum seekers to leave the country as fast as possible; second, to ensure that asylum seekers do not have to wait for years to receive their decision so that they can be more quickly "integrated into society"[12]; and third, to cut government costs.[13] Today, the new accelerated procedure lasts for a maximum of 140 days, with sixty to seventy per cent of all asylum applications being dealt with in this way. The remaining thirty to forty per cent of all asylum applications—namely, those deemed more complicated and needing more time to be examined—are assigned to the extended procedure which works more or less the same way as the "regular" procedure did at the time of my research. The accelerated procedures take place in so-called "federal centres" (*Bundeszentren*) located in six different regions in Switzerland. Apart from accommodating the asylum seekers, these centres also house SEM decision-makers and legal advisors. Asylum seekers have access to free legal advisors who accompany the former throughout the whole procedure. Before the 2019 reform, it was uncommon for asylum seekers to have legal representation during the first-instance proceedings with legal advice services being provided by different NGOs mainly at the appeal level. However, there used to be so-called "social aid representatives" (*Hilfswerksvertretungen*) present during the asylum interviews in the old procedures. These social aid representatives—whose function I will describe in more detail below—have now been replaced by the new "in-house" legal advisors. Moreover, another substantial

[11]This last reform was set in motion after it had been "accepted by two-thirds of [the] voters in a nationwide ballot in 2016" (https://www.swissinfo.ch/eng/explainer-_how-well-does-the-new-swiss-asylum-system-work--/45360318, last accessed 31.01.2020).

[12]https://www.swissinfo.ch/eng/explainer-_how-well-does-the-new-swiss-asylum-system-work--/45360318, last accessed 31.01.2020.

[13]See: https://www.swissinfo.ch/eng/explainer-_how-well-does-the-new-swiss-asylum-system-work--/45360318, last accessed 31.01.2020 and https://sem.media-flow.ch/asylverfahren-de#12, last accessed 31.01.2020.

change induced by the reform has been to drastically cut the deadline for appealing first-instance asylum decisions to the Federal Administrative Court: from thirty days down to seven days for those asylum seekers going through the accelerated procedure. For those assigned to the extended procedure, the deadline remains at thirty days.[14]

In the remaining parts of this book, I will not deal with this accelerated procedure but rather look at the "regular" procedure as it existed until early 2019. Most steps of the decision-making procedure and the legal requirements for receiving asylum have remained the same. What I describe in this book is, therefore, still relevant for understanding asylum decision-making in Switzerland today. Furthermore, the Swiss asylum decision-making procedure shares many characteristics with other initial asylum decision-making proceedings in the Global North: the proceedings are inquisitorial in design, credibility determination plays a crucial role and is based on a special standard of proof, and the legal refugee definition is based on the one from the 1951 Refugee Convention and 1967 Protocol (see Johannesson 2017: 13; Poertner 2018: 6). Hence, my analysis also contributes to understanding processes and practices of asylum decision-making more generally.

The Decision-Making Procedure

The SEM is, according to its website, "responsible for all matters covered by legislation on foreign nationals and asylum seekers in Switzerland".[15] The organisation defines its main tasks as follows:

> The SEM determines under what circumstances a person may enter Switzerland to live and work. It also decides who is granted protection from persecution. In collaboration with the cantons, the SEM organises the accommodation of asylum seekers and the return of people who do not need protection to their country of origin. It also co-ordinates the integration of foreign nationals into Switzerland, is responsible for naturalising foreigners and works actively at an international level to control migration movements.[16]

In "*Economy and Society*", Max Weber identifies both the "clearly defined hierarchy of offices" and the clear division of competences and tasks as typical

[14]See: https://www.swissinfo.ch/eng/explainer-_how-well-does-the-new-swiss-asylum-system-work--/45360318, last accessed 31.01.2020 and https://sem.media-flow.ch/asylverfahren-de#12, last accessed 31.01.2020, https://www.fluechtlingshilfe.ch/asylgesetzrevision.html, last accessed 31.01.2020.

[15]https://www.sem.admin.ch/sem/en/home/ueberuns/sem/aufgaben.html, last accessed 02.02.2020.

[16]https://www.sem.admin.ch/sem/en/home/ueberuns/sem.html, last accessed 02.02.2020.

characteristics of bureaucracy (Weber 2013 [1978]: 220). Both these features are characteristic of the SEM.

This book considers the work which is done within one of the SEM's four directorates: the asylum directorate. More specifically, I did all my fieldwork in three of this directorate's divisions: "Asylum I", "Asylum II" and "RPC". "RPC" stands for reception and processing centres, whose function I will describe in detail below. The directorate "Asylum" is the biggest directorate in the SEM and the three divisions I studied were, at the time of my research, those with the most staff. This was clearly evident when I attended a "welcome day" for new SEM employees in early 2014. There were twenty-five new employees present that day of whom twenty were destined for the asylum directorate while the other five were headed to the other three directorates.

The asylum directorate is responsible for first-instance asylum proceedings in Switzerland. It is charged with examining all asylum applications and reaching first-instance decisions. At the second instance, these decisions can then be appealed at the Federal Administrative Court. The Federal Administrative Court is the first, and simultaneously the last, appeal board in Switzerland. Negative judgements by the court cannot be appealed on a national level any further. Thereafter, the only remaining possibility is to file an appeal against Switzerland at the European Court of Human Rights.[17] The SEM's asylum directorate's duties are, to a great extent, limited to the asylum decision-making proceedings. Consequently, the provision of accommodation for asylum seekers and providing social welfare, for example, are duties which are carried out by other actors. Organisations (both profit and non-profit) are commissioned by the SEM to provide these "services" in the RPCs (or today in the *Bundeszentren*) or they are commissioned by the cantons once asylum seekers have been assigned to them. The cantons are also responsible for executing removal orders—or, to put it more bluntly, for detaining and deporting rejected asylum seekers—and for many questions concerning asylum seekers' stay (such as their right to employment).

At the time of my research, the majority of asylum applications were filed at the RPCs. Even if the RPCs have now been replaced by the *Bundeszentren* and do not exist as such anymore, I will proceed to describe the proceedings in the RPCs in the present tense for better readability. In RPCs, asylum seekers' personal data is recorded, their photos and fingerprints are taken, and a medical examination is carried out by security, medical or otherwise

[17]In some cases, asylum seekers can make use of what are called "extraordinary legal remedies" (*ausserordentliche Rechtsmittel*): a request for a revision of the judgement by the Federal Administrative Court or for a "reconsideration" (*Wiedererwägung*) of the claim by the SEM on the basis of article 66 of the Federal Act on Administration Procedure (APA).

specialised staff. Their fingerprints are then checked against the EuroDac (European Dactyloscopy) database in order to see whether the applicant has been registered in any of the other signatory states of the Schengen Agreement. On the basis of this, a case file is opened up, which is randomly assigned to a decision-maker at the RPC. Days, or sometimes weeks later, this decision-maker summons the asylum seeker to the first (short) asylum interview: the *Befragung zur Person* (the interview about the applicant's identity). Other than the decision-maker and the asylum seeker, only an interpreter may be present during these interviews. Thus, the decision-makers themselves write the minutes of the interview. In these first interviews, the asylum seekers are questioned about their personal data (e.g. family ties, education, place of residence, etc.) as well as their reasons for applying for asylum and their travel routes. Often in these interviews, decision-makers probe with a detailed "country test" to try and ascertain whether the asylum seekers "really" are from where they claim. This is because, after the first interview, the decision-maker has to assign the 'case' to one of three identity categories: A, B or C. Category A indicates that there is "valid" (*rechtsgenüglich*) proof of identity. Category B concedes that, although there is no valid proof of identity, the caseworkers have no serious doubts about the applicant's country of origin. Category C, on the other hand, indicates that caseworkers suspect the applicants' declared "country of origin" to be untrue because they question the authenticity of identity documents and/or find that the asylum seekers have "insufficient knowledge" about their "country of origin" or that there are "linguistic indicators" that the asylum seekers might be from somewhere else other than what they have said. My analysis of random case files suggests that the majority of case files are assigned to category B, or at least that was true at the time of my fieldwork. The classification of 'cases' into the category C usually leads to a so-called LINGUA report being requested before the case file is passed on to a decision-maker for taking further procedural steps. LINGUA reports are done by so-called external experts, which are contacted by the LINGUA unit of the SEM, "a specialised unit for analysis of origin". The unit's—or rather its experts'—task is to

> carry out analyses of origin for people seeking asylum and for other foreigners. [...] It is the aim of the analysis of origin to determine the country and/or region or, at least, the milieu, which have had the biggest influence on the subject in his/her process of socialization. It is for this purpose that the subject's

speech as well as his/her cultural knowledge of the region concerned are examined.[18]

In addition to assigning 'cases' to the three identity categories, after the first interview, decision-makers also have to indicate if (they think) the 'case' they are dealing with falls within the Schengen/Dublin regulation or is a so-called *GespeVer* (gender-based persecution) 'case'. All forms of violence, harm and discrimination experienced by the applicants on the basis of their gender identity and sexual orientation are considered gender-based persecution by the SEM.[19] According to Article 6 of the *Asylverordnung 1 über Verfahrensfragen* ("Regulation 1 on Asylum"), in the case of gender-based persecution, the asylum interview must be conducted by a decision-maker of the same gender as the applicant and only in the presence of people (the social aid representative, interpreter and minute-taker) of the same gender (see Art. 6, AsylV1).

All these assessments—what identity category a 'case' is assigned to and whether it is a *GespeVer* or Dublin 'case' or not—impact upon where the case file is next sent and how it is dealt with further. This first "triage", as it is called, falls within the jurisdiction of the heads of the different units at the RPCs. They decide whether the file is sent to the headquarters, stays at the RPC or goes to the Dublin unit. Exactly which 'cases' are kept at the RPCs and which are sent to the headquarters remained a slight puzzle to me throughout my fieldwork. Mostly, this was because my interaction partners—including the heads—were often confused themselves about the current practice, which they told me kept changing. The heads at the RPCs triage the files according to a list which states for each "country of origin" whether the case file has to be sent to the headquarters or not. On the lists, the countries are classified into different "priority categories". When I first started doing research in the SEM, there were three such "priority categories".[20] "Priority 1" were countries, to which applicants could ('easily') be deported back. In turn, countries were classified as "priority 2" if deportations were possible but complicated and costly (*aufwändig*). "Priority 3" countries were those to which deportations were not possible, and only so-called "voluntary returns" (see Loher 2020) could be affected. Decision-makers at the reception centres mostly dealt with "priority 1 cases", while the 'cases'

[18]https://www.sem.admin.ch/sem/en/home/publiservice/service/sprachanalysen/lingua.html, last accessed 02.02.2020.

[19]See SEM manual "*Asyl und Rückkehr*", article D2, https://www.sem.admin.ch/dam/data/sem/asyl/verfahren/hb/d/hb-d2-d.pdf, last accessed 02.02.2020.

[20]See also Ephraim Poertner (2018: 172–173, 283–284) for a discussion of the priority categories in the SEM.

assigned to the other two categories were sent to the headquarters. Later on during my research the situation changed, with the three "priority categories" being reduced to two categories. "Prio 1 cases" then became those 'cases' that would most likely be decided negatively (e.g. claims by applicants from countries with very low recognition rates, claims by applicants coming from so-called "safe countries" or through a "Dublin country", claims by applicants who have committed a crime, etc.), while all others became "second priority cases". With "prio 1 cases", the decision-makers were requested to work according to the principle "last in, first out". With second priority 'cases', in turn, the guiding principle was "first in, first out". Ephraim Poertner has argued that these principles function as measures of deterrence. Thus, "for the first group of claimants, deterrence is considered to work best with a prompt negative decision and a threat of expulsion [...]. And for the second group of claimants, who are likely to receive protection, deterrence works through the suspension of benefits until asylum is finally granted" (2017: 19).

During my research, it seemed that many of the "prio 1 cases" remained at the RPCs to be dealt with while a large proportion of the other priority categories were sent to the headquarters. However, as officials, both at the headquarters and at the RPCs, told me repeatedly, this division was not as strict as it had formerly been, leading to "everyone doing everything". Nevertheless, my impression was that 'cases' submitted by applicants from countries where fewer asylum seekers come from were often sent to the headquarters as well as 'cases' which were deemed to be "very complex" and "time-consuming".

Once the files are assigned to a specific section, either at the headquarters or the RPCs, it is up to the head of this section to allocate the 'cases' to one of their employees or to send them to the archives for a while. Some cases, instead of going directly to a decision-maker, are first given to a so-called "pooly". The name "pooly" derives from the fact that these people belong to a pool of interviewers who only conduct asylum interviews but do not take any decisions. "Poolies" do not belong to the SEM's regular staff, but are rather paid by the hour to conduct asylum interviews. Like decision-makers, "poolies" carry out the second longer asylum interviews—which may take place weeks, months or, in some cases, even years after the first short interview. In these interviews, the decision-makers or "poolies" interrogate the asylum seekers in detail about their reasons for fleeing and for applying for asylum in Switzerland. In rare cases, a third supplementary interview is carried out. A minute-taker and a social aid representative join the decision-maker (or "pooly"), the asylum seeker and the interpreter in the longer second and third interviews. As the job title indicates, social aid representatives work for different NGOs active in the field of asylum. Their job is to "observe the procedure from a neutral perspective". Furthermore, they can "have the SEM [officials] ask the asylum seekers about certain issues or pose the questions themselves, express objections and urge additional clarifications".[21] At the end of the interview, they fill in a form, which is stapled to the minutes of the interview and goes in the case file. On the forms they can note any particular observations they made during the interview, suggest further investigations (e.g. a medical examination), and state any objections they might have to the minutes. Finally, they write a report for the organisation they work for and for the Swiss Refugee Council (*Schweizerische Flüchtlingshilfe*) which is the umbrella organisation of all refugee organisations in Switzerland, coordinating social aid representatives' work in the asylum procedures. On these forms, the social aid representatives must, amongst other things, assess the 'case' (and indicate if they think it was credible or not and predict whether it will probably lead to asylum or not). These forms are sometimes used by lawyers and legal advisors when filing an appeal against a negative decision with the Federal Administrative Court. At the end of the second and sometimes third asylum interviews, the minutes are read back to the asylum seeker by the interpreter. The asylum seeker has to sign every page in order to prove the veracity of the recorded statements. The signed minutes, together with the report form from the social aid representative and any material evidence the applicant might have handed in, are then included in the case file, which normally remains with the same caseworker or, in the case of a "pooly-interview", is passed on to the official responsible for taking the decision. During the process of taking the written decision, caseworkers might undertake further investigations with the Swiss embassies in the applicants' countries of origin, have documents tested for their authenticity, order a LINGUA report or a wrist bone analysis (the latter is done in order to find out whether the applicant is "really" a minor)[22] or consult a "country analyst", for instance.[23] Once the caseworker has made the decision, it must be checked and double-signed by the head of the section or their proxy before it is sent by post to the asylum seeker or their legal representative. The SEM official's involvement is then usually over except in case of an appeal. In case of an appeal, the FAC invites the SEM (through the official in charge of the 'case') to hand in an official statement concerning the

[21] https://www.refugeecouncil.ch/asylum-law/asylum-procedure-until-march-2019/social-aid-representation.html, last accessed 02.02.2020.

[22] For a description of this method, see Andreas Schmeling et al. (2003: 164).

[23] These kinds of investigations are discussed in more detail in Chapter 4.

SEM's stance on the applicant's reasons for appeal. If the SEM's original decision is upheld by the court or if the decision is not appealed against in the first place (e.g. because it is a positive decision, the deadline for appeal is too short or the applicants do not find a legal advisor willing to help and/or represent them), the decision obtains legal force (*Rechtskraft*). If asylum or temporary protection is granted, the responsibility is primarily passed on to the cantons. In case of a negative decision without temporary protection, the directorate of "International Cooperation" (a different directorate of the SEM) becomes responsible for organising the "return" of the rejected applicants and the cantons become responsible for organising the deportations.

From the above description, we can see that asylum determination in the SEM fits an inquisitorial style of decision-making, one of two main types of decision-making which Mirjan Damaška distinguishes, the other one being adversarial decision-making (1986: 3). Rebecca Hamlin contrasts the two styles as follows:

> The adversarial style takes the shape of a triad: two disputants arguing their respective cases before a passive judge, who must resolve the dispute by deciding which case is more persuasive [...] Unlike this courtroom-like setting, inquisitorial hearings are designed to be nonadversarial and nonlegalistic, taking the form of a dyad between the person whose fate is to be decided and the person deciding it. The inquisitorial decision maker engages in a conversation with the parties, and the facts must be discovered through a collaborative process of research and questioning. (2014: 18)

The inquisitorial style appears to be common for the initial stages in most asylum determination procedures in the Global North (see Hamlin 2014; Johannesson 2017: 13). Second-instance proceedings, in turn, tend to be more adversarial. In Switzerland, on appeal level, the appellant and the SEM both submit their opinions or "versions of the story" (Hamlin 2014: 18) in writing to the Federal Administrative Court, with the whole proceedings from then on taking place via written documents and briefs. While in theory the judges at the Federal Administrative Court would have the possibility to conduct court hearings, in practice this is not done. Instead, the judges sometimes send out written questionnaires to the appellants, but, mostly, their work consists of analysing the documents handed in at appeal level as well as those from the first-instance proceedings, including the minutes from the asylum interviews. Furthermore, they sometimes also request information or ask for assessments from the in-house "country analysts". Hence, in this regard, their role to some extent also remains inquisitorial.

Robert Kagan suggests an additional way of distinguishing between different models of decision-making, namely according to how "formal" or "informal" they are and whether they are organised in a more "hierarchical and centralised" or "fragmented and participatory" way, the latter referring to "multiple disputing parties" participating in the proceedings (Hamlin 2014: 19; see Kagan 2001: 9–10). By "informal" he means that decision-making is mainly "based on discretion and case-by-case considerations" while "formal" decision-making is "based on legal rules and precedents" (Hamlin 2014: 19; see Kagan 2001: 9–10). Apart from being clearly inquisitorial, I would argue that asylum decision-making in the SEM tends more towards being "formal" as well as "hierarchical and centralised", which Robert Kagan refers to as "bureaucratic legalism" (2001: 10). Rules, institutional guidelines—or "secondary application norms", as Jonathan Miaz calls them (2017: 291–297)—as well as precedents set by the Federal Administrative Court significantly guide SEM decision-makers' everyday practices. However, at the same time, decision-making in the SEM is also to some extent what Kagan calls "informal": officials deal with asylum applications on a case-by-case basis, actively investigating the 'cases' they are dealing with, selecting which rules to apply in particular situations and interpreting those rules in the course of their application. With its centralised organisation that is then segmented into "decentralised branch-offices" (Schneider 2019: 288) and rather clear-cut institutional hierarchies, the SEM, furthermore, seems to closely resemble first-instance asylum organisations in other Western European civil law countries, such as the *Bundesamt für Fremdenwesen und Asyl* in Austria (see Dahlvik 2018), the *Bundesamt für Migration und Flüchtlinge* in Germany (see Probst 2012; Schneider 2019) or the *Office Français de Protection des Réfugiés et Apatrides* in France (Probst 2012).

The Swiss Asylum Act

Decision-making in the SEM ultimately comes down to assigning asylum claimants to one of four legal categories, each of which is attached to a set of rights and obligations. As Fig. 3.4 shows, these categories are: refugee with asylum, refugee with temporary admission, non-refugee with temporary admission (mostly on the basis of so-called "humanitarian grounds") and non-refugee without temporary admission.

In order to assign asylum seekers to one of the four categories a sequence of yes or no questions must be answered by the decision-makers. The two main eligibility questions decision-makers deal with are: Are applicants eligible to

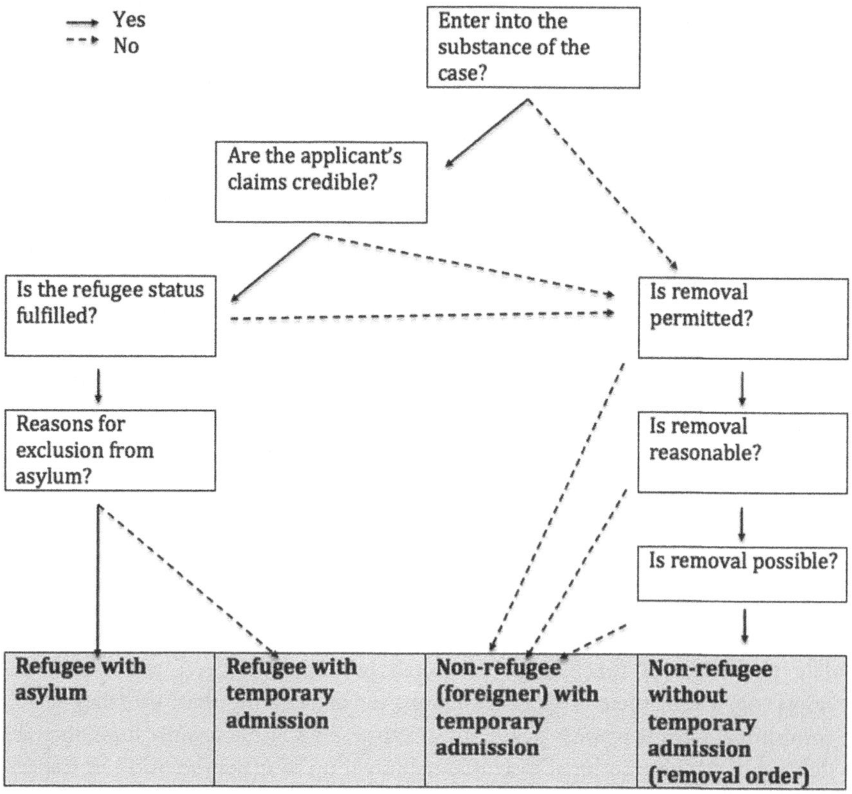

Fig. 3.4 Flowchart of asylum decision-making based on the Swiss Asylum Act (*Source* Own diagram). This diagram is my synthesis of flowcharts I received in three separate training modules that I attended in the SEM

asylum and, if not, are they eligible to temporary protection? Both these eligibilities are enshrined in the Swiss Asylum Act (AsylA). In order to receive asylum, asylum seekers must be recognised as refugees. Drawing on the 1951 Refugee Convention, refugees in the Swiss Asylum Act are defined as "persons who in their native country or in their country of last residence are subject to serious disadvantages or have a well-founded fear of being exposed to such disadvantages for reasons of race, religion, nationality, membership of a particular social group or due to their political opinions" (Art. 3, paragraph 1, AsylA). Article 3 AsylA, furthermore, elaborates on what is included in "serious disadvantages": namely "a threat to life, physical integrity or freedom as well as measures that exert intolerable psychological pressure" (Art. 3, paragraph 2, AsylA). In addition, it notes that "[m]otives for seeking asylum specific to women must be taken into account" (ibid.). In 2012, following a public referendum, the refugee category was made more restrictive by excluding certain groups of people from it. For this purpose, two new paragraphs were added to Article 3 of the Asylum Act. Paragraph 3 now states that "[p]ersons who are subject to serious disadvantages or have a well-founded fear of being exposed to such disadvantages because they have refused to perform military service or have deserted are not refugees" (Art. 3, paragraph 3, AsylA). And paragraph 4 lays down that "[p]ersons who claim grounds based on their conduct following their departure that are neither an expression nor a continuation of a conviction already held in their native country or country of origin are not refugees" (Art. 3, paragraph 4, AsylA). These restrictions mainly came about as a reaction to applications from Eritreans seeking protection after having deserted from the military and, thus, having fled from probable life-long service, and as a reaction to people claiming asylum on the basis of persecution due to their conversion to Christianity, for example.

In Fig. 3.4, we can see that in some cases, while people are recognised as refugees, they are, nevertheless, excluded from asylum. This is, on the one hand, done on the basis of Article 1F of the 1951 Refugee Convention which states that

> The provisions of this Convention shall not apply to [...] person[s] with respect to whom there are serious reasons for considering that: (a) [they have] committed a crime against peace, a war crime, or a crime against humanity, as defined in the international instruments drawn up to make provision in respect of such crimes; (b) [they have] committed a serious non-political crime outside the country of refuge prior to his admission to that country as a refugee; (c) [they have] been guilty of acts contrary to the purposes and principles of the United Nations. (Article 1F, 1951 Convention relating to the Status of Refugees)

On the other hand, the Swiss Asylum Act itself sets out reasons for excluding refugees from asylum. Thus, Article 53 determines that "[r]efugees shall not be granted asylum if: a. they are unworthy of it due to serious misconduct; b. they have violated or endangered Switzerland's internal or external security" (Art. 53, AsylA) and Article 54 states that "[r]efugees shall not be granted asylum if they became refugees in accordance with Article 3 only by leaving their native country or country of origin or due to their conduct after their departure" (Art. 54, AsylA).

A major precondition for being recognised as a refugee and receiving asylum is that applicants "prove or at least credibly demonstrate their refugee status" (Art. 7, paragraph 1, AsylA). Article 7 stipulates that one's "[r]efugee status is credibly demonstrated if the authority regards it as proven on the balance of probabilities [and that] [c]ases are not credible in particular if they are unfounded in essential points or are inherently contradictory, do not correspond to the facts or are substantially based on forged or falsified evidence" (Art. 7, paragraphs 2 and 3, AsylA). "On the balance of probabilities" seems to be a comparatively high standard of proof in asylum proceedings compared to that of other countries and the standard set by international law which 'merely' demands "a reasonable degree of likelihood" (see Good 2015; Kelly 2012; Sweeney 2009). Commonly, "on the balance of probabilities" is the standard of proof in civil law proceedings, and not in asylum procedures (see Kelly 2012: 764). Whether this is a translation problem – since English is not an official language of the Swiss Confederation – or whether the standard of proof is, at least in formal terms, indeed higher in Switzerland than in other countries is not possible for me to determine with certainty, but may be an important issue to be addressed by legal scholarship. In any case, being credible is "different both from 'being proven' and from 'being true'" (Sweeney 2009: 711). Claimants' eligibility to refugee status does not have to be "proven beyond reasonable doubt" and is not "immediately susceptible to positivistic proof" (Kelly 2012: 759, 264; see also Kelly 2011: 194). Hence, material evidence and witnesses that corroborate the ill treatment of asylum seekers are not a necessary requirement for being granted asylum (see Good 2011: 94).[24]

If asylum seekers are regarded as not being eligible to asylum, for instance because the claims are deemed non-credible, the caseworkers must decide whether the applicant should receive temporary admission on the basis of Article 83 of the Federal Act on Foreign Nationals (FNA). Temporary admission is granted to applicants "[i]f the enforcement of removal is not permitted [under international law],[25] not reasonable [for humanitarian reasons][26] or not possible [for 'technical' reasons]"[27] (Art. 83, paragraph 1, FNA). If any of these questions are answered with yes, the applicant is granted subsidiary protection. If the answer to all these questions is no, applicants receive a letter

[24]See also Anthony Good (2003: 4), Walter Kälin (1990: 299), Cécile Rousseau et al. (2002: 44) as well as the SEM "Asylum and Return Compendium": https://www.sem.admin.ch/dam/data/sem/asyl/verfahren/hb/b/hb-b3-d.pdf, last accessed 10.02.2020.

[25]"Enforcement is not permitted if Switzerland's obligations under international law prevent the foreign national from making an onward journey to their native country, to their country of origin or to a third country" (Art. 83, paragraph 3, FNA). The relevant international treaties this refers to are the European Convention on Human Rights, the United Nations Conventions relating to the Status of Refugees and the United Nations Convention on the Rights of the Child.

[26]"Enforcement may be unreasonable for foreign nationals if they are specifically endangered by situations such as war, civil war, general violence and medical emergency in their native country or country of origin" (Art. 83, paragraph 4, FNA).

[27]"Enforcement is not possible if the foreign national is unable to travel or be brought either to their native country or to their country of origin or a third country" (Art. 82, paragraph 2, FNA).

informing them that they must leave Switzerland within a certain amount of time. With such "removal orders", the responsibility for the 'case' is passed on to another directorate of the SEM, that of "International Cooperation", and to the cantonal authorities who must decide whether to detain or to deport the people whose asylum applications have been rejected, and hence organise these actions. Thus, this no longer falls within the responsibility of asylum decision-makers.

References

Asylum Act, (AsylA), of 26 June 1998 (Status as of 1 January 2020). 142.31.

Asylverordnung 1 über Verfahrensfragen, (Asylverordnung 1, AsylV 1), of 11 August 1999 (Status as of 1 January 2020). 142.311.

Boswell, Christina. 2003. *European Migration Policies in Flux: Changing Patterns of Inclusion and Exclusion*. London: Wiley-Blackwell.

Boswell, Christina. 2007. "Migration Control in Europe After 9/11: Explaining the Absence of Securitization." *Journal of Common Market Studies* 45 (3): 589–610. https://doi.org/10.1111/j.1468-5965.2007.00722.x.

Convention on the Rights of the Child, adopted on 20 November 1989. https://www.ohchr.org/en/professionalinterest/pages/crc.aspx, last accessed February 10, 2020.

Convention relating to the Status of Refugees, adopted on 28 July 1951. https://www.ohchr.org/en/professionalinterest/pages/statusofrefugees.aspx, last accessed February 10, 2020.

Dahlvik, Julia. 2018. *Inside Asylum Bureaucracy: Organizing Refugee Status Determination in Austria*. IMISCOE Research Series. Cham: Springer.

Damaška, Mirjan R. 1986. *The Faces of Justice and State Authority*. New Haven: Yale University Press.

D'Amato, Gianni. 2008. "Une revue historique et sociologique des migrations en Suisse." *Annuaire Suisse de politique de développement* 27 (2): 169–187. http://journals.openedition.org/aspd/511, last accessed February 10, 2020.

Däpp, Heinz. 1984. "Bankrott einer staatspolitischen Maxime." In *Asylpolitik gegen Flüchtlinge*, edited by Heinz Däpp, and Rudolf Karlen, 211–226. Basel: Lenos.

Efionayi-Mäder, Denise. 2003. Asylpolitik der Schweiz 1950–2000. *ASYL* 2/03: 3-9.

Eule, Tobias G. 2014. *Inside Immigration Law: Migration Management and Policy Application in Germany*. Farnham: Ashgate.

Eule, Tobias G., Lisa Marie Borrelli, Annika Lindberg, and Anna Wyss. 2019. *Migrants Before the Law: Contested Migration Control in Europe*. Cham: Palgrave Macmillan.

European Convention on Human Rights. https://www.echr.coe.int/Documents/Convention_ENG.pdf, last accessed February 10, 2020.

Fassin, Didier. 2005. "Compassion and Repression: The Moral Economy of Immigration Policies in France." *Cultural Anthropology* 20 (3): 362–387. https://doi.org/10.1525/can.2005.20.3.362.
Fassin, Didier. 2007. "Humanitarianism as a Politics of Life." *Public Culture* 19 (3): 499–520. https://doi.org/10.1215/08992363-2007-007.
Fassin, Didier. 2012. *Humanitarian Reason: A Moral History of the Present.* Berkeley: University of California Press.
Fassin, Didier. 2016a. "Vom Rechtsanspruch zum Gunsterweis. Zur moralischen Ökonomie der Asylvergabepraxis im heutigen Europa." Translated by Frank Jakubzik. *Mittelweg 36* 1: 62–78.
Fassin, Didier. 2016b. "From Right to Favor: The Refugee Question as Moral Crisis." *The Nation.* https://www.thenation.com/article/from-right-to-favor/, last accessed February 11, 2020.
Fassin, Didier, and Carolina Kobelinsky. 2012. "How Asylum Claims Are Adjudicated: The Institution as a Moral Agent." *Revue française de sociologie* 53 (4): 444–472. https://doi.org/10.3917/rfs.534.0657.
Federal Act on Administrative Procedure, (Administrative Procedure Act APA), of 20 December 1968 (Status as of 1 April 2019). 172.021.
Federal Act on Foreign Nationals, (Foreign Nationals Act, FNA), of 16 December 2005 (Status as of 1 December 2019). 142.20.
Fuglerud, Oivind. 2004. "Constructing Exclusion: The Micro-Sociology of an Immigration Department." *Social Anthropology* 12 (1): 25–40. https://doi.org/10.1111/j.1469-8676.2004.tb00088.x.
Gill, Nick, and Anthony Good. 2019. "Introduction." In *Asylum Determination in Europe: Ethnographic Perspectives*, edited by Nick Gill, and Anthony Good, 1–26. Cham: Palgrave Macmillan.
Good, Anthony. 2003. "Anthropologists as Experts: Asylum Appeals in British Courts." *Anthropology Today* 19 (5): 3–7. https://doi.org/10.1111/1467-8322.00215.
Good, Anthony. 2011. "Witness Statement and Credibility Assessments in the British Asylum Courts." In *Cultural Expertise and Litigation*, edited by Livia Holden, 94–122. Abingdon, New York: Routledge.
Good, Anthony. 2015. "'The Benefit of the Doubt' in British Asylum Claims and International Cricket." In *Of Doubt and Proof: Ritual and Legal Practices of Judgement*, edited by Daniela Berti, Anthony Good, and Gilles Tarabout, 119–140. London: Routledge.
Hamlin, Rebecca. 2014. *Let Me Be a Refugee: Administrative Justice and the Politics of Asylum in the United States, Canada, and Australia.* Oxford: Oxford University Press.
Haug, Werner. 1984. "Asylpolitik im historischen Rückblick." In *Asylpolitik gegen Flüchtlinge*, edited by Heinz Däpp, and Rudolf Karlen, 127–175. Basel: Lenos.
Huysmans, Jef. 2000. "The European Union and the Securitization of Migration." *Journal of Common Marked Studies* 38 (5): 751–777. https://doi.org/10.1111/1468-5965.00263.

Johannesson, Livia. 2017. *In Courts We Trust: Administrative Justice in Swedish Migration Courts*. Stockholm University. http://www.diva-portal.org/smash/get/diva2:1072557/FULLTEXT01.pdf, last accessed February 3, 2020.
Jubany, Olga. 2017. *Screening Asylum in a Culture of Disbelief: Truths, Denials and Sceptical Borders*. Cham: Palgrave Macmillan.
Kagan, Robert. 2001. *Adversarial Legalism: The American Way of Law*. Cambridge: Harvard University Press.
Kälin, Walter 1990: *Grundriss des Asylverfahrens*. Basel: Helbing & Lichtenhahn.
Kelly, Tobias. 2011. "The Legalization of Human Rights and the Protection of Torture Survivors: Asylum, Evidence and Disbelief." In *Are Human Rights for Migrants? Critical Reflections on the Status of Irregular Migrants in Europe and the United States*, edited by Marie-Bénédicte Dembour, and Tobias Kelly, 1–22. New York: Routledge.
Kelly, Tobias. 2012. "Sympathy and Suspicion: Torture, Asylum, and Humanity." *Journal of the Royal Anthropological Institute* 18 (4): 753–768. https://doi.org/10.1111/j.1467-9655.2012.01790.x.
Kobelinsky, Carolina. 2015. "In Search of Truth: How Asylum Applications Are Adjudicated." In *At the Heart of the State: The Moral World of Institutions*, edited by Didier Fassin, 67–92. London: Pluto Press.
Kopp, Elisabeth. 1987. "Die Schweiz im weltweiten Flüchtlingsproblem." In *Zeit der Flüchtlinge*, edited by Urs Gfeller, 109–124. Zürich: Edition M.
Liodden, Tone Maia. 2016. "The Burdens of Discretion: Managing Uncertainty in the Asylum Bureaucracy." PhD diss. (unpublished), University of Oslo.
Loher, David. 2020. "Governing the Boundaries of the Commonwealth: The Case of So-Called Assisted Voluntary Return Migration." In *The Bureaucratic Production of Difference*, edited by Julia Eckert, 113–134. Bielefeld: transcript.
Maillard, Alain, and Christophe Tafelmacher. 1999. *"Faux réfugiés"? La politique Suisse de dissauasion d'asile, 1979–1999*. Lausanne: Editions d'en bas.
Meiner, Beat. 2007. "Asyl im Würgegriff der Politik: Aktuelle Probleme der Flüchtlingshilfe." In *Verdrängung, Verklärung, Verantwortung: Schweizerische Flüchtlingspolitik in der Kriegs- und Nachkriegszeit 1940–2007*, edited by Helena Kanyar Becker, 119–122. Basel: Universitätsbibliothek Basel.
Miaz, Jonathan. 2017. "Politique d'asile et sophistication du droit: Pratiques administratives et défense juridique des migrants en Suisse (1981–2015)." PhD diss. (unpublished), University of Lausanne and University of Strasbourg.
Parini, Lorena, and Matteo Gianni. 2005. "Enjeux et modifications de la politique d'asile en Suisse de 1956 à nos jours." In *Histoire de la politique de migration, d'asile et d'intégration en Suisse depuis 1948*, edited by Hans Mahnig, 189–252. Zurich: Editions Seismo.
Piguet, Etienne. 2006. *Einwanderungsland Schweiz: Fünf Jahrzehnte halb geöffnete Grenzen*. Bern: Haupt.

Piguet, Etienne. 2009. *L'immigration en Suisse. Soixante ans d'entrouverture.* Lausanne: Presses polytechniques et universitaires romandes.
Poertner, Ephraim. 2017. "Governing Asylum through Configurations of Productivity and Deterrence: Effects on the Spatiotemporal Trajectories of Cases in Switzerland." *Geoforum* 78: 12–21. https://doi.org/10.1016/j.geoforum.2016.11.004.
Poertner, Ephraim. 2018. "Re-cording Lives: Governing Asylum in Switzerland and the Need to Resolve." PhD diss. (unpublished), University of Zurich.
Probst, Johanna. 2012. *Instruire la demande d'asile: étude comparative du processus décisionnel au sein de l'administration allemande et française.* Science politique, Université de Strasbourg. https://tel.archives-ouvertes.fr/tel-00985215/document, last accessed February 03, 2020.
Rousseau, Cécile, François Crépeau, Patricia Foxen, and France Houle. 2002. "The Complexity of Determining Refugeehood: A Multidisciplinary Analysis of the Decision-making Process of the Canadian Immigration and Refugee Board." *Journal of Refugee Studies* 15 (1): 43–70. https://doi.org/10.1093/jrs/15.1.43.
Schmeling, Andreas, Andreas Olze, Walter Reisinger, Friedrich W. Rösing, and Gunther Geserick. 2003. "Forensic Age Diagnostics of Living Individuals in Criminal Proceedings." *HOMO—Journal of Comparative Human Biology* 54 (2): 162–169. https://doi.org/10.1078/0018-442X-00066.
Schneider, Stephanie. 2019. "Becoming a Decision-Maker, or: 'Don't Turn Your Heart into a Den of Thieves and Murderers'." In *Asylum Determination in Europe: Ethnographic Perspectives*, edited by Nick Gill, and Anthony Good, 285–305. Cham: Palgrave Macmillan.
Schweizerische Flüchtlingshilfe SFH, ed. 2009. *Handbuch zum Asyl- und Wegweisungsverfahren.* Bern: Haupt.
Sille, Irina. 2016. "Die Konstruktion der vorläufigen Aufnahme im Asyl- und Ausländergesetz: Eine Analyse des Gesetzgebungsdiskurses zwischen 1985 und 2012." Master thesis. Neuchâtel: Université de Neuchâtel, Faculté des lettres et sciences humaines. http://doc.rero.ch/record/277779/files/Sille_Irina_-_Die_Konstruktion_der_vorl_ufigen_Aufhnahme_UNINE_MEMOIRE_2016.pdf, last accessed February 10, 2020.
Stünzi, Robin. 2010. "La migration, une menace? Contexte et enjeux autour de la 'sécuritisation' de la migration." *Tangram* 26: 97–101.
Sweeney, James A. 2009. "Credibility, Proof and Refugee Law." *International Journal of Refugee Law* 21 (4): 700–726. https://doi.org/10.1093/ijrl/eep027.
UNHCR. 1992. *Handbook on Procedures and Criteria for Determining Refugee Status under the 1951 Convention and the 1967 Protocol Relating to the Status of Refugees.* Geneva: United Nations High Commissioner for Refugees.
Weber, Max. 2013 (1978). *Economy and Society.* Edited by Guenther Roth, and Claus Wittich. Berkeley: University of California Press.

Zetter, Roger. 2007. "More Labels, Fewer Refugees: Remaking the Refugee Label in an Era of Globalization." *Journal of Refugee Studies* 20 (2): 172–192. https://doi.org/10.1093/jrs/fem011.

Zimmermann, Susan E. 2011. "Reconsidering the Problem of 'Bogus' Refugees with 'Socio-economic Motivations' for Seeking Asylum." *Mobilities* 6: 335–352. https://doi.org/10.1080/17450101.2011.590034.

4

Knowledge as Practice: Producing Decisional Certainty

> Over lunch Julie tells me that she still really struggles with assessing the credibility of asylum claims. She has only started working in the SEM a couple of weeks ago and so far, finds credibility determination the most difficult part of her job. "I keep having doubts", she tells me. She knows that stories 'only' have to be "predominantly credible" to fulfil the requirements, but she finds this incredibly difficult to assess. She explains that, at the moment, she is luckily only dealing with asylum applications by Eritreans and they "anyway always receive temporary admission [on humanitarian grounds] or temporary admission as refugees. So, either way they are in safety". But in other cases assessing credibility "must be so much more difficult", she fears.[1]

Julie's statements are characteristic for what new decision-makers experience on the job. Many told me that they found reaching final decisions very difficult, especially regarding the assessment of asylum seeker's credibility—or, more precisely, the credibility of asylum seekers' statements.[2] Julie's statement hints at one important reason for this: Asylum caseworkers' decisions have very serious consequences for asylum seekers' lives. In case of a "wrong decision", asylum seekers may experience further traumatisation, be imprisoned, tortured or even killed, a fact that decision-makers are well aware of. This creates a high emotional burden for decision-makers,

---

[1] Julie, caseworker, headquarters, field notes, my own translation.

[2] In German, a distinction is made between "*glaubwürdig*" and "*glaubhaft*" which in English both translate as "credible". "*Glaubwürdig*" refers to the credibility of a person whereas "*glaubaft*" relates to the credibility of statements. In the Swiss asylum procedure, the focus is explicitly on "*Glaubhaftigkeit*" and not on "*Glaubwürdigkeit*". However, in practice these evaluations intersect and the words were often interchangeably used in the office.

L. Affolter, *Asylum Matters*, Palgrave Socio-Legal Studies,
https://doi.org/10.1007/978-3-030-61512-3_4

making it important for them to reach as much certainty as possible that—to the best of their knowledge—they are taking "the right decision" (see Liodden 2016: 235, 277; Sweeney 2007: 31). This emotional burden is not something that goes away, however, as I will show in this and the following chapter, credibility assessment is something that becomes easier over time, with decision-makers gaining experience and professional-practical knowledge.

That Julie finds credibility assessment so difficult, moreover, has to do with the "fundamental unknowability" (Poertner 2018: 218) inherent in asylum decision-making or what Tobias Kelly (2012) calls "known unknowns". The term stands for the things decision-makers are aware of that they can never truly know but which, nevertheless, play a crucial role in decision-making. In asylum decision-making, I identify four such major "known unknowns". In order to be recognised as refugees, applicants must have been persecuted (or—in the words of Article 3 AsylA—have been subject to serious disadvantages) in the past or have a "well-found fear" of being persecuted in the future. The first "known unknown" therein is that decision-makers can never know for sure what will happen to an applicant in the future, of which they are well aware. Assessing the probability of future persecution and, connected to this, the well-founded-ness of fear of future persecution is, therefore, highly challenging for decision-makers. A second "known unknown" is that decision-makers realise they cannot know for sure what "really happened" to the applicant in the past (see Poertner 2018: 218). The fact that they do not and cannot know this is mostly put down to the particular standard of proof in asylum procedures (see Chapter 3). Since credibility assessments are mainly done on the basis of applicants' statements, decision-makers know that there is always the possibility that applicants could lie—this is something they themselves would probably do, I was often told (see also Kelly 2012). The third "known unknown" is that decision-makers are conscious that they can never—and are also not required to—know for sure whether what the asylum seekers are telling them is "the truth" or not. According to Article 7 of the Asylum Act, the veracity of a story must "just" be probable, that is what credibility means. Many decision-makers told me that, in theory, this meant that a claim must be regarded as 51 per cent probable in order to be deemed credible, which again leaves a lot of room for uncertainty. The fourth "known unknown" in this is that decision-makers are aware of the fact that one can never really know what it means for something to be 51 per cent probable because it is not something that can be measured in numerical terms. Nevertheless, despite these uncertainties, as is characteristic of legal categorisations, asylum decision-makers must in the end reach clear-cut either/or decisions: asylum applicants must either be recognised as refugees and be granted asylum or not, or they must be granted subsidiary protection or not. Hence, as Tobias Kelly claims, a "forced migrant" cannot be "half a refugee" just like a "convict is not a little bit guilty [and] a couple is not partially divorced" (2015: 188). This is illustrated by the statement made by Alexandra when describing her task as a decision-maker to me. Alexandra is a decision-maker close to retirement, who has been working at the SEM for most of her adult life.

> Decision-making, well, that's our trade, […] that's our main business […]. This might be a bad comparison, but it's a bit like Caesar in the arena going like this [thumbs up] or like that [thumbs down]. We either say yes or no. There is a little bit of grey area in-between, but in the end we say yes or no, that's the decision.[3]

What I am mainly concerned with in this chapter is how SEM officials like Alexandra attempt to overcome the uncertainties described above in order to reach such clear-cut either/or decisions. Thus, rather than dwelling on what these uncertainties are and how they are experienced by the decision-makers, in this chapter I focus on the techniques they devise to overcome these uncertainties and to manage their doubts (see Kelly 2012: 765–766; 2015: 188). By doing so, I follow Tobias Kelly who argues that

> [t]he sense of known unknowns and, more importantly, the techniques we devise to try to overcome such ignorance, whilst also being aware of the limits of our knowledge, are central to the ways in which we try to make important decisions. […] The key point […] is not that things are uncertain. Rather, it is that we need to grasp the conditions under which attempts are made to overcome these uncertainties in the full knowledge of their existence. (2012: 765–766)

That decision-making is about reducing uncertainties and doubt is not specific to asylum administrations, but appears to be characteristic of bureaucratic decision-making in general (see Lahusen and Schneider 2017: 12; Liodden 2016: 274; Lipsky 2010: xiii). It is also typical that doubt and uncertainties can never be fully eradicated (see Downs 1967: 3). However, for caseworkers to be able to feel sufficiently confident about their decisions, doubt must be reduced as much as possible. In the SEM, as my analysis in this chapter shows, different factors contribute to this. These

[3]Alexandra, caseworker, reception and processing centre, interview transcript, my own translation.

include: practice doctrine, "country knowledge", the production of "on-file facts"—mostly through the questioning techniques in asylum interviews but sometimes also in form of so-called "expert reports"—and, very importantly, decision-makers' professional-practical knowledge.

This chapter contributes to the overall argument of the book in a threefold way. First, by shedding light on how uncertainties, ambiguities and doubt are reduced in and through the decision-making processes while never being fully eradicated, I contribute to gaining a better understanding not only of how asylum administrations work but also of bureaucracies in general. Nevertheless, it is worth noting that while not being unique to asylum decision-making, the "psychological weight" of taking asylum decisions in the light of their potential consequences for asylum seekers' lives appears to be particularly elevated in asylum administrations (Rousseau et al. 2002: 44). Furthermore, the specific "known unknowns" arising from the standard of proof in asylum determination constitute another particularity of asylum administrations. Second, this chapter brings out the ways in which structural constraints posed by the law itself—or, more precisely, arising from the clear-cut form necessarily required of legal categorizations—as well as regulatory frameworks in the form of practice doctrine, shape what decision-makers do. Third, as Julia Dahlvik argues, from a praxeological perspective "every practice is first and foremost a knowledge-based activity" (2018: 57). This means that if we want to understand what administrative caseworkers do, we need to pay attention to the knowledge that constitutes their practices. Much of this knowledge is implicit, embodied and non-verbalisable. As I show in this chapter, this kind of non-verbalisable, implicit knowledge—which, building on Andreas Reckwitz's (2003: 289–294) definition, I call professional-practical knowledge—plays a crucial role in credibility determination by guiding decision-makers' practices, but also by providing them with the necessary conviction or "sense of security" that they are taking "the right" decision (see also Dahlvik 2018: 57–62). In other words, it shapes what decision-makers do. Drawing on Julia Dahlvik (2018: 58), I argue that this kind of knowledge, on the one hand, shapes the meanings ascribed to certain objects, persons and situations. On the other hand, it provides decision-makers with a sense of what the procedural steps are and of "how a chain of action is competently produced" (ibid.). Finally, it gives decision-makers an understanding of what they want; of what seems appropriate and desirable (ibid.). As such, it becomes clear that professional-practical knowledge—and, more generally, knowledge decision-makers have acquired through experience—constitutes part of caseworkers' institutional habitus, their schemes of thinking, acting, feeling and desiring that arise from belonging to and working in the SEM.

This chapter mainly focuses on the first above-mentioned aspects of knowledge: how it shapes the meanings ascribed to certain objects, persons and situations. The other two aspects are addressed in Chapters 5 and 6. I start this chapter by introducing a case example to provide an image of what dealing with uncertainties may look like in practice. Following this, the chapter sets out the different means and moments through which uncertainty is turned into decisional certainty, allowing decision-makers to take clear-cut either/or decisions, and the role different types of knowledge play.

Ben's Case

Ben is a decision-maker in his early thirties, who had been working in the SEM for a couple of months at the time I first met him. It was by chance that I sat in on his interview one morning. Originally, it was planned that I would spend the day with one of Ben's more experienced co-workers. However, this decision-maker suddenly decided he did not want me attending his asylum interview after all so the head of the asylum unit took me to Ben's office.[4] At this point, Ben is just about to start an asylum interview so he hurriedly briefs me on the 'case'. He tells me that the applicant is a young man from Afghanistan, who claims to have been persecuted due to his former occupation as a bodyguard for an official of the Afghan authorities. He explains that he has already interviewed the same applicant once before, but, because he still does not know how to decide on the case, he has decided to conduct a supplementary interview. The difficulty, he says, lies in the credibility assessment. He explains that while the applicant has told his asylum story in a very detailed manner, there are also serious contradictions in his story. That is why, he says, he just does not know whether to believe the applicant or not. Ben hopes that after the second interview he will finally be able to reach a decision. I ask him how he has prepared for the interview and he tells me that, as usual, he has prepared questions he wants to ask the applicant and that he also wants to confront the applicant with some of the contradictions in the story to see if they can be resolved. Also, because Ben is not very familiar with 'cases' from Afghanistan yet, he has read the *Asyl- und Wegweisungspraxis* (APPA) for Afghanistan. APPAs are institutional guidelines

[4] I do not know why the caseworker did not want me there; he did not tell me himself but informed his boss before I arrived at the office in the morning. This is a good example of how "fieldwork does you" which I described in Chapter 2 (see Simpson 2006: 125).

on how to decide asylum cases from specific countries or regions and with specific flight motives. Furthermore, they provide internal "country of origin information". Studying the APPA, he explains, is important in order for him to have something to compare the applicant's statements to. He adds that if one already knows the country well, it is not necessary to read and prepare an interview as much as he has in this case. He explains that "knowing the country" is important, because it helps to assess whether what the applicant is saying could be true or not.

Then, Ben gets a phone call from a security guard at the main building, informing him that the applicant, the interpreter and the social aid representative have all arrived. Together we go to collect them, while the minute-taker stays behind in Ben's office. When we return to Ben's office everyone takes their assigned seats around a square table on which there are glasses of water and a box of tissues. The interview starts as usual. Ben introduces all the people present and asks the applicant whether he knows what his rights and duties are. The applicant—through the interpreter—confirms that he does. Then, Ben asks the applicant about his family and his education. Next, he questions the applicant thoroughly about his activities as a bodyguard and then requests that the applicant tell him about the different threats he experienced in a chronological order. In his account the claimant says that he and his family had received several death threats from the Taliban; that once he was beaten up by a group of four men who he identified as being Taliban; and that once he was abducted for three days by his persecutors but was released after his father paid a significant amount of ransom money. Ben then continues to ask specific follow-up questions on the different threats. At the end, as is common practice in the SEM, he confronts the applicant with the contradictions he has "found" in the applicant's narrative.

After the interview, and also during breaks, I ask Ben what he thinks about the 'case' and what decision he is going to take. Ben tells me that he still finds it a very difficult 'case' and that he is pretty sure not everything the asylum seeker has told him is true, especially not the part about being abducted. Noticing from my puzzled look that the reasons for this are not as clear to me as they are for him, he goes on to explain: "He got really worked up there, emotionally, that just did not seem very authentic". However, Ben tells me that he does believe the applicant was a bodyguard and that he might really have been threatened a couple of times. And since the requirements for Afghanistan are "quite low", as he puts it (which is something he considers to be "not so fair"), believing the applicant when he says that he used to be a bodyguard for a government official would probably be enough to give him asylum. Ben also points out that, as a consequence, there is no need for him to "find out the truth about everything". But, because he still feels unsure about this 'case', and says that the second interview has produced even more contradictions in the asylum narrative, he decides to weigh all the credible elements against the non-credible ones. He also thinks that he will probably take another look at the APPA before making the decision.

Unfortunately, by the time Ben writes his decision, I have already left his unit. However, I return a couple of months later for the final decision. Ben has, indeed, taken the decision to grant asylum. On the internal request form for positive decisions—forms which must be counter-signed by a superior but never leave the institution to prevent applicants learning from them how to present a successful claim—Ben has, as requested, identified a persecutor (the Taliban), a "persecutee" (the applicant), a motive for persecution (that the applicant worked for the Afghan authorities) as well as measures of persecution the applicant had suffered (the death threats, beating and abduction). He has also quoted a passage from the APPA to justify his decision: "Intentional attacks on people collaborating with the Afghan government or seen to do so occur frequently".[5] In addition, with reference to the claimant's credibility, he has written that the claimant told his story with a lot of detail and that the story seemed largely plausible, coherent and substantiated. However, he also notes that there were a lot of contradictions in the story, which probably meant that the applicant had invented parts of the story (especially the part about being abducted). But, he writes, the contradictions could have also arisen from the fact that a lot of time has passed between the events in Afghanistan and the asylum interviews. These remarks are followed by a long list of material evidence the applicant has submitted, such as identity documents, a death threat the applicant had received by email as well as a letter confirming that he used to work as a bodyguard for the government official.

Ben's case is illustrative in many ways. It exemplifies the unease arising from the above-mentioned uncertainties in decision-making. Ben feels equally uneasy about either taking a positive decision in spite of the "severe contradictions" or else taking a negative decision on the basis of these contradictions, even though the applicant had told his story in a "very detailed manner". Although Ben and I did not talk about this, I assume that one reason for his unease with taking a negative decision despite his uncertainties has to do with him knowing what potential consequences his decision could have on the asylum seeker's life. Likewise, as I will discuss in more detail in Chapter 5, he wants to avoid having the decision quashed by the Federal Administrative Court. The reason for his unease with taking a

[5] Internal form for positive decisions, field document, my own translation.

positive decision in spite of his uncertainties, have to do with the ideological environment in which Ben works or, in other words, with the ethics and ethos of the office (see Eckert 2020). For Ben, it is important not to be perceived as "too easily" taking a positive decision and not "too naively" believing applicants. Also, in order to get the decision past his superior, Ben needs to convince the latter that his decision is "correct". All these issues are discussed in Chapters 5 and 6. What is of interest for this chapter, in turn, is rather *how* Ben goes about overcoming his uncertainties.

The unease Ben feels is something I often encountered in the SEM. Commonly, in order to turn ambiguous situations into unambiguous decisions, caseworkers turn to so-called experts for help or ask colleagues—and sometimes their superiors—for their opinion and advice. The latter they usually do by orally describing the 'case' to their colleagues or superiors and asking them for their impression, but occasionally they also ask them to take a look at the minutes of the asylum interview or at the whole case file. Ben has chosen a different solution here, namely to conduct a third supplementary interview. This is not a very popular strategy since supplementary interviews are often perceived as hindering effective decision-making because they cost both time and money, but it is also not uncommon for decision-makers to opt for this solution.

Ben's case shows how the APPA on Afghanistan helps him manage his uncertainties in two different ways. First, the APPA provides him with "country knowledge" that helps him assess whether what the applicant has told him is likely to have happened in that way or not. Second, it provides him with an "on-file fact", a fragment of text that can be used for writing and reasoning the final decision. Furthermore, Ben's case draws attention to the important role the asylum interview plays in helping decision-makers gain enough certainty for taking clear-cut either/or decisions. This has mainly to do with the production of what I call "on-file facts" in the interviews through the usage of specific questioning techniques. The technique Ben uses of starting with questions about family, education and life "at home", then going on to more and more specific questions about the reasons for applying for asylum and finally to confronting the applicant with contradictions is exemplary of how I observed all but two—very experienced—decision-makers proceed and plays a crucial role in the production of "on-file facts". But interviews are not only important because of that. They are also vital for decision-makers to develop a better "feeling" of the 'case' and to gain a personal impression of the asylum applicant, which Ben's example also hints at.

In the end, Ben's final written decision was not quite unambiguous, since on the internal form for positive decisions Ben noted that he had doubts about some parts of the applicant's story. This is not uncommon for positive decisions. However, final negative decisions never make reference to such ambiguities. This has to do with the fact that, different to positive decisions, the reasoning for negative decisions is sent out to the applicants, leaving no room for ambiguities. Any ambiguities, I was told, would leave the SEM vulnerable to attack and open the door to an easy appeal. This does not mean that there are never any ambivalences and doubts which arise while taking negative decisions. However, in the process of fitting 'cases' into legal categories, they are made to disappear. With positive decisions, in turn, if decision-makers feel that there are "still" ambiguities, they will often mention them in case their superior examines the case file closely before the final decision is counter-signed or in case someone else reads the case file. They want to make sure that anyone who appraises the case file sees that they were aware that there were "indicators of non-credibility" in the applicant's statement—and, thus, possible reasons for rejecting the claim—but that, in the light of the overall picture, they considered these to be irrelevant for the decision.

"Country Knowledge"

Where applicants come from is crucial for decision-making because the applicants' so-called "country of origin" constitutes an important factor of eligibility. Both the "evaluation of their 'well-founded fear of persecution' [...] and the possibility of enforcing an expulsion in case of a negative decision" greatly depend on the "country of origin" applicants are associated with (Poertner 2018: 182; see also Bohmer and Shuman 2008; Cabot 2014; Poertner 2017). My sample of case files provides a clear picture of this. The decisions were taken for applicants from nineteen different countries. The claimants who in the end received a positive decision came from only six different countries. Hence, this shows that where the asylum seekers are from is a very strong factor in determining whether they will (or could even) receive asylum (and temporary protection) or not. In this sense, APPAs provide decision-makers with significant guidance. APPAs are internal guidelines on how to decide asylum cases from specific countries or regions and with specific flight motives. They identify certain profiles of people at risk of future persecution. There are APPAs for all the most common "countries of origin" in the SEM. They are created and kept up to date by the *Federführungen*. In the SEM, the term *Federführungen* refers to a person or group of people in the SEM responsible for a particular "country of origin".[6] They are involved in setting the institution's decision-making practice for dealing with 'cases' from "their" country and—to some extent—try to monitor other decision-makers' practices regarding 'cases' by applicants from the country they are responsible for.[7]

APPAs are always built up the same way. They consist of an introductory part with general remarks on the situation in the country at issue, one part each on how to conduct the first short asylum interviews and the second longer interviews, a section on different asylum motives and the corresponding decisions, and the same for the issue of removal where, for example, the (un-)reasonableness of return for certain groups of people or to certain regions within the country is determined. The part on asylum motives usually includes different possible motives for claiming asylum. Each motive is followed by a guiding principle as to whether in that particular case asylum should be granted or not. The principle is then explained in more detail and recommendations are made on what needs to be examined. In order to create these APPAs and keep them updated, the *Federführungen* try to keep track of all the relevant judgements by the FAC regarding cases from the country they are responsible for and to see whether they have any effect on the institution's practice. They also work closely together with the SEM's country analysts and use the information the latter produce in their so-called country of origin reports to upgrade the APPAs. The country analysts work in a different division of the SEM, namely the division "analysis and services", and are responsible for writing and updating the internal country of origin reports (COIs) as well as for making COIs written by their counterparts in other countries internally available.[8] They do not take any decisions and do

[6]In German, the phrase "'*die Federführung haben*' means 'to have the lead'" (Affolter et al. 2019: 270).

[7]Changes to practice doctrine with potential major impacts are, however, "negotiated in higher-level meetings" in which senior officials not only from the SEM but also "from other Federal Departments, notably that of Foreign Affairs, [...] [as well as] senior staff of the UNHCR and the Swiss Refugee Council" take part in (Poertner 2018: 240).

[8]Country of origin reports (COIs) are expert reports on the "political, economical, and human rights situation" in particular countries. According to the SEM website, the reports offer "an in-depth view on gender-based issues and health care in countries of origin". Furthermore, the information in the reports is stated to be "[c]urrent, factual and impartial" and findings in them are "documented in keeping with scientific practice" (https://www.sem.admin.ch/sem/en/home/internationales/herkunftslaender.html, last accessed 11.02.2020). For academic research on (the production of) COI reports, see Robert Gibb and Anthony Good (2013), Damian Rosset (2015) as well as Damian Rosset and Tone Liodden (2015).

not set the institution's decision-making practice. However, decision-makers can consult the analysts in individual cases, as I will show below.[9]

As Ben's case indicates, APPAS—and "country knowledge" in general—may not only be useful for assessing asylum seekers' eligibility to refugee status or subsidiary protection, but may also help decision-makers assess the credibility of asylum claims. Country knowledge is mainly used in three different ways for determining the credibility of asylum claims. Firstly, it is used to assess whether applicants are 'really' from the place/country they claim to be from. Secondly, they are used to assess whether what the applicants are saying is plausible or, in other words, whether what they claim happened to them could feasibly have taken place in the way described. Thirdly, decision-makers use country knowledge in order to know what kind of behaviour (for instance, concerning manner of speaking or topics of conversation) can or cannot be expected from applicants from different countries. The type of country knowledge used for this varies. There is the country knowledge decision-makers themselves hold. It is knowledge they have acquired through experience on the job, by having dealt with many 'cases' from a particular country; and through their preparation work for individual 'cases', by having read APPAs and country of origin reports; from having studied maps (nearly all the offices I entered at the SEM had at least one map of the world or a particular region hanging on the wall); and from having done research on the Internet. Furthermore, many decision-makers also try to keep up to date on countries they are dealing with by reading news reports and watching TV documentaries. There is also county knowledge so-called experts hold, which caseworkers can refer to for decision-making. These experts are mainly the SEM's country analysts, the external language specialists employed by the LINGUA unit of the SEM and to some extent also the *Federführungen.*

Determining Applicants' "Country of Origin"

"Finding out" where asylum seekers are from is crucial for the reasons discussed above. Or rather, what is important to "find out" is whether asylum seekers are "really" from where they say they are since, if the applicants are, in the end, considered *not* to be from that place by the decision-makers, their "actual" origin becomes irrelevant for decision-making. All that matters then is that their stated "country of origin" is not credible. Usually, the assessment of applicants' "country of origin" is done in the first short asylum interviews which take place at the reception and processing centres (RPC). If asylum

---

[9]Occasionally, country analysts and sometimes also the *Federführungen* go on so-called "fact-finding missions" to the countries they are responsible for (see also Dahlvik 2018: 134).

seekers do not hand in identity documents which decision-makers believe to be genuine, this assessment is done through what Thomas Scheffer calls an examination of applicants' "membership knowledge" (2001: 146–127; see also Griffiths 2012; Poertner 2018: 183–185). This test consists of questions about things that people coming from a certain country or place are expected to know, as this extract from the minutes of a first asylum interview illustrates:

> *Q*: What is the international dialling code of Morocco?
> *A*: 00212.
> *Q*: What is the name of the king of Morocco?
> *A*: (asylum seeker smiles) That's Mohammed the sixth. I am a real Moroccan.
> *Q*: What's the name of his wife, the queen?
> *A*: I know she's from Fes. When he got married, I wasn't in Morocco.
> *Q*: What are the places surrounding Kneitra called?
> *A*: Kneitra lies about 40 km away from Rabat. There's an American base camp in Kneitra. The surrounding places are called Sidi Yahia, Sidi Suleiman and Sidi Kassem.[10]

The decision-makers then check asylum seekers' answers against their own country knowledge that they have acquired from previous experience or from doing research on the Internet and studying maps, often as part of the preparation of the interview, but occasionally I also observed decision-makers directly checking the asylum seekers' answers on the Internet during the interview. It is then up to the decision-makers to set the bar for applicants to pass this test, which in the case cited above, the applicant did (see also Poertner 2018: 183). For caseworkers, it is often more important how applicants answer their questions rather than whether their answers are correct or not as indicated in the following statement made by Angela, a SEM official working in one of the RPCs: "I might ask the claimant how far it is from village A to village B. This is not something I can check, that we can find out whether it is true or not, but that doesn't really matter. What is much more decisive is how the claimants react and whether what they then say seems realistic".[11] Nevertheless, sometimes the "correctness" of the answers does play a decisive role. Yet, because the information decision-makers use to assess applicants' answers is potentially also available to the latter—anybody can look it up on the Internet, I was often told—decision-makers do not always automatically equate "correct" answers with credibility. This becomes apparent in the following statement made by Klaus:

[10]Minutes of a first asylum interview, field document, my own translation.
[11]Angela, caseworker, reception and procedure centre, field notes, my own translation.

> I have this case, a Somali, but I'm not sure he's Somali. [...] He could tell me the colour of the number plates; he could name villages, the distances between them [...]. He could tell me where the buses leave from, where to buy the ticket [...]. All this he knew. But there are two radio stations in Somalia and one TV station and those he didn't know. Maybe he was in Somalia a long time ago. Maybe he's not even Somali, but Kenyan and just went to visit someone in Somalia, maybe he has relatives there, maybe he was there, but didn't grow up there. So how can we evaluate this? I mean, you can look the number plate up. Maybe he heard that we were doing country tests and looked up a couple of things on Wikipedia. But the radio stations he should know. And he gave me the international dialling code of Ethiopia. So what I did then was to look at the minutes and to underline everything in green that was correct and everything in red that wasn't. And now I have to make an evaluation of it and that is difficult. But according to the interpreter I asked, he should really know the two radio stations.[12]

Because decision-makers, like Klaus, often suspect asylum seekers of having prepared for the "country tests", it is common practice to regularly keep changing the questions asked during the interviews, with ideas for new questions being frequently exchanged amongst colleagues. In Klaus's case, it was very important for him to know whether the applicant was from Somalia or not because it determined whether the latter was to be granted temporary protection or not. Therefore, Klaus's solution was to weigh all the things the applicant had known against the things he had not known and he had also turned to the interpreter for help. The latter is something decision-makers are officially not supposed to do, but, at least in the two RPCs I did fieldwork in, this was quite a common practice. While the opinions provided by the interpreters cannot be used for reasoning final decisions in writing, decision-makers nevertheless perceive them as useful guidance for determining the credibility of applicants' stated "countries of origin".[13] What Klaus could have done instead of asking the interpreter for help, would have been to request a so-called LINGUA test. However, as he explained to me, he had decided against that because for applicants from Somalia there was quite a long waiting list and he wanted to decide the 'case' as quickly as possible since it had already been on his desk for quite a while.

LINGUA reports are done by so-called external experts, which are commissioned by the LINGUA unit of the SEM, "a specialised unit for

[12]Klaus, caseworker, reception and processing centre, interview transcript, my own translation.

[13]This seems to be different in the Austrian first-instance asylum procedure where interpreters can be officially requested to provide reports (see Dahlvik 2018: 137).

analysis of origin". These experts examine the applicants' speech and their "culture knowledge" in order to "determine the country and/or region or, at least, the milieu, which have had the biggest influence on the [...] [asylum applicants] in [...] [their] process of socialization".[14] They then send a report with their assessment to the decision-maker in charge of the 'case'. From what I observed in the SEM, the LINGUA experts' assessments are generally accepted as a fact, meaning that they are not challenged and are used as "facts" to legitimise and reason final written decisions (see also Dahlvik 2018: 134). Finally, decision-makers also have the possibility to ask the Swiss embassy in the applicant's "country of origin" to try and find out whether the applicant is really from a particular place in that country. However, as Ephraim Poertner writes, embassy enquiries are "considered the *ultima ratio* of clarification" because they are "a very costly and time-consuming form of gathering information" (2018: 185). Furthermore, such embassy enquiries can themselves potentially "create a well-founded fear of persecution by placing the applicant on the radar of local authorities" (ibid.). Caseworkers can, therefore, only request that such enquiries be carried out with the permission of their superiors.

Assessing Reasonable Likelihood

Country knowledge is not just used to determine asylum seeker's "country of origin". It is also put to use in trying to find out whether what the applicants are saying could have happened in the way they describe and, to some extent, assess asylum seekers' "overall credibility". Often, decision-makers rely on country information they themselves have access to and knowledge they have acquired through "experience in the service" (Weber 2013 [1978]: 225) in order to appraise whether what the applicants have told them could be possible or not. This was one of the reasons why Ben read the APPA for Afghanistan before conducting the interview. He said he needed information he could then compare with the applicant's answers. He also said that if one already knew the country well—which in this case he did not—it was not necessary to read the APPA and prepare oneself as extensively as he had for the interview. Thus, often country knowledge for assessing the plausibility of stories also comes from decision-makers' experience (see Dahlvik 2018: 57; Jubany 2017: 146). As an example, in one 'case' I observed, the decision-maker did not test credibility at all in the asylum interview. When I asked

[14]https://www.sem.admin.ch/sem/en/home/publiservice/service/sprachanalysen/lingua.html, last accessed 11.02.2020.

her about it she said: "I just looked at the minutes [of the first interview] and knew it was credible. [The applicant] mentioned so many things we know about Sri Lanka".[15] However, while stories fitting with what decision-makers know from experience about a country are—as in the example above—usually considered as an indicator of credibility, stories which are seen to be "too standard" are sometimes also read as a sign of non-credibility.[16] At the time of my research, examples of what were commonly referred to as "standard stories" were Iranians claiming to have become known to the authorities due to their political activities in exile, Nigerians claiming to have been persecuted on the grounds of their homosexuality and Tibetans claiming to have been persecuted after participating in a rally: "They were all at a rally, waved around a Dalai Lama flag and then heard that they were being persecuted. That's the standard story with Tibetans".[17] Decision-makers took such "standard stories" to mean that they were not true but had been prepared by the asylum seekers because the latter knew that with such stories they could be granted asylum.

Like with the assessment of asylum seekers' "country of origin", decision-makers sometimes also turn to so-called experts for help in determining the probability of something having happened in the way it was described by the applicants. Hence, they might go to the *Federführung* and ask them what they think or they might request help from a country analyst. Decision-makers are not allowed to ask the country analysts for recommendations on how to decide a particular case or for assessments of whether something could be "true" or not, but they can ask them for specific information, for instance, if it is possible to buy a certain medicine in a particular county or if documents are (or could be) genuine and official. In one 'case', for example, the decision-maker posed the following questions to the country analyst:

> Is marriage forbidden in Egypt between a Christian [man] and Muslim [woman]? If so, does the law order punishment for people trying to enter into such a marriage? [...] If a Christian [man] and a Muslim [woman] have children together, who is regarded as the legal guardian of those children? Can an unmarried couple live together in Egypt and have children?[18]

---

[15]Ursula, caseworker, reception and processing centre, field notes, my own translation.

[16]This is something Thomas Scheffer also found in his ethnographic research on German asylum administrations (2001: 165–167; 2003: 443–444), Tone Liodden has shown with regard to asylum decision-making in Norway (2016: 224) and Olga Jubany describes for asylum decision-making in the UK as well (2017: 159).

[17]Klaus, caseworker, reception and processing centre, interview transcript, my own translation.

[18]Internal consultation form, field document, my own translation.

The decision-maker was, thereby, trying to find out whether it was likely that the applicants had been persecuted due to their "mixed-religion" marriage. In this case, the decision-maker furthermore decided to request an embassy enquiry, asking the officials at the Swiss embassy in Egypt to investigate the following:

> Does the copy of the family register which the applicants have handed in correspond with the records of the registry office in X, respectively is the family register genuine? What can be found out about the people named on the family register (stay, current residence, job, identity, etc.)? Are the applicants known at the above-mentioned address in Y? What can be found out on-site about the time of departure, their reasons for leaving and other useful [aspects], such as professional activities, family background, religious affiliation?[19]

The decision-maker finally ended up rejecting the asylum claim following the response she received from the embassy, namely that the family register which the applicants had handed in was a fake.[20]

Assessing Demeanour

Officially, caseworkers in the SEM are instructed to ignore asylum seekers' demeanour and emotions and to not let them influence their decision-making. However, caseworkers' stance towards this is ambivalent. Many agreed that this should be the aim, while several others explicitly stated that they found applicants' behaviour a useful source of information for assessing credibility. However, regardless of these different opinions conveyed to me, in practice I observed that applicants' demeanour does very often serve as an indicator and useful source of information for assessing credibility, even if this is not something that can be used to reason final written decisions with (see also Jubany 2011, 2017: 157).

> [T]he more you have seen, the better you can judge… Especially with nations - Asians just behave differently to Africans [laughs], Arabs different to Persians. […] [A]t the beginning I found this very difficult. […] But the longer you do this kind of thing, the better you feel what is culturally driven and what just simply isn't true.[21]

---

[19]Embassy enquiry form, field document, my own translation.

[20]Written asylum decision, field document, my own translation.

[21]Patricia, caseworker, headquarters, interview transcript, my own translation.

Regarding applicants' manner of speaking I was, for instance, told by several decision-makers that Iranians spoke in an over-embellished way, but that did not necessarily mean that what they were saying was true, that one could expect Sri Lankans to give detailed accounts of what had happened to them and that Eritreans were not very talkative and could not always be expected to provide many details. This type of country knowledge may, therefore, also influence how high decision-makers set the bar for different groups of asylum seekers to fulfil the credibility requirements.

So far, I have shown how "institutional practice"—or practice doctrine—in the form of APPAs as well as country knowledge help decision-makers' reduce uncertainties, providing them with what Thomas Scheffer (2003) calls "power of judgement" (*Urteilskraft*) which allows them to take and justify decisions. Whereas the country knowledge which exists in writing—the LINGUA and embassy reports, country analysts' answers to consultations, COIs and country of origin information in the APPAs—can be used to reason final decisions, country knowledge decision-makers have themselves acquired through "experience in the service" (Weber 2013 [1978]: 225)—for instance, knowledge of what "standard" or typical stories are or of how people from certain places typically speak and/or behave—cannot. However, this does not mean that this kind of knowledge does not play an essential role in overcoming uncertainty and producing clear-cut either/or decisions. On the contrary, it plays an important part in guiding decision-makers' practices: what arguments they dig for in the interviews; how they do so (e.g. if they ask many questions to test an applicant's credibility or if they refrain from doing so because they "already" believe an applicant); and what arguments they look for in the minutes when writing decisions, for instance. But country knowledge is not the only type of knowledge to do so, as the next section of this chapter brings to light.

Producing Decisional Certainty: The Role of Professional-Practical Knowledge

This part of the chapter is essentially about decision-makers' "gut feeling", which plays a crucial role in assessing asylum seekers' credibility as numerous researchers writing about asylum administrations have shown (see, for instance, Dahlvik 2018; Fassin and Kobelinsky 2012; Fassin 2013; Johannesson 2017; Jubany 2011, 2017; Kelly 2012; Liodden 2016; Macklin 1998; Miaz 2017; Thomas 2009). However, this is not specific to asylum administrations. Anne Lavanchy (2014), for instance, describes how "feeling" essentially guides officers' work in Swiss registry offices when trying to assess the genuineness of marriages—or to "debunk" so-called "bogus marriages"—and Vincent Dubois shows how "instinct" shapes how French welfare workers engage with their "clients" (2010: 98–100).

"Gut feeling", I argue, can be understood as an expression of what Andreas Reckwitz calls "practical knowledge". He defines "practical knowledge" as a type of know-how which already forms part of what the practice itself is. It cannot be thought of independently from the practice. It is embodied and incorporated knowledge; a conglomerate of everyday techniques; and a practical sense of self-evident understanding (Reckwitz 2003: 289–294; see also Dahlvik 2018: 57–62; Wagenaar 2004: 651).[22] Thus, this knowledge forms part of "the doing" itself (Dahlvik 2018: 57). The "gut feeling" which guides asylum decision-makers' credibility assessments constitutes precisely this kind of knowledge. This is nicely exemplified by a SEM decision-maker saying to Jonathan Miaz that she could not really explain to him how she took decisions, that was just something one did, just like skiing (Miaz 2017: 212; see also Bloch 1991: 189). Hence, this is why I draw on Reckwitz's term. However, I add the word "professional" to Reckwitz's term, making it professional-practical knowledge, to stress the fact that the type of knowledge I am referring to develops on the job and grows out of decision-makers' profession.

Professional-practical knowledge is not something that can be used for reasoning final decisions. This means that decision-makers cannot write in the final decision: "The claim is credible (or non-credible) because I just know or I can feel that it is". However, like I described for country knowledge above, it essentially guides decision-makers' practices. Furthermore, it plays a crucial role in helping decision-makers feel certain about their decisions. More explicit knowledge—like country knowledge—can over time also turn into professional-practical knowledge once it becomes so incorporated by decision-makers that it becomes self-evident and, through this, very difficult to verbalise (see also Miaz 2017: 213).

Since the data I draw on in this book is "conversational in nature" (Affolter et al. 2019: 266), approaching professional-practical knowledge is methodologically challenging (see also Chapter 2). Hence, as soon as we ask a person to put such "gut feelings" into words, we provoke a kind of ex-post rationalisation. Nevertheless, I argue that we should try and come as close as

---

[22]This is similar to what Michael Polanyi has called "tacit knowledge", which he understands as a type of knowledge that is more about "knowing how" than "knowing that" (Polanyi 1962 [1958], 1966; see also Ryle 1951).

possible to analytically describing this type of knowledge and the role it plays in bureaucratic decision-making because, as Georg Breidenstein et al. (2013: 36) argue, what counts as "normal" and "self-evident" is precisely what we should attempt to grasp as researchers. Furthermore, such ex-post rationalisations can tell us a lot about what decision-makers think they should be doing which is important for understanding bureaucratic work (see Eckert 2020).

All the decision-makers I spoke to in the SEM told me that they preferred interviewing asylum seekers themselves rather than having to decide upon 'cases' in which the interview was conducted by a "pooly" or another case-worker.[23] One important reason for this is the "feeling" they get when listening to asylum seekers' stories during the interviews. During breaks in asylum interviews when I asked decision-makers if they already knew what decision they were going to take, it was common that they explained their decision by referring to their impressions about authenticity, like Ben did. They would claim that an applicant's story (or parts of a story) was either "authentic" or "not-authentic", that a story was "clearly true" or that there was something "off" about a story. This was also reflected in the answers I got from many officials when I asked them in a more abstract way how they knew—in general—whether a claim was credible or not. The following statement by Andrea represents a common response I got to this question: "It's more like a feeling. And then I look for it in the text".[24] What Andrea means by "And then I look for it in the text" is that she looks at the minutes of the asylum interviews to see if she can find any fragments of texts in them that confirm her "feeling" and allow her to develop legal arguments for reasoning her decision with. Professional-practical knowledge structures how and what arguments are looked for in the minutes but also what questions are asked in the interviews, and when and how thoroughly credibility is tested. My reaction to officials telling me that credibility decisions usually started with a feeling was to ask them: "Well ok, yes, but how do you feel this?" The following two statements by Theodor and Ralph indicate how difficult it often was for decision-makers to articulate this feeling:

> I don't really know, maybe some who's new could [explain how to assess credibility to you] better. I just do it "out of feeling or intuition" (*aus dem Gefühl heraus*). [...] With experience you just somehow know, for instance, that it is "incompatible with practical experience" (*erfahrungswidrig*), or I don't know,

[23]"Poolies" are people employed by the SEM who only conduct interviews (and are paid by the hour to do so) but do not take any decisions (see Chapter 3).

[24]Andrea, caseworker, headquarters, field notes, my own translation.

> you just know what arguments there are for non-credibility. […] I mean, it's not just "intuitive" (*gefühlsmässig*). Your common sense also develops.[25]

> Well, I have to say, in interviews you realise quickly if it's credible or not, if a person has experienced something or not. Um, it's difficult to put into words. It has substance and, you know, such "reality criteria" and the narrative is just different from a person's who is lying.[26]

Apart from showing how Theodor and Ralph struggle to verbalise their professional-practical knowledge, their statements also attest that professional experience is crucial for developing professional-practical knowledge. Furthermore, in the explanations they offered me, they rationalise their decisions just like they would in writing final decisions, as I show later on in this chapter. By stating that there are "arguments for non-credibility" and that if something was "incompatible with practical experience" then that was an indicator of non-credibility, Theodor makes reference to criteria from the Swiss Asylum Act and case law. Ralph, in turn, refers to the reality criteria from Criteria-Based Content Analysis. What I mean by criteria from the Asylum Act and case law is the following: article 7 of the Asylum Act sets out the subsequent denominations of *non*-credibility: "unfoundedness in essential points", meaning that asylum seekers cannot speak in a detailed manner about events relevant for asylum; "inherent contradictions"; "contradictions to facts" (*Tatsachenwidrigkeit*) and "forged or falsified evidence" (Art. 7, paragraph 3, AsylA). Thus, credibility is defined negatively. Further criteria are provided by case law, most notably by a judgement made in 2004 by the Commission for Asylum Appeals (now the Federal Administrative Court). In the judgement, it is declared that applicants' statements are credible if they are sufficiently substantiated, coherent and plausible. Their statements should not be limited to vague descriptions and there should not be any contradictions in the main issues of their stories. Moreover, they should not lack what is called an "inner logic" and should also not contradict facts and "general experiences" (EMARK 2004/1). Finally, the judgement reads that the applicants themselves must appear credible, which is particularly declared not to be the case if they base their claims on forged evidence; conceal or deliberately change important facts (*Tatsachen*); change or up their claims and add parts to their stories without good cause; do not show sufficient interest in the procedure; or refuse to cooperate (ibid.). For all of these criteria, decision-makers have boilerplates at their disposal for reasoning negative asylum decisions.

[25]Theodor, caseworker, reception and processing centre, interview transcript, my own translation.
[26]Ralph, caseworker, reception and processing centre, interview transcript, my own translation.

Boilerplates are fragments of pre-written text that can be used to develop legal arguments.[27]

The reality criteria Ralph, in turn, refers to are indicators of credibility rather than of *non*-credibility. They come from Criteria-Based Content Analysis (CBCA), a method/theory from forensic psychology which was originally developed to evaluate testimonies of "victims of child sexual abuse" (Amado et al. 2016: 201). CBCA identifies nineteen "reality criteria" (*Realkennzeichen*) which are seen as indicators of the statements being based on events that the narrator has experienced.[28] At the time of my research, all new decision-makers learnt about these reality criteria in their initial training; and professional development courses were regularly taught by Swiss university forensic psychologists on the method.[29] In theory, according to CBCA, narratives need to be systematically analysed in order to see whether any reality criteria can be found, which should then be read as an indicator for credibility. However, this is not how credibility is done in practice in asylum proceedings, with the focus being on trying to find markers of non-credibility and, rather in the absence of these, finding accounts credible, as I will show later on in this chapter.

What role exactly CBCA plays in credibility determination in the SEM remained somewhat of a puzzle to me. One impression I got was that pre-eminently CBCA gives credibility determination a scientific legitimation. This is clearly illustrated in a comment made by Hannah, a head of an asylum unit at an RPC, when I told her what I was working on: "Credibility determination, that is truly an interesting topic. Especially if you take into account how it has developed. In the past, we just did it any old way. Today it is done on the basis of scientific findings", she said.[30] Nevertheless,

[27]In the SEM, there are boilerplates for the following criteria: "unfoundedness", "contradictions to known facts", "contradictions to general experience", "contradictions to the inner logic of acting", "inherent contradictions", "belated assertions", "no longer mentioned assertions", "forged evidence" and "unqualified evidence". "Contradictions to general experience" and "contradictions to the inner logic of actions" are usually used together and stand for the plausibility of certain actions.

[28]These nineteen criteria are: "1. Logical structure, 2. Unstructured production, 3. Quantity of details, [...] 4. Contextual embedding, 5. Descriptions of interactions, 6. Reproduction of conversation, 7. Unexpected complications during the incident, [...] 8. Unusual details, 9. Superfluous details, 10. Accurately reported details misunderstood, 11. Related external associations, 12. Accounts of subjective mental states, 13. Attribution of perpetrator's mental state, [...] 14. Spontaneous corrections, 15. Admitting lack of memory, 16. Raising doubts about one's own testimony, 17. Self-deprecation, 18. Pardoning the perpetrator, [...] 19. Details characteristic of the offence" (Amado et al. 2015: 4).

[29]As Stephanie Schneider describes, this also applies to decision-makers working in the German asylum administration (2019: 295).

[30]Hannah, head of asylum unit, reception and processing centre, interview transcript, my own translation.

I also found that to some extent knowledge of the reality criteria is incorporated into decision-makers' professional-practical knowledge as my encounter with Theodor illustrates:

> *Laura*: Could you tell me what makes a case so clearly credible for you? [...]
> *Theodor*: There are documents for that. If you want to, I can send them to you. I'm not so up to date (*à jour*) with that. Well, credible [accounts] are, for instance, nuanced, really well described, and mention minor matters. [...] If it's not just a smooth story, if there are stumbling blocks (*Stolpersteine*) and irrelevant details. For instance, if [the applicant] says that the light flared and suddenly the light went out. You know, things like that. [...] And substance, particularly with events that had a traumatising effect. Not with regard to the traumatising event, but with what happened around it; that one focuses on a particular [aspect] of the man appearing, for instance: "I saw that he had sweat beads on his forehead". You know, something special like that. But I would have to [look for] some [documents]. I can't tell you just like that.[31]

In his description, Theodor brings up the narration of "minor matters", "stumbling blocks" and the applicant mentioning some of the perpetrator's physiological responses (the sweat beads on his forehead). Each of these issues bears resemblance with one of the nineteen reality criteria. Thus, the mentioning of "minor matters" fits with the reality criterion of "superfluous details" and the "stumbling blocks" can be read as the reality criterion "unexpected complications during the incident". As a further point, Theodor's "sweat beads" reminded me of one of the training courses when the participants were told that the narration of perpetrators' physical responses (like the sweat beads) formed part of the reality criterion "attribution of perpetrator's mental state". Theodor himself did not use the word "reality criteria" and did not make any explicit reference to CBCA. However, the documents he kept referring to were about CBCA and reality criteria. The way I interpret this quote, is, therefore, that Theodor, like many other decision-makers, has selectively internalised this knowledge of the reality criteria; not necessarily by memorising it, but possibly by using the documents on CBCA to assess the credibility of asylum claims when he was new to the job and had not acquired enough professional-practical knowledge to "simply" know whether a claim was credible or not and by learning from others, who had also been schooled in CBCA, in what credible accounts "looked like". Theodor struggles to verbalise what exactly characterises credible stories. That is why he

[31]Theodor, caseworker, reception and processing centre, interview transcript, my own translation.

wants to show me the documents on CBCA because they explicitly describe this. However, it becomes apparent that for his day-to-day work, he does not need the documents. Despite looking for them on the SEM's internal server for over ten minutes, he is unable to find them, indicating that in his daily practice he never, or at least only very rarely, needs to look them up. He already knows due to his practical experience and internalised knowledge what makes a story credible. Many other decision-makers, like Louis for example, defined credible accounts as creating a feeling as if one were in a film: "[…] if a story's credible, it's just a flood of words. Everything just figures. When you listen to them talk it's just like being in a film. These stories, they really live".[32] Furthermore, credible stories were said to be told "straight from the heart" and that, therefore, in such 'cases' it was not necessary to ask many questions, because those stories "just came pouring out". Hence, in the words of one official, all one had to do was to "lean back and listen to them talk"[33] (see also Pelosi 1996: 59).

By allowing decision-makers to intuitively know whether asylum claims are (probably) credible or not, such knowledge provides caseworkers with a kind of "felt certainty", which is crucial in the light of the "known unknowns" introduced at the beginning of this chapter. Professional-practical knowledge helps decision-makers feel certain that they are taking the "right decision". This becomes apparent in the following example in which caseworker Andrea—a caseworker who had at the time already been working at the SEM for a couple of years—has lost faith in her "feeling":

> Andrea and I are sitting together during a coffee break. She tells me that there's soon going to be a training session on credibility assessment that she recommends me to attend. She tells me that she would really like to go, but that she's not allowed to because only two people from each section can take part. She says she would have really liked to have gone, because she was going through a bit of a crisis at that time because she couldn't really trust her intuition anymore: "Not so long ago I had this woman from Turkey", she tells me. "She didn't know anything and she barely spoke any Turkish. I was so sure that she wasn't from Turkey. But then I asked for an 'embassy report' and it turned out that it was all true". Andrea explains that this has really thrown her off balance, because she had been so sure about it not being true. If she hadn't had this possibility for investigation she would have said it wasn't credible. She tells me that, because of this, she currently feels so insecure about her assessments that the other day she told a colleague who had wanted her opinion on

[32]Louis, caseworker, headquarters, field notes, my own translation.

[33]Daniel, caseworker, reception and processing centre, interview transcript, my own translation.

> a 'case' because he thought he might be biased, to go and ask someone else for help.[34]

For Andrea, no longer being able to trust her "feeling" was a problem, hindering her from carrying out her everyday credibility assessment tasks as she used to. She therefore hoped that she would soon regain confidence in her "intuition" again.

Producing On-File Facts: The Asylum Interview

Even though professional-practical knowledge plays a vital role in caseworkers' decision-making, it does not appear in the final written decisions. Hence, if we were to solely analyse final written decisions, we would not learn much about the reasons for reaching a certain decision. What we would instead learn about are the justifications for the decision at stake (see Kelly 2012: 762; Miaz 2017: 327; Poertner 2018: 194). Thus, every decision a caseworker takes, must be justified in writing. There are two main formats for this. In the case of positive decisions, applicants are informed about the decision and what this means in terms of rights and obligations, but not about the "reasons" for the decision. These "reasons", or rather justifications, are listed solely on the internal application form that goes into the applicant's case file and might potentially be checked by the head of the asylum unit before the positive decision is sent out. With negative decisions, a letter is sent to the applicants informing them of the outcome of the decision, but also providing them with the decision's legal reasoning. The part which outlines the legal arguments for the decision in these letters is always structured in the same way:

> The considerations always begin (in the case of decisions that enter into the substance) with an introduction: "The decision of the SEM on your asylum application is based on the following considerations: Switzerland grants asylum to applicants if they make a persecution in the sense of Art. 3 Asylum Act at least credible (Art. 7 Asylum Act) and no grounds for exclusion exist". The next set phrases state the legal content of Article 3 or 7 of the Swiss Asylum Act or both [...]. The argumentative part consists commonly of a number of syllogisms – formal legal arguments – that have the structure of: (A) the legal norm (major premise) → (B) the specific facts of the case [...] (minor premise)

[34] Andrea, caseworker, headquarters, field notes, my own translation.

> → the application of the legal norm on the specific case (consequence or legal subsumption). (Poertner 2018: 200–201)

The "specific facts of the case" Ephraim Poertner refers to are fragments of texts decision-makers can use to reason their decisions with as well as documents they can refer to, which is why I have opted to call them "on-file facts". The previous parts of this chapter have brought to light some potential on-file facts: the LINGUA and embassy reports, country analysts' answers to consultations and country of origin information reports. Furthermore, any material evidence asylum seekers hand in may also become an on-file fact. An observation I made in the SEM—similar to what Julia Dahlvik describes for the Austrian Federal Asylum Office (2018: 141)—is that material evidence handed in by asylum seekers is often met with suspicion and that the authenticity of such documents is frequently doubted. This does not necessarily mean that such material evidence no longer functions as an on-file fact, but rather that it is turned into a different kind of "fact", namely one which attests the non-credibility of the applicant rather than what is stated on the documents themselves (see also Jubany 2017: 166). The most important on-file facts, however, are asylum seekers' statements as they are recorded in writing in the minutes of asylum interviews (see also Jubany 2017: 134). In the SEM, during the first short asylum interview at the RPCs, it is the decision-makers themselves who write the minutes on a standardised form at their disposal for this purpose. During the second (and potential third) longer asylum interviews, the minutes are written by minute-takers who are employed by the hour for their work and are often university students. At the end of the interviews, asylum seekers are requested to sign each page of the minutes—after they have been read back to them by the interpreters—to confirm the veracity of the recorded statements. Through this, the recorded statements become authoritative facts (Dahlvik 2018: 133), enabling the justification of final decisions. That is why decision-makers are very reluctant to question the veracity of such recorded facts. For example, Mauro, deputy head of an asylum unit at the headquarters, explained to me that, of course, sometimes when asylum seekers complained that something had not been correctly translated in the first interview and one could see from the minutes that there really were communication problems, then once could not use this against the asylum seekers. But, he added,

> on the other hand, we have to be really careful when asylum seekers claim things like that, we cannot really accept that. We say: "We have the written minutes, we translated everything back to you, you have signed the minutes so

> now they are legally valid (*rechtsgültig*) and can be used". Because if we start questioning everything then we might as well just stop.[35]

Mauro's statement shows that the authoritative character of the minutes is vital for decision-making. Without such "facts", turning uncertain situations into decisional certainty would be impossible. But for minutes to be viable for decision-making they must meet certain expectations. This is one of the reasons why decision-makers prefer interviewing asylum seekers themselves rather than relying on interviews conducted by "poolies" or other caseworkers. That way they can steer the interview better and ask questions that will produce the arguments they need for the final decision; this is what is called "goal-oriented questioning" (*zielorientiertes Fragen*). Many decision-makers, furthermore, explained to me that during the interviews they always had the decision in mind and, only when they thought they had enough arguments for reasoning, stopped the interview.

Writing about asylum procedures in different countries such as Canada, Germany, Spain, Sweden, the UK and the USA, scholars have argued that the focus of asylum interviews is on uncovering lies (Jubany 2017: 137), "checking for discrepancies" (Bohmer and Shuman 2008: 136), identifying weaknesses inherent in asylum stories (Jubany 2017: 135) and "searching for untruth" (Kelly 2012: 765).[36] Thus, decision-makers focus more on finding indicators of non-credibility than of credibility (see also Johannesson 2017: 12). This is something I also observed in the SEM and is a practice I have elsewhere opted to call "digging deep" (Affolter 2020; see also Affolter 2017: 155). Digging deep refers to the practice whereby decision-makers interrogate asylum seekers until they have enough arguments to reject an asylum claim on the basis of non-credibility, or are convinced that the applicant's story is true "after all". This is how asylum interviews are usually done, but in some cases decision-makers might also decide not to dig deep because they already know from professional experience that the asylum seeker is telling "the truth". Samuel's statement illustrates this practice of "digging deep". Talking about how to properly conduct asylum interviews he explained: "And then you have to probe [the asylum seekers]. You can't content yourself with an answer that doesn't convince you. But then there might still be something to [what they have told you]. So you have to probe them until you're either

[35]Mauro, deputy head of an asylum unit, headquarters, interview transcript, my own translation.

[36]See also Jessica Anderson et al. (2014), Rosemary Byrne (2007), Ilene Durst (2000), Olga Jubany (2011), Michael Kagan (2003), Audrey Macklin (1998), Thomas Scheffer (2001: 184; 2003: 455), James Souter (2011), Robert Thomas (2009) and Trevor Trueman (2009: 296).

convinced that it's true or that it isn't.[37] Two distinct metaphors were used by decision-makers to describe what I have called "digging deep": "It is like a funnel (*Trichter*)",[38] one said and another one compared it to the "tightening of a noose (*Zuziehen einer Schlinge*)".[39] The first metaphor seems to indicate that through this kind of questioning one gets closer and closer to the heart of the matter; "the truth" (or "non-truth") of what happened.[40] The second metaphor fits with the prevalent "institutional mistrust" I encountered, with the assumption that asylum seekers can and will often lie, which is an issue I deal with in detail in Chapter 6.

In what follows, I now turn to how "digging deep" works in practice and how through "digging deep" on-file, facts are created in order to justify written decisions. I do so by showing on the basis of a specific example, how *one* such a viable on-file fact is generated in the asylum interview. The case concerns a man in his early-forties from Eritrea. The caseworker in charge, Bernard, who is an "old stager" working in one of the RPCs, rejected the man's asylum claim on the grounds of "non-credibility". The sole legal criterion Bernard used to justify his decision was that of "inherent contradictions", which, as my research showed, is the criterion must commonly applied for reasoning negative credibility decisions. One of the on-file facts Bernard refers to in justifying his decision is this one:

> Whilst in your free narrative you said that about 20 days to a month passed between the first time the authorities came to your house and the time the military searched your house (see file A9, p. 8), you later said that only two to three days had passed between the questioning by the authorities and the searching of the house. (see file A9, p. 22)[41]

---

[37] Samuel, caseworker, headquarters, interview transcript, my own translation.

[38] Tom, caseworker, reception and processing centre, interview transcript, my own translation.

[39] Gabriel, caseworker, headquarters, interview transcript, my own translation.

[40] Decision-making is, of course, not really about "finding out the truth", as I was repeatedly told by caseworkers and is nicely exemplified by Peter's statement: "In the training courses – but that was mere provocation, you have to understand – I used to always say: 'If someone manages to convince you of their eligibility to asylum even if they are lying they deserve to be granted asylum according to the law and if someone tells you the truth, but does not manage to render their story credible, then they deserve a negative decision'. I always used this to teach the new caseworkers that they should not look for the truth. No-one requires us to do that. The law just requires us to assess whether something is credible or no. We don't have to find out the truth, otherwise we could never take a decision. […] If you look for the truth, you will never find it, [or] hardly ever" (Peter, caseworker, headquarters, interview transcript, my own translation). However, a few newcomers confided in me that not trying to find out "the truth" was something they really struggled with and that they often, nevertheless, tried to do so even if they were aware they could never fully achieve that.

[41] Asylum decision, field document, my own translation.

But how was this particular on-file fact created? When Bernard brought me the applicant's case file a few days prior to the interview, he told me that he thought his 'case' would probably lead to a negative decision (with temporary admission). He told me that he had already found a couple of contradictions in the minutes of the first short interview and, therefore, thought there was probably nothing to the applicant's story. Because of this he planned on asking some "mean questions"—as he called them—in order to see whether they would lead to further contradictions in the second interview. On the day of the interview, Bernard, as usual, started the part about the applicant's reasons for applying for asylum in the interview with an open question: "Ok, so now you can freely tell me about what happened to you personally in Eritrea and why you left Eritrea".[42] In his narrative, the asylum seeker mentioned the following event: "Two or three armed people came to my home. They asked me questions. They insulted me verbally. Then they beat me. I don't remember what happened after that [...]. They left us alone for roughly 20 days to a month. [...] The soldiers then searched our house".[43] Later on in the interview, Bernard began asking the asylum seeker "wh-"[44] and "yes or no questions":

Q: To confirm, just a quick question: If I've understood you correctly, the authorities came to your house twice. The first time you were interrogated and beat and the second time your house was searched. Is that correct?
A: Yes. They knew I had contact with X. The government has spies everywhere.
Q: How much time passed in-between these two events, roughly?
A: A short time; about two or three days. They really wanted to know what X had said to me.
Q: Can you name the date your house was searched and you left [your home town]?[45]

Finally, at the end of the interview, Bernard confronted the applicant with contradictions:

Q: You said today that you were left alone for about 20 days after the first interrogation by the authorities. Later you said that two or three days passed between the two interrogations. Which one is true?

---

[42] Minutes of second asylum interview, field document, my own translation.

[43] Minutes of second asylum interview, field document, my own translation.

[44] "Wh- questions usually start with a word beginning with wh-, but 'how' is also included. The wh-words are: what, when, where, who, whom, which, whose, why, and how" (https://dictionary.cambridge.org/de/worterbuch/englisch/wh-question, last accessed 13.02.2020).

[45] Minutes of second asylum, field document, my own translation.

A: It was two or three days. If last time I said 20 days I was referring to the time span when I left [my home town]. There were so many problems. That's why I can't remember everything too clearly.[46]

Bernard already had an idea what decision he was going to take before the interview. Thus, he already knew what "direction" his questions would go in, before even starting the interview. This is something I came across frequently. What makes decision-makers already have such preconceptions differs. Sometimes, as with Bernard, it is because they have found contradictions in the minutes of the first interview or because of a particular "feeling" when reading the minutes of the first interview. And sometimes it is related to what—from experience—they expect from applicants "belonging" to certain groups.

Another typical aspect the example brings to light is the questioning technique used to test credibility. It is common for decision-makers to start the part about applicants' reasons for leaving their country and applying for asylum in the interviews with an open question such as "Why did you leave country XY and apply for asylum in Switzerland?".[47] After that the decision-makers follow-up up with specific "wh-questions" and some yes or no questions. And, at the end of the interview, decision-makers usually confront asylum seekers with contradictions they have found in their story, which already counts as granting applicants the right to be heard (*rechtliches Gehör gewähren*). This technique is taught to all decision-makers in the initial training they receive. The open question at the beginning is intended to give asylum seekers the opportunity to tell their stories. At the same time, several decision-makers told me that this strategy of starting with an open question was useful because in their "free narrative" (*freien Erzählung*) asylum

[46]Minutes of second asylum interview, field document, my own translation.

[47]The part on applicants' reasons for applying for asylum usually constitutes the second part of the interviews. In the first part, asylum seekers are asked questions about their "life at home"; their family, living situation, occupation, educational background, etc. These questions serve three different purposes. First, decision-makers need this kind of information for assessing the "reasonableness" of return in order to know, for example, if applicants have a support network "at home" and/or the means to survive. Second, many decision-makers told me that these questions served to create a "friendly", "unthreatening" atmosphere in which asylum seekers would feel more comfortable to talk. Thus, I frequently observed decision-makers stopping asylum seekers who, right at the beginning of the interview, started taking about their reasons for leaving their countries and telling them that they "would come to that later". Third, several decision-makers told me that those questions were useful because one could compare the applicants' ways of narrating the answers to those "unthreatening" questions with the ways in which they talked about their reasons for applying for asylum. This fits the method of "structure comparison" (*Strukturvergleich*) from forensic psychology which is taught in the training modules both for new and "old" employees (for the method of structure comparison, see, for instance, Greuel et al. 1998; Volbert and Steller 2009).

seekers tended to get tangled up in contradictions—"if the story was not true" (see also Jubany 2017: 136; Poertner 2018: 161–162). One purpose of the follow-up questions (the wh-questions in particular) then is to enable the decision-makers to collect all the necessary information for taking their decisions (e.g. who exactly the persecutors were and what might have been motives for persecution). Another purpose of these questions is to see whether asylum seekers can talk in detail about certain events they are asked about (e.g. "please tell me in detail about the daily routine in prison") or to generate answers the decision-makers can then compare with "facts" they can look up (e.g. "what was the name of your church that was bombed?"). Both these things—depending on whether asylum seekers manage to answer them adequately or not—serve as indicators of credibility or non-credibility; if they are found as non-credible, the corresponding criteria would be "unfoundedness" and "contradiction to facts". Finally, as Bernard's example shows, these questions allow for comparisons.[48] Hence, in order to "be able to" reason non-credibility decisions on the basis of contradictions, decision-makers need on-file facts that they can compare with. Three possibilities for comparison are created through the asylum procedure. Decision-makers can compare asylum seekers' recorded statements from the first interview with those from the second (and possibly third) interview. They can compare the statements of people who share certain experiences, such as siblings or spouses, for example, and they can make comparisons between statements from the one and the same interview, as Bernard did (see also Dahlvik 2018: 144; Scheffer 2001: 160–165; 2003: 438–443).

Writing Asylum Decisions: The Final Creation of Legal Facts

If interviews are "done well", writing asylum decisions is usually not very difficult anymore I was often told by decision-makers, as exemplified by Ralph's statement: "If the interview and your preparation work was good, then the decision itself does not require so much effort. I mean, then it's just committing to paper what you've found out. […] The most elaborate and time-consuming part happens before. By the time you write the decision, you've already made up your mind" (see also Kelly 2012: 762).[49] Yet, occasionally, even after having carried out the asylum interview, decision-makers

[48]This fits the method of "consistency analysis" (*Konstanzanalyse*) from forensic psychology (see, for instance, Greuel et al. 1998; Volbert and Steller 2009).

[49]Ralph, caseworker, reception and processing centre, interview transcript, my own translation.

are still unsure how to decide. I never observed this happening in practice during my fieldwork, but several caseworkers told me that in such cases they usually just started writing a decision to see if they could find enough arguments for it and, if not, they would try taking a different type of decision until they found one that worked (see also Poertner 2018: 194). Thus, as Jonathan Miaz argues, "in sum, the civil servants take a certain decision because they have the arguments for justifying it" (cited and translated by Poertner 2018: 196; see Miaz 2017: 327).

Asylum decisions consist of two main parts. The first part describes the "facts of the case" (*Sachverhalt*) and, in the second part, the legal justifications for taking a particular decision are outlined. All decision-makers I observed writing decisions kept going back and forth between writing the two parts, adding bits and pieces that they had found from reading through the documents in the case file and adapting the first part which describes the "facts of the case" so that it would fit the reasoning part. This is important because, in the end, the first part should only indicate aspects that are then also mentioned in the legal justifications part. Ephraim Poertner fittingly calls this process "decision-editing" rather than "decision-making" (2018: 194). The example below shows how Manuela, a historian who, when I met her, had been working at the SEM for just over two years, struggles but finally succeeds in finding the necessary on-file facts in the minutes for justifying her decisions:

> I am sitting next to Manuela at her desk. She is writing a decision for a woman from Sri Lanka. Manuela tells me that for her it is clear what the decision is going to be. She will not grant the woman asylum, but temporary admission. She says that the 'case' is clearly not credible; the woman's statements completely unfounded. However, she explains that upon every question the applicant added some more information, which makes it difficult for her to take a negative decision solely on the basis of "unfounded-ness". Manuela regrets that there aren't any contradictions in the asylum seeker's story, because this, she says, would have made reasoning the 'case' with non-credibility much easier. She tells me that she has also had a quick look at the applicant's brother's case file, just to see whether it confirms her feeling, which it does.
>
> Manuela starts by summarising the "facts of the case". Then she selects two boilerplates: one for Article 3 and one for Article 7. She starts working on the Article 7 argument, selecting the boilerplate for "unfoundedness". For this, she then starts looking for on-file facts which show the "unfoundedness" of the applicant's claims in the minutes of the asylum interviews. Every time she finds one, she makes a bullet point of it in the reasoning part of the decision and then goes back to the part on the "facts of the case" to make some

> changes. When looking for such text passages she discovers some contradictions between statements in the minutes from the applicant's case file and those from the applicant's brother's. She makes a note of those contradictions and adds the boiler plate for "inherent contradictions" to the decision. She explains to me that this comparison is important because otherwise she would not have enough arguments for the decision. Other [caseworkers] might have already been satisfied with "unfoundedness", she says, but she just didn't feel secure enough about it. Because she has to grant the applicant the right to be heard on these contradictions if she wants to use them for her decision, she can't finish the decision just yet. Thus, she sets the case file aside and starts working on something else.[50] (field notes)

What does this example show us? Although for Manuela it was clear from the beginning what the decision was going to be (even before she started writing it), she could, at first, not find sufficient on-file facts to reason her decision. Her professional-practical knowledge told her this story was "unfounded"; a credible story sounded different; it was much more detailed—she was sure about that. However, at the same time, Manuela struggled to find arguments for justifying, on the basis of specific examples from the minutes, that the applicant had been unable to provide any detailed information on what she had experienced. In this 'case', she found this particularly difficult because whenever she had asked the applicant about "details" (e.g. by asking her how she had received the job as a secretary to a LTTE general; how she had met this general; and why he had given her this job), the applicant had added new information, but this information still did not seem detailed enough to Manuela. However, she did not really know how to show this. In the end, Manuela managed to find some contradictions (her favourite non-credibility criterion as she told me) because she was able to use the brother's case file for comparison. With the contradictions she discovered, her justification became complete. Manuela did not know what had "really happened" to this woman in Sri Lanka. She suspected that the applicant maybe had experienced problems in Sri Lanka due to being a single woman or maybe she had been forced to get married. But for Manuela it did not matter that she did not know this. Her duty was to achieve enough decisional certainty for producing a clear-cut, justifiable either/or decision. And that she had done.

[50] Field notes, my own translation.

Managing Uncertainty: The Importance of Credibility Determination

So far, this chapter has evidenced that professional-practical knowledge, country knowledge decision-makers themselves have acquired, expert knowledge and reports, the production of on-file facts in asylum interviews through the use of specific questioning techniques and the assembling of on-file facts with legal criteria in the process of writing decisions all enable asylum caseworkers to overcome the uncertainties inherent in asylum decision-making. This then allows them to take clear-cut either/or decisions that they feel comfortable with, in the light of the emotional burden asylum decision-making poses, and which for them also seem justifiable towards "the outside", as I will show in more detail in Chapter 5. In this final part of the chapter, I want to argue that credibility determination in itself constitutes an important means for dealing with and overcoming uncertainty.

Because negative asylum decisions are registered with the same code regardless of whether they are taken on the basis of non-credibility or on the basis of asylum seekers being regarded as not eligible to refugee status or a combination of both, it is not possible to draw statistics on the frequency of these different decisions. However, all the decision-makers I spoke to were of the impression that the majority of negative decisions are based on non-credibility, which is also something that has been described for other asylum administrations in the Global North (see introduction to this book). In accord with this, the SEM online manual on asylum and return states that the majority of rejections are attributable to asylum seekers' claims lacking credibility.[51] The argument presented here by the SEM, therefore, at least implicitly, suggests that the reason for the majority of asylum seekers being refused refugee status is that most of them lie (see Affolter 2018). However, this seemingly tautological assumption is something I question. As this chapter has demonstrated, so-called "liars", "lies" and elements of non-credibility are produced through the questioning techniques used in asylum interviews themselves, independent of asylum seekers' motivations (see also Crawley 1999: 52; Sbriccoli and Jacoviello 2011: 184–185; Scheffer 2001, 2003).

One reason why the majority of asylum claims are rejected on the basis of non-credibility has to do with the "official" policy in the SEM to take negative decisions on the basis of Article 7 whenever possible. Or, at least,

---

[51] https://www.sem.admin.ch/dam/data/sem/asyl/verfahren/hb/c/hb-c61-d.pdf, last accessed 14.02.2020. Furthermore, the analysis of my sample of case files shows that out of forty-two negative decisions, twenty-nine were inter alia argued on the basis of Article 7 AsylA.

that seemed to be the case in most of the asylum units during my fieldwork, while some decision-makers from one of the RPCs told me that they had never heard of this policy. The reason that was commonly given to me for this policy was that Article 7 arguments were much more difficult to challenge successfully on appeal level by the asylum seekers (and their lawyers). Hence, the decision-makers claimed that if they argued on the basis of the applicant's recorded statements in the minutes that there were contradictions in the narrative or that what the applicant had said contradicted "given facts" (*Tatsachen*) that was then very difficult to confound. The policy is, therefore, linked to fact creation and, as I will outline in the following, creating non-refutable facts for Article 7 decisions is often easier than for Article 3 decisions. At the same time, and in seeming contradiction to what I have just claimed, I argue that the "subjective quality" ascribed to credibility assessments by decision-makers additionally reinforces this policy. I observed in the SEM that having an Article 3 decision quashed by the Federal Administrative Court was often valuated as significantly worse than having a decision quashed by the court because of an "erroneous" credibility assessment. In the latter case, it was deemed expectable that in some cases the judges might "subjectively" evaluate an applicant's credibility differently.

Basing negative decisions on Article 7 AsylA rather than on Article 3 AsylA is, however, not just an institutional policy. Most caseworkers I spoke to claimed that this was also their personal preference. I argue that there are two main reasons for this. The first reason is that uncertainties are more easily overcome with such decisions. Or, in other words, it is often easier to achieve decisional certainty for non-credibility decisions than for negative decisions based on non-eligibility to refugee status:

> Testing the credibility is especially important if they [the asylum seekers] come from states that act in an arbitrary manner [*willkürliche Staaten*]. [...] Or broadly speaking, the worse the situation in a country, the more we have to focus on the credibility of the claim, or the more we tend to argue on the basis of credibility. I guess we have to. Because in such countries even a minor political activity can quickly result in the person being persecuted.[52]

> For instance, a mafia story: is it relevant for asylum or not? [...] Because [...] the state [of origin] is not really capable of protection (*schutzfähig*). [Yet,] there is no real motive for asylum behind it. [...] But if you just say, this is all not credible, then you kind of cover your back.[53]

[52]Samuel, caseworker, headquarters, interview transcript, my own translation.

[53]Daniel, caseworker, reception and processing centre, interview transcript, my own translation.

In their statements, Samuel and Daniel insinuate that often as a decision-maker one has no way of knowing whether an applicant might be in danger of future persecution in their "country of origin" or not—anything could in some countries potentially lead to someone being persecuted. In contrast, for the reasons presented in this chapter, for them there is a way of sufficiently knowing whether an asylum seeker's claims are credible or not. The second reason why decision-makers prefer rejecting asylum claims on the basis of non-credibility rather than on non-eligibility to refugee status is because it is emotionally easier. One caseworker, for instance, told me that it sometimes felt so cynical to her to say to someone from Syria, for example: "You have no reason to be afraid" of going back to Syria. But she felt that pointing out the contradictions in asylum seekers' statements and raising doubt about a whole story instead was easier.[54] Another decision-maker, Helen, too expressed this in an even more explicit way: "But I can also tell you why [I prefer arguing negative decisions on the basis of non-credibility]. It's for my conscience. If someone tells you rubbish [*dir einen Stuss erzählt*], then you don't have such a guilty conscience".[55] Helen and Patricia's statements indicate how, through reasoning with Article 7, the responsibility for the outcome of the decision is shifted to the asylum seekers: it is their fault for not telling "the truth".[56] Thereby, the emotional burden of taking such life-changing decisions is lessened.

Concluding Remarks

Decision-makers are requested to reach clear-cut either/or decisions. Thus, they must classify asylum seekers into one of four categories: refugee with asylum, refugee with temporary admission, non-refugee with temporary admission and non-refugee without temporary admission. These classifications have major impacts on asylum seekers' lives since they lead to different rights and obligations. Not only do they have an impact on whether a person is legally allowed to reside in Switzerland or not, they also affect whether a person has the right to immediately apply for family reunification or whether they must first wait for at least three years before they can apply for it. Hence,

[54] Patricia, caseworker, headquarters, interview transcript, my own translation.

[55] Helen, caseworker, headquarters, interview transcript, my own translation.

[56] This allocation of responsibility can also clearly be seen in the standard way asylum seekers are informed about their "duty to collaborate" at the beginning of asylum interviews: "You have the duty to say the truth and the duty to collaborate in the process of gathering the facts for the evaluation of your application. You bear responsibility for your statements. If you make untrue statements, this might have negative consequences for you" (Poertner 2018: 153–154).

if asylum seekers' stories are classified as non-credible and, due to this, the applicants are granted temporary admission rather than asylum, this means that they can only apply for their spouses and unmarried children under the age of eighteen to be granted temporary admission after three years, and only if they do not depend on social welfare and are, thus, able to provide for their families by themselves.[57] For recognised refugees who have been granted asylum, on the other hand, there are no such restrictions.

This chapter has shown how decision-makers go about reaching such clear-cut decisions and how, in order to do so, they try to overcome the uncertainties inherent in asylum decision-making. Law requires clear-cut categorisations. As such, it constitutes a fundamental structural condition of bureaucratic decision-making. The chapter has brought to light how this structural condition shapes SEM caseworkers' practices. Furthermore, it has shown how through the classification into clear-cut legal categories, in the process of which ambiguities and doubts are reduced and often become hidden from sight, new legal facts and "truths" are created. And it has pointed to the crucial role intuitive and incorporated knowledge plays in decision-making. It helps decision-makers acquire enough certainty for reaching decisions in a twofold way. On the one hand, decision-makers very much trust their intuitive knowledge, gaining a sense of "felt security" from it. On the other hand, by guiding decision-makers' actions in dealing with case files, conducting asylum interviews and writing decisions, it also plays an essential role in overcoming uncertainties through the production of legal facts.

This knowledge, which lies in "the doing" of actions itself (see Dahlvik 2018: 57), constitutes part of decision-makers' institutional habitus. But not only is the institutional habitus constituted in this way by decision-makers' everyday practices, it is also constitutive of the latter, as this chapter has shown. By creating the legal "truths" decision-makers intuitively set out to look for through their everyday practice, the institutional habitus is continuously reaffirmed. However, it is important to note that this self-sustaining production of "truths" is not something that is (for the most part) carried out consciously and mean-spiritedly, but should rather be understood as the workings of the institutional habitus. Nevertheless, decision-makers' practices are, of course, not structured in a deterministic way (see also Hitchings 2012). They are also—and must to some extent always remain—creative; allowing decision-makers to deal with asylum applications on a case-by-case

[57] https://www.refugeecouncil.ch/asylum-law/legal-status/temporary-admission-of-foreigners.html, last accessed 28.02.2020.

basis, dealing with the particular uncertainties as they arise from the individual 'cases' and situations (see also Bourdieu 1990: 55; Dahlvik 2018: 62; Shove and Pantzar 2007). Yet, what for decision-makers comes to constitute "normal", acceptable and doable ways of dealing with and assessing 'cases' is shaped by what they know (and can and cannot know) as well as the organisational, legal and ideological structures they are embedded in. It is set by the limits of their institutional habitus (Wacquant 1992: 19).

References

Affolter, Laura. 2017. "Asyl-Verwaltung kraft Wissen: Die Herstellung von Entscheidungswissen in einer Schweizer Asylbehörde." In *Asyl verwalten. Zur bürokratischen Bearbeitung eines gesellschaftlichen Problems*, edited by Christian Lahusen, and Stephanie Schneider, 145–171. Bielefeld: transcript.

Affolter, Laura. 2018. "Der grösste Teil von [unserem] Job ist Unglaubhaftigkeit." *Terra Cognita – Schweizer Zeitschrift zu Integration und Migration* 32: 92–94.

Affolter, Laura. 2020. "Keeping Numbers Low in the Name of Fairness. Ethos and Ethics in a Swiss Asylum Administration." In *The Bureaucratic Production of Difference*, edited by Julia Eckert, 27–57. Bielefeld: transcript.

Affolter, Laura, Jonathan Miaz, and Ephraim Poertner. 2019. "Taking the 'Just' Decision: Caseworkers and Their Communities of Interpretation in the Swiss Asylum Office." In *Asylum Determination in Europe. Ethnographic Perspectives*, edited by Nick Gill, and Anthony Good, 263–284. Cham: Palgrave Macmillan.

Amado, Barbara G., Ramon Arce, and Francisca Fariña. 2015. "Undeutsch Hypothesis and Criteria Based Content Analysis: A Meta-Analytic Review." *The European Journal of Psychology Applied to Legal Context* 7 (1): 3–12. https://doi.org/10.1016/j.ejpal.2014.11.002.

Amado, Barbara G., Ramon Arce, Francisca Fariña, and Manuel Vilariño. 2016. "Criteria-Based Content Analysis (CBCA) Reality Criteria in Adults: A Meta-Analytic Review." *International Journal of Clinical and Health Psychology* 16 (2): 201–210. https://doi.org/10.1016/j.ijchp.2016.01.002.

Anderson, Jessica, Jeannine Hollaus, Annelisa Lindsay, and Collin Williamson. 2014. *The Culture of Disbelief: An Ethnographic Approach to Understanding an Under-Theorised Concept in the UK Asylum System.* Working Paper Series No. 102. Oxford: Refugee Studies Centre. https://www.rsc.ox.ac.uk/files/files-1/wp102-culture-of-disbelief-2014.pdf, last accessed February 3, 2020.

Asylum Act, (AsylA), of 26 June 1998 (Status as of 1 January 2020). 142.31.

Bloch, Maurice. 1991. "Language, Anthropology and Cognitive Science." *Man* (New Series) 26 (2): 183–198. https://www.jstor.org/stable/pdf/2803828.pdf, last accessed March 13, 2020.

Bohmer, Carol, and Amy Shuman. 2008. *Rejecting Refugees: Political Asylum in the 21st Century*. London: Routledge.

Bourdieu, Pierre. 1990. *The Logic of Practice*. Translated by Richard Nice. Stanford: Stanford University Press.

Breidenstein, Georg, Stefan Hirschauer, Herbert Kalthoff, and Boris Nieswand. 2013. *Ethnografie. Die Praxis der Feldforschung*. Stuttgart: UTB.

Byrne, Rosemary. 2007. "Assessing Testimonial Evidence in Asylum Proceedings: Guiding Standards from the International Criminal Tribunals." *International Journal of Refugee Law* 19 (4): 609–638. https://doi.org/10.1093/ijrl/eem056.

Cabot, Heath. 2014. *On the doorstep of Europe: Asylum and Citizenship in Greece*. Philadelphia: University of Pennsylvania Press.

Crawley, Heaven. 1999. *Breaking Down the Barriers: A Report on the Conduct of Asylum Interviews at Ports*. London: Immigration Law Practitioners' Association (ILPA).

Dahlvik, Julia. 2018. *Inside Asylum Bureaucracy: Organizing Refugee Status Determination in Austria*. IMISCOE Research Series. Cham: Springer.

Downs, Anthony. 1967. *Inside Bureaucracy*. Boston: Little, Brown and Company.

Dubois, Vincent. 2010. *The Bureaucrat and the Poor: Encounters in French Welfare Offices*. Translated by Jean-Yves Bart. Farnham: Ashgate.

Durst, Ilene. 2000. "Lost in Translation: Why Due Process Demands Deference to the Refugee's Narrative." *Rutgers Law Review* 53: 127–179. https://papers.ssrn.com/sol3/papers.cfm?abstract_id=269166, last accessed February 26, 2020.

Eckert, Julia. 2020. "The Office. Ethos and Ethics in Migration Bureaucracies." In *The Bureaucratic Production of Difference*, edited by Julia Eckert, 7–26. Bielefeld: transcript.

EMARK. 2004/01. https://ark-cra.rekurskommissionen.ch/assets/resources/ark/emark/2004/01.htm, last accessed February 26, 2020.

Fassin, Didier. 2013. "The Precarious Truth of Asylum." *Public Culture* 25 (1 (69)): 39–63. https://doi.org/10.1215/08992363-1890459.

Fassin, Didier, and Carolina Kobelinsky. 2012. "How Asylum Claims Are Adjudicated: The Institution as a Moral Agent." *Revue française de sociologie* 53 (4): 444–472. https://doi.org/10.3917/rfs.534.0657.

Gibb, Robert, and Anthony Good. 2013. "Do the Facts Speak for Themselves? Country of Origin Information in French and British Refugee Status Determination Procedures." *International Journal of Refugee Law* 25 (2): 291–322. https://doi.org/10.1093/ijrl/eet015.

Greuel, Luise, Susanne Offe, Agnes Fabian, Peter Wetzels, Thomas Fabian, Heinz Offe, and Michael Stadler. 1998. *Glaubhaftigkeit der Zeugenaussage: Theorie und Praxis der forensisch-psychologischen Begutachtung*. Weinheim: Beltz.

Griffiths, Melanie. 2012. "'Vile Liars and Truth Distorters'. Truth, Trust and the Asylum System." *Anthropology Today* 28 (5): 8–12. https://doi.org/10.1111/j.1467-8322.2012.00896.x.

Hitchings, Russel. 2012. "People Can Talk About Their Practices." *Area* 44 (1): 61–67. https://doi.org/10.1111/j.1475-4762.2011.01060.x.

Johannesson, Livia. 2017. *In Courts We Trust. Administrative Justice in Swedish Migration Courts*. Stockholm University. http://www.diva-portal.org/smash/get/diva2:1072557/FULLTEXT01.pdf, last accessed February 03, 2020.

Jubany, Olga. 2011. "Constructing Truths in a Culture of Disbelief: Understanding Asylum Screening from Within." *International Sociology* 26 (1): 74–94. https://doi.org/10.1177/0268580910380978.

Jubany, Olga. 2017. *Screening Asylum in a Culture of Disbelief: Truths, Denials and Sceptical Borders*. Cham: Palgrave Macmillan.

Kagan, Michael. 2003. "Is Truth in the Eye of the Beholder? Objective Credibility Assessment in Refugee Status Determination." *Georgetown Immigration Law Journal* 17 (3): 367–415. https://scholars.law.unlv.edu/facpub/633, last accessed February 03, 2020.

Kelly, Tobias. 2012. "Sympathy and Suspicion: Torture, Asylum, and Humanity." *Journal of the Royal Anthropological Institute* 18 (4): 753–768. https://doi.org/10.1111/j.1467-9655.2012.01790.x.

Kelly, Tobias. 2015. "Afterword." In *Of Doubt and Proof: Ritual and Legal Practices of Judgement*, edited by Daniela Berti, Anthony Good, and Gilles Tarabout, 183–192. Farnham: Ashgate.

Lahusen, Christian, and Stephanie Schneider. 2017. "Asyl verwalten: Eine Einleitung." In *Asyl verwalten. Zur bürokratischen Bearbeitung eines gesellschaftlichen Problems*, edited by Christian Lahusen, and Stephanie Schneider, 7–24. Bielefeld: transcript.

Lavanchy, Anne. 2014. "Die Gefühlswelt des Gesetzes. Die kritische Umsetzung von eherechtlichen Vorschriften im Zivistandsamt." *FAMPRA* 1: 92–117.

Liodden, Tone Maia. 2016. "The Burdens of Discretion. Managing Uncertainty in the Asylum Bureaucracy." PhD diss. (unpublished), University of Oslo.

Lipsky, Michael. 2010. *Street-Level Bureaucracy, 30th Anniversary Edition: Dilemmas of the Individual in Public Service*. New York: Russel Sage Foundation.

Macklin, Audrey. 1998. "Truth and Consequences: Credibility Determination in the Refugee Context." Conference Paper. Ottawa: International Association of Refugee Law Judges. http://refugeestudies.org/UNHCR/97%20-%20Truth%20and%20Consequences.%20Credibility%20Determination%20in%20Refugee%20Context.%20by%20Audrey%20Macklin.pdf, last accessed February 03, 2020.

Miaz, Jonathan. 2017. "Politique d'asile et sophistication du droit: Pratiques administratives et défense juridique des migrants en Suisse (1981–2015)." PhD diss. (unpublished), University of Lausanne and University of Strasbourg.

Pelosi, Anna. 1996. "Intercultural Communication in the Refugee Determination Hearing." Master Thesis. Montreal: School of Social Work, McGill University. http://digitool.library.mcgill.ca/R/?func=dbin-jump-full&object_id=27480&local_base=GEN01-MCG02, last accessed July 15, 2017.

Poertner, Ephraim. 2017. "Governing Asylum through Configurations of Productivity and Deterrence: Effects on the Spatiotemporal Trajectories of Cases in Switzerland." *Geoforum* 78: 12–21. https://doi.org/10.1016/j.geoforum.2016.11.004.

Poertner, Ephraim. 2018. "Re-Cording Lives: Governing Asylum in Switzerland and the Need to Resolve." PhD diss. (unpublished), University of Zurich.

Polanyi, Michael. 1962 (1958). *Personal Knowledge: Towards a Post-Critical Philosophy*. London: Routledge.

Polanyi, Michael. 1966. *The Tacit Dimension*. Chicago: University of Chicago Press.

Reckwitz, Andreas. 2003. "Grundelemente einer Theorie sozialer Praktiken: Eine sozialtheoretische Perspektive." *Zeitschrift für Soziologie* 32 (4): 282–301.

Rosset, Damian. 2015. "Les informations sur les pays d'origine dans les procédures d'asile: construction et négociation institutionnelle de la réalité." *Jusletter* 16 (3). http://jusletter.weblaw.ch/en/juslissues/2015/794/le-savoir-sur-les-pa_097022417f.html, last accessed July 13, 2017.

Rosset, Damian, and Tone Liodden. 2015. "The Eritrea Report: Symbolic Uses of Expert Information in Asylum Politics." *Oxford Monitor of Forced Migration* 5 (1): 26–32.

Rousseau, Cécile, François Crépeau, Patricia Foxen, and France Houle. 2002. "The Complexity of Determining Refugeehood: A Multidisciplinary Analysis of the Decision-making Process of the Canadian Immigration and Refugee Board." *Journal of Refugee Studies* 15 (1): 43–70. https://doi.org/10.1093/jrs/15.1.43.

Ryle, Gilbert. 1951 (1949). *The Concept of Mind*. London: Hutchinsons University Library.

Sbriccoli, Tommaso, and Stefano Jacoviello. 2011. "The Case of S: Elaborating the 'Right' Narrative to Fit Normative/Political Expectations in Asylum Procedure in Italy." In *Cultural Expertise and Litigation*, edited by Livia Holden, 172–194. Abingdon and New York: Routledge.

Scheffer, Thomas. 2001. *Asylgewährung: Eine ethnographische Analyse des deutschen Asylverfahrens*. Stuttgart: Lucius & Lucius.

Scheffer, Thomas. 2003. "Kritik der Urteilskraft: Wie die Asylprüfung Unentscheidbares in Entscheidbares überführt." In *Migration steuern und verwalten: Deutschland vom späten 19. Jahrhundert bis zur Gegenwart*, edited by Jochen Oltmer, 423–458. Göttingen: Vandenhoeck & Ruprecht.

Schneider, Stephanie. 2019. "Becoming a Decision-Maker, or: 'Don't Turn Your Heart into a Den of Thieves and Murderers'." In *Asylum Determination in Europe. Ethnographic Perspectives*, edited by Nick Gill, and Anthony Good, 285–306. Cham: Palgrave Macmillan.

Shove, Elizabeth, and Mika Pantzar. 2007. "Recruitment and Reproduction: The Careers and Carriers of Digital Photography and Floorball." *Human Affairs* 17 (2): 154–167. https://doi.org/10.2478/v10023-007-0014-9.

Simpson, Bob. 2006. "'You Don't Do Fieldwork, Fieldwork Does You': Between Subjectivation and Objectivation in Anthropological Fieldwork." In *The SAGE*

Handbook of Fieldwork, edited by Dick Hobbs, and Richard Wright, 125–137. London: Sage.

Souter, James. 2011. "A Culture of Disbelief or Denial? Critiquing Refugee Status Determination in the United Kingdom." *Oxford Monitor of Forced Migration* 1 (1): 48–59.

Sweeney, James A. 2007. "The 'Lure' of Facts in Asylum Appeals: Critiquing the Practice of Judges." In *Applying Theory to Policy and Practice: Issues for Critical Reflection*, edited by Steven R Smith, 19–35. Hampshire: Ashgate.

Thomas, Robert. 2009. "Refugee Roulette: A UK Perspective." In *Refugee Roulette: Disparities in Asylum Adjudication and Proposals for Return*, edited by Jaya Ramji-Nogales, Andrew I. Schoenholtz, and Philip G. Schrag, 164–186. New York: New York University Press.

Trueman, Trevor. 2009. "Reasons for Refusal: An Audit of 200 Refusals of Ethiopian Asylum-Seekers in England." *Journal of Immigration, Asylum and Nationality Law* 23 (3): 281–308.

Volbert, Renate, and Max Steller. 2009. "Die Begutachtung der Glaubhaftigkeit." In *Psychiatrische Begutachtung: Ein praktisches Handbuch für Ärzte und Juristen*, edited by Klaus Foerster, and Harald Dressing, 817–850. München: Elsevier, Urban & Fischer.

Wacquant, Loïc J.D. 1992. "Toward a Social Praxeology: The Structure and Logic of Bourdieu's Sociology." In *An Invitation to Reflexive Sociology*, edited by Pierre Bourdieu, and Loïc J.D. Wacquant, 1–59. Cambridge: Polity Press.

Wagenaar, Hendrik. 2004. "'Knowing' the Rules: Administrative Work as Practice." *Public Administration Review* 64 (6): 643–656. https://doi.org/10.1111/j.1540-6210.2004.00412.x.

Weber, Max. 2013 (1978). *Economy and Society*. Edited by Guenther Roth, and Claus Wittich. Berkeley: University of California Press.

5

Getting in Line with the Office

The habitus—people's dispositions of thinking, acting, feeling and desiring—is, according to Pierre Bourdieu, "socialized subjectivity" (Bourdieu and Wacquant 1992: 126). This chapter is about how (new) decision-makers are socialised in the SEM and thereby acquire an institutional habitus or, in other words, "socialised subjectivity". It looks at how decision-makers learn the appropriate ways of fulfilling their role and how they learn to "properly" interpret the law.

In their famous article "*Toward a theory of organizational socialization*", John Van Maanen and Edgar Schein define organisational socialisation as "the process by which one is taught and learns 'the ropes' of a particular organizational role. In its most general sense, organizational socialization is then the process by which an individual acquires the social knowledge and skills necessary to assume an organizational role" (1979: 211).[1] Moreover, in a more general sense, Christina Toren describes socialisation as "the process through which people [...] are made to take on the ideas and behaviour appropriate to life in a particular society" (2002: 512). Hence, socialisation stands for the process through which people, particularly novices, appropriate "acceptable"

[1] For further theoretical approaches to "organisational socialisation" see Blake Ashforth et al. (2007), Sue Ashford and Samir Nurmohamed (2012), Georgia Chao (2012), Roy Lewicki (1981), Peter Manning and John Van Maanen (1978) as well as Connie Wanberg (2012). Several authors, such as Julia Dahlvik (2018), Josiah Heyman (1995), Olga Jubany (2011, 2017), Tone Liodden (2016), Jonathan Miaz (2017a, b), Zachary Oberfield (2014), Johanna Probst (2012) Stephanie Schneider (2019) as well as Stephanie Schneider and Kristina Wottrich (2017) have also dealt with officials' socialisation in asylum administrations and street-level bureaucracies in more empirical terms. These authors' work has been crucial to informing my way of approaching institutional socialisation in the SEM in this chapter.

L. Affolter, *Asylum Matters*, Palgrave Socio-Legal Studies,
https://doi.org/10.1007/978-3-030-61512-3_5

ways of acting, thinking and desiring. If we want to understand how novices come to appropriate such ways, we thus need to look closely at three crucial points, salient in the definitions above.

First, the definitions show that socialisation is essentially about learning. Novices must learn the necessary skills and (social) knowledge for fulfilling their role within the organisation and they must learn the acceptable and appropriate ways to behave within their "society". Thus, we must concern ourselves with how new decision-makers learn to do their job and what is expected from them. Second, Toren writes that people are made to take on certain ideas and behaviours. This does not necessarily mean that novices are intentionally and explicitly forced to adopt particular ideas and behaviours, but rather that the appropriation of these ideas and behaviours may also be the outcome of the powerful influence which some actors have over others. Hence, we must pay attention to the influence the different actors involved in asylum decision-making have over each other. Third, the definitions show that socialisation is necessarily linked to belonging. Thus, in order for novices to learn the acceptable and appropriate ideas and the behaviours of their "society", there must be a "society" they affiliate themselves with (or are affiliated with) and are trying to fit into. Consequently, we need to explore what belonging means for decision-makers in the SEM. The chapter is structured around these three different aspects. In the first part, I explore how people become members of the office; the different affiliations and allegiances they develop within the office; as well as what this means in terms of "belonging". The second part of the chapter then sets out how newcomers to the office acquire the necessary knowledge and skills to fulfil their roles as decision-makers. And in the third part, I show how accountability towards superiors and peers, but also beyond that towards politicians, media and "the public", shapes what decision-makers do. Finally, I argue that only by looking at these above-mentioned processes together can we come to understand how certain things become self-evident for decision-makers to do, think and want.

Becoming a Member of the Office

In order to become socialised in the office, decision-makers must first become part of it. This section of the chapter explores who the people working in the asylum units of the SEM are and what their motives for doing the job are. I set forth patterns in decision-makers' profiles that I observed and link them to recruitment procedures in the SEM. I thereby show what qualities the (different) heads of asylum units look out for in new recruits. This provides a first image of what, in the eyes of superiors, constitutes a "good decision-maker" and what is, therefore, expected from new caseworkers once they have joined the office. Because it is mainly the heads of the individual asylum units themselves (together with the deputy heads) that recruit new decision-makers, this has a substantial impact on the composition of their teams, which, in turn, leads to the consolidation of ideas on "how to [best] interpret the law" and best fulfil the role of decision-maker, and to the development of "'shared repertoires' of knowledge" within the different units, as I will show in the last part of this section (Affolter et al. 2019: 265; see Wenger 2003). Thus, "belonging" may mean different things to different decision-makers working in the SEM. At least in part, this has to do with the different "groups", or what elsewhere—building on Wenger (2003)—we have called "communities of interpretation" that co-exist within the office (Affolter et al. 2019).

Who Are the Decision-Makers?

Gabriel is a political scientist who works as a decision-maker at the headquarters. This is his first "proper job". During his studies, he worked as a social aid representative and therefore already knows the asylum proceedings quite well. I met him on the first day of the training session, which was his first day at his new job. Two months later I interviewed him and asked about his motivations for applying for the job at the SEM. He replied: "I am interested in foreigners, other cultures. The basic idea is to help these people, even if we do – of course – reject many of them".[2]

Claire is a jurist. When I met her she had been working at one of the reception and processing centres (RPCs) for slightly more than a year. Prior to this she had worked as a clerk at a regional court for many years. She had considered taking her bar exams before joining the SEM, but then decided instead to look for a job in which she could do "something social", while still practising law.[3]

Patricia is a social anthropologist. After completing her studies she was an intern with UNHCR in an African country. In the long term her ambition is to work for a renowned international NGO, but, at the moment, she thinks that she needs more work experience for which the job at the SEM "proved to be a good opportunity". "I mean, the job does interest me", she told me in an

[2]Gabriel, caseworker, headquarters, interview transcript, my own translation.

[3]Claire, caseworker, reception and processing centre, field notes, my own translation.

interview, "but it's mainly just an entry point". When I met her she had been working in one of the units at the headquarters for a couple of months.[4]

> Helen is a lawyer. She applied to the SEM after a friend of hers told her about an employment opportunity. At the job interview she told the employers that she could not promise that she would stay for more than a year. But now, 15 years later, she is still doing the same job. She thinks it is too late for her to change jobs now. "I have probably become too specialised in asylum law to be able to work elsewhere", she told me.[5]

The four profiles above exemplify the main patterns I found amongst decision-makers in the SEM's asylum units.[6] First, with the exception of one person, all the decision-makers I spoke to in the SEM held a degree from university, which is hardly surprising since having a university degree is nowadays a formal requisite for becoming a caseworker in the SEM. Out of the thirty-one decision-makers from my sample, thirteen had a law degree. The same number had a background in humanities, with more than half of those being social anthropologists. Thus, social anthropology was second to law as the most common educational background in my sample. A second salient point is that for half of my interaction partners, the job at the SEM is their first "proper job" (see also Miaz 2017a: 187–188). However, many of them had done one or several internships previously, mostly "in the field of migration". This connects with the third pattern I observed, namely that prior to working in the SEM, many decision-makers had already gained experience in the "field of migration and asylum". Several had worked part-time in some capacity in the asylum process while they were still at university: as social aid representatives, minute-takers or "poolies". Others had worked for the UNHCR, the International Organization for Migration (IOM) or different cantonal migration offices. And others had come into contact with asylum proceedings through internships in Swiss embassies. My material shows that this is especially true for non-jurists. While several of my interaction partners with a legal background were employed as decision-makers without having any previous experience in the "field of migration", this was only the case for very few non-jurists.

[4] Patricia, caseworker, headquarters, interview transcript, my own translation.

[5] Helen, caseworker, headquarters, interview transcript, my own translation.

[6] Similar patterns are also described by Jonathan Miaz who did research in the SEM between 2010 and 2012 (see Miaz 2017a: 188–190).

People apply for the job as a decision-maker for several different reasons.[7] Many decision-makers stated a general interest in migrants and asylum seekers and in wanting to help them. A couple mentioned that this interest came from their personal experience: their parents had come to Switzerland as refugees. For most, however, this interest came from having worked with refugees (or migrants in general) previously. A main reason for applying for the job for those people was that they wanted to have a say in asylum decision-making and to not remain passive bystanders. Thus, they wanted to take on more responsibility themselves. Furthermore, several found the job appealing because it enabled face-to-face contact with people. The latter was especially often mentioned by decision-makers with a legal background. Many of whom had come to the SEM because they had wanted to do a job that contained not only legal but "social" aspects. Finally, for several, the job was a convenient entry-point into the professional world. For jurists in particular the job represents one of the few opportunities for directly going into practising law without taking the bar exams.

In my interviews with "old stagers" of the office, I would often ask them somewhat provocatively not why they had applied for the job, but why there were still there. Some of the reasons given for remaining closely resemble the initial motivations—or rather, as Jonathan Miaz has argued, the ex post rationalisations of motivations (2017a: 193, 201)—described above, but there are also others:

> Because I think my job is great. Every job is monotonous in a way, no matter what you do. But the situation in the world keeps changing. There are always adjustments and so you must always make sure to keep yourself up to date. The situation in Kosovo isn't the same as it used to be 15 years ago, but instead we've got other "trouble spots" (*Krisenherde*) now. [...] And then every person is different. Even if you've heard the same story a hundred times, you're still always dealing with an individual being and I find this having to engage with people very interesting. If we didn't have this customer contact I don't think I'd be working here anymore. [...] And, of course, the working conditions are great. We've got a lot of holidays, which I think we really need and the salary is good.[8]

Like Klaus, many officials mentioned "contact with people" as one of the things they like most about their job and, therefore, as one of the main

---

[7]What I describe here closely matches Jonathan Miaz's findings from his research in the SEM (see Miaz 2017a: 192–201, 219). Furthermore, Johanna Probst shows that decision-makers in France have very similar motivations (2012: 226–227).

[8]Klaus, caseworker, reception and processing centre, interview transcript, my own translation.

reasons for remaining in the job. Another thing they enjoy is the variability and the changing nature of their job. Hence, they like that they do not just have various different tasks to fulfil, but that the situation in the world keeps changing and that, by being required to keep up to date, they learn so much about the current situation. Another reason that came up frequently in the discussions—particularly with jurists—was that, after a while, one could no longer really leave the job because the prospects of finding a job elsewhere were relatively low. Many jurists explained to me that once one had become too specialised in asylum law, it became difficult to gain a foothold in a different legal field. Furthermore, they said that asylum law had low status in the legal sphere and, hence, once one had got into it, it was difficult to get out of it again (see also Miaz 2017a: 203). Finally, the good working conditions were amongst the main reasons many of my interaction partners gave as to why they stay on the job. They thought that elsewhere—especially outside Federal administration—it would probably be difficult to encounter such good working conditions.

Recruiting New Decision-Makers

It being an attractive job for the above-mentioned reasons, many people usually apply for the role of asylum decision-maker when jobs are advertised. In the last ten to fifteen years, a large volume of new caseworkers have been employed in the SEM's asylum units as the sample of my interaction partners clearly indicates (see Chapter 2). On the one hand, this has to do with a relatively stable rate of turnover in the office. On the other hand, it has to do with recent reorganisations and with the fact that the SEM's asylum directorate has been growing constantly since 2007. Or, at least, that was the case between 2007 and 2017, with the number of decision-makers increasing every year in an attempt to reduce the number of pending 'cases'.[9] As stated above, it is the heads and the deputy heads of the different asylum units who decide whom to employ. However, the final decision is not entirely up to them. The heads must provide their direct superiors with a justification of their reasoning for employing a particular person. Only if the latter agree is the applicant eventually employed.

Although the wording of the recruitment advertisement is consistent and always states that applicants with a law degree are preferred, in practice the individual heads have divergent preferences about educational background and previous experience. Thus, some heads told me that for them it was

[9]Hence, during that time the full-time equivalent of the directorate doubled from 254.0 in 2007 to 512.4 in 2017 (numbers given to me by the statistical service of the SEM, 15.06.2017).

essential that decision-makers have already gained some sort of experience working with migrants or asylum seekers. For others, in turn, it is central that decision-makers have travelled and know how "things work elsewhere", while for others it is more important that decision-makers are experienced jurists:

> *Laura*: What is important to you when employing new people? What do you look for?
> *Nadia*: That is quite subjective. Every head of division has different preferences. For me it isn't mandatory that this person is a jurist and versed in law (*rechtlich sattelfest*). Maybe that they have a bit of an idea, but that is really secondary. I prefer someone with life experience, someone who knows how things work abroad and not just in Russia, America or France, but in Bangladesh or Uganda for example. [...] Someone who can free themselves from a euro-centric perception and who has life and people skills.[10]
> Well, I try to evaluate their social competence. [...] I look at what kind of experience they have. I don't like taking people fresh from university. I think that for the work we do here it is important that someone has work experience. On the other hand, I don't find it important whether people have travelled around the world much or not. I like jurists, because we deal with juridical questions here and I think that someone with a legal background is better equipped for dealing with these things.[11]

Job applicants that are shortlisted are not just invited to a job interview but also are required to do a test which consists of two parts. In the first part, applicants have to write an asylum decision within a limited time. For that they receive a copy of the Swiss Asylum Act (AsylA) and the Federal Act on Foreign Nationals (FNA) as well as the minutes from an initial short asylum interview and its corresponding second longer interview. In the second part, the job candidates are requested to write a letter in the name of the Federal Councillor in charge of the SEM (for instance, as a response to a letter "from the public"). These tests are used to assess what are perceived as essential qualities for the job. One such quality is "decisiveness"; a job applicant's ability to take a decision and to assume responsibility for it. The tests are also intended to reveal the ability of an applicant to make a decision in a particular direction and argue it through to a conclusion. Furthermore, an applicant's capacity to capture the aspects deemed crucial for taking a decision, to use

[10]Nadia, head of asylum unit, headquarters, interview transcript, my own translation.

[11]Oliver, head of asylum unit, reception and processing centre, interview transcript, my own translation.

the law correctly and to write well and error-free (mistakes are counted) are qualities assessed through these tests. Moreover, the tests are about showing whether an applicant is capable of performing as the office and, thus, is able to speak in the name of the SEM. Finally, as Jonathan Miaz has argued, the tests are also perceived by the superiors as being a useful indicator of whether job applicants are able to reach a decision without letting their "ideological views interfere" and/or their "conscience getting in the way" (see Miaz 2017a: 204–206).[12]

When new decision-makers are employed, they first work on temporary contracts. Thus, during the first three years of their employment, caseworkers get fixed-term contracts, which have to be renewed annually. Only after three years do they receive an open-ended contract. This enables the office to flexibly react to rising and falling numbers of asylum seekers, with respect to pending 'cases'. Furthermore, it has an impact on how new employees are disciplined in the office, as I will show later on in this chapter.

Communities of Interpretation

Socialisation is "the process through which people [...] are made to take on the ideas and behaviour appropriate to life in a particular society", Cristina Toren argues (2002: 512). In this case, the "society" is the SEM. However, as we have shown elsewhere, "[i]t is important not to perceive the office solely as a unified whole. Rather, it appeared to us to be divided along complicated and evolving lines of affiliations and allegiances" (Affolter et al. 2019: 276). Building on Etienne Wenger (2003), we opted to call these lines of affiliation "communities of interpretation". Such communities may arise situationally, but they can also take on a more permanent form. Furthermore, while different perceptions of what constitutes good decision-making might prevail in these communities, we should at the same time not overestimate such differences. There is also a lot of "mutual understanding" between these different communities of interpretation (Affolter et al. 2019: 276). Finally, these communities do not form dividing lines in an absolute sense. "Officials in the office are affiliated to multiple 'communities' and may 'change sides'" (ibid.). In this part of the chapter, my focus is solely on the affiliation and identification with the specific divisions decision-makers work in: the headquarters or the RPCs as well as the subdivisions within these centres. These

[12]In connection to this, Jonathan Miaz argues that a quality they look out for in the recruitment process is that potential employees are neither too left- nor too right-wing (2017a: 205–206). While this never came up in my conversations with SEM officials with regard to recruitment, it was often mentioned as part of the ethos of being a good decision-maker (see Chapter 6).

affiliations seem to have the strongest influence on decision-makers' "sense of belonging" since they are official organisational units that are each lead by a superior and that have their own place within the SEM's organisational hierarchy. In addition, many of these divisions are located physically apart from each other. Thus, at the time of my research, the RPCs were situated in five different areas in Switzerland and, at the headquarters, the different units partly worked on different floors of the same building.

In my fieldwork, I found that most decision-makers tend to primarily identify themselves with the particular centre they work in: the headquarters or (one of) the RPCs. This shapes their view of what it means to work in line with the office. Both at the headquarters and in the RPCs, officials often complain about the respective others and the ways in which they conduct their work. Officials in the RPCs also make distinctions between the different RPCs (for instance, some are said to be much stricter than others). However, those differences were stressed much less in the conversations I had with officials. Mostly they spoke of "we in the RPCs and them up there in Bern", while, at the headquarters in Bern, talk was often of "us and the RPC-ians". The most common critique I observed at the headquarters about "RPC-ians" was that the latter conducted their work in a hurried and inaccurate (*husch husch*) way and that they did not stick to institutional practice. Mostly, in their critique of RPC caseworkers' so-called *husch husch* approach, the headquarter officials referred to the "RPC-ians" as not asking enough (relevant) questions in the first short interviews, as well as to the minutes of those interviews being sketchy and inaccurate. They complained that this made decision-making more difficult for them. First, because they then lacked a solid basis for making comparisons between asylum seekers' statements at different moments in the procedure. Second, they feared that because of the sketchy minutes, when appealing a negative decision, applicants could claim that they had not actually said what was recorded in the minutes and possibly win their case. Officially, decision-makers at the headquarters are in charge (through the *Federführungen*) of developing institutional practice. However, many decision-makers working at the headquarters complained about "RPC-ians" not sticking to the practice set by them. Furthermore, some of my interaction partners at the headquarters felt that their counterparts at the RPCs were too strict or "hardline". In that respect, one decision-maker once told me that when he had gone to do his one-week "internship" at one of the RPCs he had been really taken aback by the disrespectful language the people there used to speak about asylum seekers.[13] As part of their "initial" training,

[13]Andrea, caseworker, headquarters, field notes, my own translation.

new decision-makers working at the headquarters go to work at one of the RPCs for a week and conversely new decision-makers from the RPCs spend a week at the headquarters. This usually happens after they have already been working at the SEM for a couple of months.

In many ways, the critiques I frequently heard at the RPCs about "the ones up there in Bern" were the obverse of the above-mentioned critiques. Headquarter officials are often criticised by the RPC-officials for "taking the easy way out". By "taking the easy way out", they mean that decision-makers try to avoid taking harsh, strict decisions. People at the RPCs, therefore, often make fun of the decision-makers who come from the headquarters to do their "internships" at the RPCs for being unable to look asylum seekers in the eye and inform them verbally of a negative decision[14]:

> And sometimes we feel here, and maybe also in the other RPCs, that the people in Bern take the easy way out. […] That they, how should I say, don't make very strict judgements. […] Sometimes, people from Bern come here for a week and there I've realised that they often don't want to inform asylum seekers 'directly verbally' (*direkt eröffnen*) of a negative decision like we sometimes do here. […] And that shows me that they prefer taking positive decisions. Good, I also like taking positive decisions better, but taking negative decisions is part of the job.[15]

A second common critique I often came across at the RPCs was that even though the caseworkers at the headquarters were those who supposedly set the institutional practice with their *Federführungen*, they were always "a bit behind". The caseworkers at the RPCs felt that the "close contact" they had with asylum seekers, deriving from their offices being located on the premises where the asylum seekers lived, enabled them to pick up new trends, like, for instance, that "many Eritreans are not really Eritreans, but Ethiopians pretending to be Eritreans",[16] and adapt their practice accordingly much faster than the caseworkers at the headquarters could. To give an example, one RPC official once told me that they were soon going to be trained by someone from the headquarters on how to deal with applications by Tibetans,

[14]Occasionally, decision-makers verbally inform applicants of the decision immediately after the interview. At the headquarters this is very rarely done and then mostly only in "clear positive cases". It is a bit more commonly done at the RPCs, however, more with "clear negative" and DAWES decisions.

[15]Daniel, caseworker, reception and processing centre, interview transcript, my own translation.

[16]Klaus, caseworker, reception and processing centre, interview transcript, my own translation.

because they "could" now in some cases also be rejected. He found this ridiculous because it had been his centre that had started "rejecting Tibetans" in the first place.[17] What is at stake here are

> different notions of "expertise" that are considered necessary for correct and fair decision-making. Officials in the reception centres perceive their expertise to derive from their "close contact" with asylum seekers and the vast number of conversations they have with them (since they conduct both the short and long asylum interviews, whilst the decision-makers in Bern only do the latter). Many decision-makers at the headquarters, on the other hand, consider their expertise to be greater and of more value, because they hold all the *Federführungen* and, therefore, have all the experts and their expertise "in house". (Affolter et al. 2019: 277)

The following example illustrates how Daniel, a decision-maker at one of the RPCs, challenges the expertise and authority of the *Federführungen* at the headquarters:

> *Daniel*: Those in the "country teams", they're supposed to be the specialists. But then someone who's been working at the SEM for half a year or so tells you what to do. [...]
>
> *Laura*: You mean that someone who's new takes on a *Federführung*?
>
> *Daniel*: Yes, exactly. [...] To give you a specific example; I once interviewed a woman from Somalia. She couldn't [tell me] anything. So I asked the *Federführung* in Bern how this works with Somali women, whether I could give her a removal order. And then someone [from the *Federführung*] wrote back to me and said: "As a woman she [belongs to] a vulnerable group". As a woman you're not per se vulnerable! [...] I didn't do it. I gave her a removal order anyway. And I was backed up.[18]

In this case, Daniel questions the *Federführung*'s expertise mainly because of her institutional age. Daniel has been working at the SEM for much longer and, thus, he feels that he knows better what "the right" decision to take is. He ends by saying that he was "backed up". Unfortunately, at the time of the interview I did not ask him by whom. However, as will become apparent in this chapter, it can only mean two things. Either he was referring to his decision being approved by his superior or to his original decision being

[17]Susanne, caseworker, reception and processing centre, interview transcript, my own translation.

[18]Daniel, caseworker, reception and processing centre, interview transcript, my own translation.

confirmed by the Federal Administrative Court after it had been appealed against. Thus, for him, this means his practice was "right".

While the strongest identification seems to be with the centre they work in, decision-makers, especially within the headquarters, also often affiliate themselves with their units and distance themselves from others. The individual sections have different reputations and there is a lot of internal gossip about this. There are the so-called "hardliner" and the so-called "softy" sections and those that are seen to be somewhere in-between. The same terminology is also applied to individual decision-makers. Thus, within a "hardliner" section there will again be decision-makers with a reputation of being either "softies" or "hardliners" and the same, of course, also applies to so-called "softy" sections. However, what it means in those sections to be a "softy" or a "hardliner" differs. Hence, decision-makers who are in their own "hardliner" section called a "softy" will often not be considered as such by decision-makers from a "softy" section. "Softies", in a general sense, are defined as those who "want to save the world" and "would like to grant asylum to everyone". They are criticised for not following the law strictly enough and for not "digging deep enough" when testing credibility. On the other hand, those decision-makers who "see contradictions everywhere", follow the law "too strictly" and, thus, hardly ever take positive decisions are called "hardliners" or "no-sayers" (*Neinsager*, see also Miaz 2017a). They are criticised for being "cynical". I often observed that decision-makers and units that were said to follow a "legalistic approach"—which were incidentally mostly people with a background in law and units in which many employees were jurists—were called "hardline" by people from other units. Decision-makers themselves mostly tend to position themselves and their units in the "neutral centre" and would not speak of themselves as either "hardliners" or "softies", but they might well be called that by others (see also Miaz 2017a: 374–375).[19] However, what I observed during fieldwork was that sections and individual decision-makers who had a reputation of being "hardliners" often criticised their co-workers and other sections for not following the law "strictly enough" whereas a common critique made by so-called "softy" decision-makers or decision-makers from "softy" sections was that their co-workers were cynics and behaved like the "Sherlock Holmes" of asylum. Hence, in some ways they seemed to self-identify themselves with the ascriptions made to their unit, mostly through discrediting other stances.

[19] There were very few exceptions to this. Only two of my interaction partners referred to themselves as being "a bit of a softy" and one decision-maker reluctantly "admitted" that if strictly following the law equated to being a "hardliner", then, yes, he was one.

This frequent gossiping about other sections and decision-makers and their respective stances, I argue, has an impact on what it means for decision-makers to "belong" to their part of the office; on what it means for them to fit in and, therefore, on the practices and norms of good and professional decision-making that they adopt. From an analytical standpoint, the ways in which decision-makers dissociate themselves and their units from others, therefore, brings to light the values that are associated with "good decision-making", which are discussed in Chapter 6. What is at stake here is less that different values subsist in different units, but rather that the importance given to different values may vary from one unit to another. Since it is the heads of the different units themselves that recruit new decision-makers and, as I will show in the following, institutional socialisation largely takes place within caseworkers' "local communities" (see also Jubany 2017: 121), such tendencies tend to become reinforced. Furthermore, Ephraim Poertner, who did fieldwork in the SEM between 2012 and 2014, argues that "as the office went through a series of reorganisations and caseworkers had to apply for the 'new' sections with only the heads of sections appointed, they usually chose a head of section with a similar notion of 'normalcy'. This led to a certain convergence of 'views' inside the sections, and arguably increased the divergence between the sections" (2018: 264).

What also comes out of the above discussed is that the demarcation from other decision-makers and units happens through affiliating these so-called others with certain "extremes". These "extremes" are generally recognised as constituting "bad decision-making". Thus, both "naively believing everybody" and "easily" granting asylum but also "seeing contradictions everywhere" and disbelieving nearly everybody are regarded as qualities of bad decision-making. As a consequence, such demarcations allude us to the kind of uncontested, self-evident understandings of good decision-making that are not associated with either "extreme" and that are generally—and often rather subconsciously—held by decision-makers in the SEM.

Belonging is important for many reasons. As I will show in the following parts of this chapter, novices learn a lot from their immediate surroundings, for instance by observing and imitating their co-workers as well as by listening to them tell work stories and criticise or make fun of other decision-makers' practices. Furthermore, through the monitoring and trust they experience from their superiors, they learn what acceptable and unacceptable practices are. The different stances and reputations of superiors also influence which decisions are perceived by caseworkers as being "easy" or "difficult" to get past their superiors and, thus, how decision-makers, to some extent, also come to "auto-control" their practices.

Learning the Ropes of Asylum Decision-Making

Every practice is "first and foremost a knowledge-based activity" (Dahlvik 2018: 57). Institutional socialisation is, therefore, largely about how novices acquire the necessary skills and knowledge for fulfilling their new role within the organisation. In Chapter 4, I showed how knowledge that is developed on the job plays a crucial role in allowing decision-makers to overcome the "known unknowns" inherent in asylum decision-making and reaching clear-cut either/or decisions. Such knowledge can take on a verbalisable form, like country knowledge, or a non-verbalisable form, like the more "intuitive" professional-practical knowledge. Building on Max Weber, I argue that together these types of knowledge can be termed "*Dienstwissen*". Thus, according to Weber, the main characteristic of *Dienstwissen* is that it is only accessible to "insiders". It is a form of "specialist" and "official" knowledge (Lassman and Speirs 1994: 373) acquired through "experience in the service" (Weber 2013 [1978]: 225). This kind of knowledge shapes decision-making practices in three different way: first, by allowing decision-makers to ascribe meanings to objects, persons and situations; second, by providing decision-makers with procedural know-how; and third, by enabling decision-makers to know what is appropriate and desirable (Dahlvik 2018: 58). Weber distinguishes *Dienstwissen* from *Fachwissen*, which, in turn, he defines as "technical knowledge" that decision-makers need in order to carry out their job (Weber 2013 [1978]: 225). Different to *Dienstwissen*, *Fachwissen* is publicly accessible.

This part of the chapter is about how decision-makers acquire the necessary *Dienstwissen* to carry out their job. Thus, as Olga Jubany argues, "[t]he ability to understand and distinguish elements only meaningful to the group [...] is core to the idea of becoming a 'true' group member" (2017: 155). Furthermore, Georgia Chao has called for scholars studying organisational socialisation to pay more attention to how novices acquire professional-practical knowledge (or what she refers to as "tacit knowledge") when they enter the job (2012: 607; see also Ashford and Nurmohamed 2012: 14). This is challenging because professional-practical knowledge cannot be put into words and is therefore inherently difficult to determine. Moreover, learning too is, at least in part, an invisible mental process, which remains inaccessible to us as researchers and indeed, inaccessible even to the learners themselves (see Good 2011: 116). Therefore, I adopt a twofold approach to respond to Chao's challenge. First, because it is difficult to show how decision-makers *learn* (particularly because I was not able to accompany my interaction partners over a long period of time, which would have allowed me to observe changes in their everyday practices and possibly their ways of thinking[20]), I focus instead on how the different forms of knowledge and skills are *taught* and *passed on* to the new decision-makers. Secondly, I explore how *Dienstwissen* in general (not just the non-verbalisable professional-practical knowledge) is imparted. I argue that we can infer much about the acquisition of professional-practical knowledge from analysing the passing on of verbalised *Dienstwissen* (such as when officials share "cultural knowledge" or their knowledge of questioning techniques) because *Dienstwissen* in its articulate form appears to partly become non-verbalisable professional-practical knowledge with the passage of time. To illustrate this I return to Theodor, quoted in Chapter 4. Theodor told me to go and ask someone newer about how to know whether a story was credible or not, because he just did it "out of intuition", through the "common sense" he had developed, and therefore could not really tell me anymore how he knew. This example illustrates how Theodor believes that once he would have been able to articulate how he knows what he knows but now it is inexpressible. He directs me to a newcomer because he believes they will still have words to explain what has now become professional-practical knowledge to him.

"I mainly 'learnt the trade' (*Handwerk lernen*) through one-to-one coaching. The training courses are more general education; so you get an idea of the subject matter".[21] In this statement, Joe, a caseworker at one of the RPCs, differentiates between two types of learning he experienced as a newcomer. He identifies them as knowledge of the subject matter and knowledge of the trade. Both forms of knowledge are necessary for decision-making. Knowledge of the trade for Joe means that he knows how to carry out his job. Thus, that he knows, for instance, how to carry out an asylum interview, how to assess a claimant's credibility, and how to write an asylum decision. Knowledge of the subject matter, in turn, refers to knowing what asylum decision-making is about or, in other words, knowing the legal basis of decision-making. To some extent, the two types of knowledge Joe identifies, therefore, resemble Max Weber's distinction between *Fachwissen*—knowledge of the subject matter—and *Dienstwissen*—knowledge of the trade.

Joe says he learnt what he knows through training and one-to-one coaching. By "training", Joe is referring to the 15 "A-module courses", which form part of the initial three-week training for new decision-makers. All novices are required to take part in these courses, ideally within the first

[20]However, I have privately known some decision-makers at the SEM for a few years. Our friendship and numerous conversations have given me some insights into their learning process.

[21]Joe, caseworker, reception and processing centre, interview transcript, my own translation.

month of their employment.[22] The majority of the modules teach the legal basics for taking different parts of asylum decisions while the remainder teach the underlying skills involved in fulfilling a decision-maker's duties. Modules include topics such as "determining refugee status", "credibility assessment", "issuing removal orders", "the roles of the different participants in asylum interviews", "writing decisions" and "country of origin information", for example. At a later stage of their training, new decision-makers attend B- and C-module courses. B-modules are organised internally in the individual asylum units and the content is largely administrative encompassing tasks such as how to file 'cases' and classify the different documents in the case files. C-modules (like the A-modules) are for decision-makers from all the different centres. They take place about a year after the initial A-module training and cover topics of more "advanced decision-making" such as the uses of LINGUA analyses and taking decisions on family reunification, for instance.[23] Most of the courses are taught by officials in senior positions, who have previously worked as decision-makers themselves.

The modular training is complemented by what Joe describes as "one to one coaching". Every new recruit is allocated an individual coach who is an experienced decision-maker from the same unit. However, occasionally, the heads of the asylum units will also do the coaching themselves. In their first weeks or months on the job, new decision-makers spend a lot of time working with their coaches because, as Joe told me, this is how they learn to "think the right thoughts".[24] They sit in on a coach's asylum interviews and often a coach will also organise for the novice to observe other experienced decision-makers' asylum interviews. Furthermore, it is common practice for new decision-makers and coaches in the early stages to prepare asylum interviews together and for coaches to sit in a novice's interview so that they can help out if necessary and to enable them to give the novice feedback. After the interview, the coach and novice review the interview together, discuss the potential decision and the coach checks the novice's written decision before it is passed on to the head of the section for checking and counter-signing.[25]

Joe states that he learnt the skills of the trade—the necessary *Dienstwissen*—through the one-to-one coaching rather than in the initial training

[22]When I attended the three-week training session, for roughly half of the participants the first day of training was also their first day at their new job. The other half had, at the time of the course, already been working at the SEM for a couple of weeks or months.

[23]As part of my research, I participated in 10 A-module courses and one C-module course.

[24]Joe, caseworker, reception and processing centre, interview transcript, my own translation.

[25]Similar processes of institutional learning are also described for the Federal Asylum Office in Austria by Julia Dahlvik (2018: 55) and with regard to the training of immigration officers in the UK by Olga Jubany (2017: 112, 120).

courses. However, in the following, I show that *Dienstwissen* is not only acquired through the sharing of experiences in one to one coaching, as Joe identified, but also develops whenever novices imitate their more experienced colleagues and indeed, is also formed through the modular courses whenever instructors share their personal experiences with the novices (see also Jubany 2017: 113–120). All three components play a part in shaping a novice's *Dienstwissen* and therefore in their subsequent decision-making practice. This idea is explored on the basis of two examples. In the first I look at how new decision-makers gradually learn what questions to ask in asylum interviews, and in the latter, I examine how new decision-makers learn to assess the credibility of asylum claims.

Learning What Questions to Ask

Within the SEM there is a common image of good asylum interviewing. Good decision-makers conduct asylum interviews in a goal-oriented way, meaning their questioning produces on-file facts, which can then be used for arguing a certain decision. The good decision-maker does not follow a pre-defined set of questions but is able to engage with the applicants and question them with dexterity and spontaneity. This ideal was shared with me by many of my interaction partners: new and "old" ones alike. Thus, several fairly new decision-makers quite apologetically explained to me that they were still using questionnaires with pre-defined questions when I went to sit in in their interviews, but that they were working towards becoming more spontaneous in their interviews.

What questions to ask—or how to know what questions to ask—is not really addressed in the initial training courses. There newcomers learn the three-step-questioning technique of starting with open questions, then going on to ask wh-questions and finally to asking yes or no questions if necessary (see Chapter 4). And they are warned against posing leading questions. Moreover, in one of the courses I participated in, the newcomers practised developing questions to ask in a fictional interview, but the interaction itself was not actually practised—unlike the role-plays Olga Jubany describes soon-to-be asylum officials doing in training sessions in the UK (2017: 111–112). Whenever the novices asked in the training courses how they would know what questions to ask in the actual interviews, they were told by the instructors that this was something that they would just come to know with time. Hence, several decision-makers told me that the first time they had conducted an interview by themselves, they had felt as if they had been "thrown in at the deep end". Nevertheless, by the time novices do their first interview, they have already observed a few of their coaches' interviews and possibly interviews conducted by other experienced colleagues. Many of my interaction partners told me that they had "adopted the style" of their coaches or one of the other co-workers they had observed and had copied the type of questions they had asked. Some decision-makers explained to me that, in the beginning, they had read the minutes of interviews conducted by more experienced decision-makers with the express purpose of getting some ideas on what questions to ask. Finally, the way new decision-makers ask questions is also shaped by the feedback they receive from their coaches when preparing interviews together or discussing past interviews. Thus, one coach told me that, at the start, it was important not only to teach newcomers what to ask but also when to ask certain questions and when to "dig deeper". She explained this with the following example:

> New [officials] often don't work with the criterion of "contradicts an inner logic" [for reasoning credibility decisions]. To give you an example: In one case, an applicant said that his father had asked him to deliver letters to another person. And he didn't just do that once, but more like four to five times a week for about half a year. Now the [new] decision-maker did not think to ask the applicant what was in those letters, so when we were preparing the interview together I told her she had to ask him that. When she did, the applicant said that he had never asked his father that out of respect. And that is just not logical. If I were your father and I gave you a letter to take to someone nearly every day, you would ask me, even if you respected [me]. You would say: "Of course I'll take the letter, father, but what are those letters you're asking me to deliver". That's the obvious thing to do. Now, say the applicant had asked his father and the father had said: "That's none of your business", that would have been relatively plausible. But that he didn't even ask his father is just not logical. And that's a strong argument [for the decision]. So that's what I mean when I say that [new caseworkers] need to learn to ask good and suitable questions.[26]

This example shows how coaches teach newcomers when and how to ask questions. When preparing the interview with the trainee, Teresa felt that the novice had missed a crucial "detail" which, if probed, might provide useful information for taking the decision and producing a solid argument. Thus, Teresa sees her duty in training the new decision-maker as making her spot such important "details". Through this she is also teaching the novice to be sufficiently suspicious and alert towards indicators that there might be something "off" about the story (see also Jubany 2017: 155). Furthermore, she

[26]Teresa, caseworker, headquarters, interview transcript, my own translation.

is conveying a clear idea of what merits suspicion and what assumptions are deemed common sense when defining behaviour as "normal" and "abnormal" or "logical" and "illogical". The novice is taught that this particular common-sense assumption (of it being illogical to not ask about the letters) will make for a strong argument, but that coming up with such arguments is dependent upon the questions she asks. Hence, learning how to conduct asylum interviews is very much linked to learning how to assess credibility, the issue I turn to in the next subsection of this chapter. However, before doing so, I want to briefly explore Teresa's example from another angle.

Common-sense assumptions (like the one of the letters) being used for taking decisions have received much criticism for being insensitive towards different cultural contexts (see, for instance, Good 2009; Kälin 1986; Rousseau et al. 2002; Shuman and Bohmer 2004; Spijkerboer 2000). This critique is well known and, to some extent, also shared by the decision-makers themselves. Thus, on several occasions during the training sessions for new employees, the decision-makers were warned against basing decisions on "eurocentric" assumptions. Furthermore, what exactly constitutes "normal" or "logical" behaviour is an issue that is often contested within the office. Hence, for example, while one caseworker told me that for her it was just not plausible that an applicant would stay hidden in a village where he knew his persecutors could come looking for him again at any time, another caseworker criticised precisely this kind of thinking of some of his colleagues. Moreover, I also observed different stories of how asylum seekers escaped from prison lead to discussions during coffee breaks of what were possible actions in a particular country (e.g. running out of a prison because there were only three walls) and what behaviours were normal or not (e.g. bribing a prison guard). Teresa, too, told me that as a decision-maker it was important not to base decisions on "eurocentric" common-sense assumptions. However, the example of the letters, for her, was not "eurocentric" common sense but general common sense. This shows that although decision-makers are aware of the critique of cultural insensitivity and often stress its importance, in practice they must still make use of such generally applicable pre-concepts in order to make 'cases' decidable. Furthermore, while some common-sense assumptions are highly contested within the office, there are also other common-sense assumptions which are never or only very rarely questioned by the decision-makers. One such widespread assumption is that all applicants want to tell their stories and another one is that traumatised people can to some degree also talk about their experiences (see also Good 2011: 102–103). I argue that these common-sense assumptions are widely held by the decision-makers and are rarely contested because otherwise it would inhibit credibility assessment as it is usually done and would make 'cases' undecidable (see Chapter 4).

Learning to Test Credibility

Credibility assessment, my interaction partners told me, was something else that they had learnt more on the job than in the initial training course. Thus, in the feedback round at the end of the three-week training modules, a few newcomers doubted their readiness to assess the credibility of asylum claims properly. However, they hoped that they would learn to do so over time because that was something the instructors had told them at several points during the training courses. Hence, whenever the newcomers asked things like: "But how will we know which parts of the story are true if applicants mix the truth with lies?", the instructors answered that these were things they would come to know with experience.[27]

As I showed in Chapter 4, credibility assessment in practice works through officials probing for reasons to doubt the veracity of a claim and only, if no such reasons can be found, do they assume that it is credible (unless their "intuition" clearly tells them that the story is "true"). Hence, for carrying out credibility assessments in practice, it is such testing strategies that the new decision-makers must acquire. Furthermore, they must obtain "cultural knowledge" in order, for instance, to know whether something is possible or where it is especially important to "dig deeper". And they must develop the necessary "intuition" (professional-practical knowledge), which guides their decision-making and gives them a feeling of certainty that they are taking the right decision. Once again novices develop this professional-practical knowledge by learning from the experienced decision-makers; by observing them work; by imitating them; by being coached by them and, as well, by the experienced decision-makers sharing their experiences and ideas with the novices. The views on what stories to be particularly suspicious of are frequently shared amongst co-workers. I show this with two examples.

My first example is a comment from an instructor during one of the initial training courses I took part in. We were discussing the different reasons for recognising applicants as refugees but excluding them from asylum—one of them being that "[r]efugees shall not be granted asylum if they became refugees in accordance with Article 3 only by leaving their native country

[27]What the new decision-makers do learn in the initial training are the three methods from forensic psychology which can be used to assess credibility. Those methods are "criteria-based content analysis" after Max Steller and Günter Köhnken (1989), "consistency analysis" (*Konstanzanalyse*) and "structure comparison" (*Strukturvergleich*) (see, for instance, Greuel et al. 1998; Volbert and Steller 2009).

or country of origin or due to their conduct after their departure" (Art. 54, AsylA)—when the instructor said:

> Lots of Iranians say that they have been politically active in Switzerland, participating in protest actions and rallies against their government. It's like they've invented this becoming politically active in exile. [...] There are exile-political groups here that offer this kind of service. They help you create your 'subjective post-flight grounds'. You just have to pay them a fee and then you become a member and can buy photos that you can hand in as evidence.[28]

The second example occurred at one of the RPCs. One day, when I was sitting in the break room with some decision-makers, one of their colleagues walked in somewhat bemused by a Nigerian applicant he had just interviewed. He commented "This one had the full program: ghosts, voodoo, homosexuality...", thus making it clear that he did not believe anything the applicant had told him, since the applicant's story had consisted of what "all the Nigerians were saying", for instance, that they were being persecuted on the grounds of their sexual orientation.[29]

So, what can we make out of these examples? Both suggest pejoratively that there is a "typical story". The implication is that the applicants have created stories they believe would lead to the granting of asylum. In the first example, the instructor's comments were serving as a warning to novices whereas, in the second example, the decision-maker related his story with no specific purpose: the story was merely a brief moment of office banter. Nevertheless, in both examples we can see how *Dienstwissen* is passed on whether the intention was to instruct or not. New decision-makers listening to such stories will learn to expect and to anticipate "Iranians pretending to have become politically active in Switzerland" or "Nigerians pretending to be homosexuals" for example. The "typical stories" make them sceptical possibly even before they have dealt with their first 'case' of a Nigerian or Iranian applicant themselves. Furthermore, the undercurrent in these shared experiences is that decision-makers have to "dig deep" in these 'cases' in order not to come across as being naïve (see Chapter 6). Hence, this in a way pre-shapes the experiences the decision-makers have on the job and, thus, the *Dienstwissen* they acquire.

In addition to such stories about the content of asylum seekers' narratives, decision-makers also tell each other about applicants' typical and atypical ways of narrating their stories and behaviours. Hence, if Patricia (who I quoted in Chapter 4) after only two months of working at the SEM says

[28]Training instructor, A-modules, field notes, my own translation.

[29]Field notes, my own translation.

she knows how Asians, Africans and Persians behave and, thus, whether their way of performing in the interviews is "culturally driven" or an indication of something "simply not being true", her knowledge should be understood in this context.

The examples have shown that knowledge and the requisite skills for decision-making are acquired by learning and copying from more experienced colleagues and through the informal sharing of ideas and experiences amongst co-workers. This is how decision-makers develop the knowledge and skills that make their 'cases' decidable. I have shown that the *Dienstwissen* growing out of this "experience in the service" (Weber 2013 [1978]: 225) is, therefore, knowledge which is collectively developed: through the sharing and imitation of ways in which to carry out tasks and ways of thinking about particular issues at stake. Of course, as already described in Chapter 4, this sharing is not something that simply stops after new decision-makers' first months on the job. Rather, decision-makers continue to ask each other for advice on how to proceed with "difficult cases" and share stories with each other during breaks. Hence, all these moments of sharing contribute to certain normal behaviours becoming further consolidated over time. Therefore, this is one way in which decision-making practices are regulated without this regulation being the outcome of explicit orders or written rules.

Accountability

An important aspect of socialisation, as Christina Toren argues, is how people are made to take on certain ideas and behaviours as members of a specific group (2002: 512). This pressure to conform with certain ideas and behaviours can be strong and explicit, but often it is also very subtle and barely consciously noticeable for members of the group themselves (see also Dahlvik 2018: 59; Martinez 2009: 118). In this part of the chapter, I explore how pressure to conform shapes what decision-makers do. I argue that questions such as "What will others think?", "How will others react?" and "What will or would others do?" substantially guide SEM officials' everyday practices (see also Dahlvik 2018: 59; Liodden 2016: 228; Wagenaar 2004: 650). I thereby draw on Tone Liodden who argues that

> [s]imply put, when people make a decision, they take into consideration how the social surroundings will react to it, and decisions are shaped by a desire to protect both one's social image and self-image [...]. People are "generally motivated to maintain the approval and respect of those to whom they are accountable" (Tetlock 1985: 309). Accountability is thereby the "implicit or

> explicit expectation that one may be called on to justify one's beliefs, feelings, and actions to others" (Lerner and Tetlock 1999: 225). (2016: 228)

As a consequence, I argue that decision-makers, on the one hand, orient their practices towards what their colleagues do—or what they expect them to do (see also Dahlvik 2018: 56, 59). On the other hand, when taking decisions, caseworkers try to anticipate the reactions of others—mainly their direct superiors and the Federal Administrative Court, but, to some extent, also their peers and the broader public—which leads them to auto-control their own decision-making behaviour, as Jonathan Miaz nicely shows in his work (see Miaz 2017a: 339–358; see also Liodden 2016: 231). In the first part of this chapter's section, I explore decision-makers' felt accountability towards their peers. The second part then analyses how accountability towards superiors, who are themselves tied into a chain of accountability (see Liodden 2016: 213–214), shapes caseworkers' everyday practices.

Peer Pressure

As J. Michael Martinez (2009: 118) argues, when "everyone is expected to perform certain chores or behave in certain ways, an individual is pressured, subtly and not so subtly, to conform" (cited in Dahlvik 2018: 59). To a considerable extent, pressure to conform is exerted by peers, as other authors working on asylum administrations have also argued (Liodden 2016: 293; Miaz 2017a: 340; 2017b: 274). This is exemplified in the following statement made by an interviewee in a study by Colin Campbell and Graham Wilson (1995: 225): "It's not necessarily the hierarchy, it's the peer group you account to… it's how you're seen in the eyes of your colleagues… it's actually how you're viewed by your colleagues is the thing that would drive me" (cited in Liodden 2016: 228).

My interaction partners were rarely as explicit as this. Helen's statement is an exception in this regard:

> And then this case with *in dubio pro [refugio]* ("when in doubt, for the refugee"). Sometimes you feel really bad [doing this]. Because [...] people speak about you behind your back: "Oh, she chose the easy way out; just quickly taking a positive [decision]". But maybe you really struggled with [the decision]. Because sometimes, even though the story is not at all convincing, but if you don't find any arguments – truly not and not just out of laziness – your only choice is to take a positive [decision]. Well, ok, maybe you could

> show the case to someone else first. Luckily, this hasn't happened to me so often up to now.[30]

In Helen's statement we can see that she is concerned about people—meaning her co-workers—talking badly about her decision-making behind her back. Furthermore, her statement indicates that this may have an influence on her decision-making practice. Her distress about what others might think of her clearly came across when we were having this conversation. Although other caseworkers did not share this concern with me as explicitly as Helen did, I observed that in their everyday practices they often appeared to be affected by what others might think of them.

During my fieldwork I observed decision-makers gossiping about others on numerous occasions, both about people from the same sections and about officials working in other sections and centres. Such talk often emanates from officials coming across decisions taken by colleagues and their corresponding case files. Furthermore, some decision-makers (and units) over time gain a certain reputation, which is continually reinforced through gossip. For instance, I once heard some decision-makers fret over the "juridical weakness" of decisions from another asylum unit and, on another occasion, I overheard some caseworkers' making fun of the "silly questions" some of their co-workers posed in interviews.[31]

In addition to gossip, which is something that decision-makers are well aware of, I argue that peer pressure is also exerted through decision-makers openly making fun of each other, mostly in a joking way, as Lucy's quote indicates:

> We sometimes tease each other a bit. If one of us takes a rather strict decision: "Oh, what a hardliner". And if someone says that they had to turn a blind eye or take an *in dubio pro [refugio]* decision: "Oh my *(oh jöh)*, what a wimp you've become". I think it's important to find a middle ground somewhere. So, that you don't slide towards one extreme, you see?[32]

What decision-making behaviours or attitudes are more prone to be criticised or made fun of varies according to how certain decision-makers identify themselves and their unit's style of decision-making in comparison with that of others, or, in other words, according to the "communities of interpretation" they affiliate themselves or others with. Hence, regardless of whether

---

[30] Helen, caseworker, headquarters, interview transcript, my own translation.

[31] Field notes, my own translation.

[32] Lucy, caseworker, headquarters, interview transcript, my own translation.

it is through gossip or making fun of each other in a joking way, ideas are conveyed about what it means to behave in an appropriate way and, thus, to fit into the office. As Helen's statement above indicated, such ideas have an impact on decision-makers' practices, leading caseworkers to adopt certain norms of what it means to do one's job well.

Helen fears being judged by her colleagues for not adhering to an important norm: that of "digging deep"—and, hence, of taking the time and trying hard enough—to find arguments for reasoning the non-credibility of a claim. She is afraid of being pegged as "lazy"; as someone who likes choosing "the easy way out". Because of that she feels pressured not to take an *in dubio pro* decision for the above-mentioned reasons. It is not that she fears being judged by her colleagues for taking a positive decision per se. If she herself feels certain that a claim is credible, she does not have a problem with taking a positive decision. But with *in dubio pro* decisions, where she herself is unsure whether to believe the applicant or not, she fears being judged by her colleagues for not having put enough effort into decision-making in order to find out whether the story really can or cannot be believed. Moreover, Helen's quote shows that this pressure is not just something which is exerted through her co-workers; she has also internalised it. She knows that her co-workers are unlikely to read her decision: thus, so long as she does not tell them about her decision, they will not know about it. However, she still feels uneasy taking such a decision, because "lightly" taking a positive decision is not the right thing to do. And, while she might know that this was not the case, and that she had tried really hard to find reasons for rejecting the case, her fear is still that her colleagues will not.

Interestingly, Lucy too uses the example of *in dubio pro* decisions as an example of bad decision-making. Taking this kind of decisions makes caseworkers "wimps" (even if it is only meant in a teasing way). Her expression "*Oh jöh*" indicates that she uses "wimp" in a belittling sense; for someone who does not have the courage to take strict decisions.[33] Since being belittled is not something the decision-makers want, here we can also see pressure not to take such decisions.

Accountability Towards Superiors and Beyond

Before final decisions are sent out to asylum seekers, they must be signed not only by the decision-maker in charge of the 'case' but also by the head of the

[33]The Swiss German expression "*jöh*" is very difficult to translate. It is often used, for example, if small children do something cute (e.g. "*Oh jöh*, the baby has just smiled at me").

respective asylum unit. On the occasions when I observed superiors check and counter-sign decisions, I noted marked differences in the way the decisions were treated. With some, the superiors just glanced at the letter, checking to see who had written the decision and who it was for before signing them, with others they quickly read through the decision, checking the arguments and, in a few cases, they opened the case file and leafed through the documents inside it (including the minutes of the asylum interviews). If the heads agree with the decision and its reasoning, they sign it and it is sent out. If not, they take the decision back to the decision-maker to work on again. In general, this does not happen very often and, when it does, superiors usually just ask a decision-maker to work on particular arguments rather than change the decision. However, the latter does occasionally also happen as I show in Chapter 6.

It is difficult to discern general patterns of whose decisions are checked more closely. One superior, for instance, told me that he tended to check the decisions of some of his employees who granted positive decisions "too readily" more closely.[34] Another superior (himself a jurist) told me that he usually looked at his non-jurists' decisions a bit more closely than those of his jurists[35] and yet another head said that he usually took a quick look at the decisions taken by a couple of his employees who tended to become quite cynical.[36] One pattern, however, I observed generally; namely that institutional age is a decisive factor in determining how thoroughly a caseworker's decisions are checked.

> With those who haven't been here long I look a bit more closely. We monitor them carefully especially regarding credibility. There I do look at the minutes once in a while and check whether the arguments work, whether they are correct and whether they are really the best ones to use. Because I think you can still form these people; you can put certain principles through. [...] With experienced caseworkers who are three years away from retirement I don't try to change the decision in such [...] things that they have always done like that.[37]

[34]Chris, head of asylum unit, reception and processing centre, interview transcript, my own translation.

[35]Nora, head of asylum unit, headquarters, interview transcript, my own translation.

[36]Jenny, head of asylum unit, reception and processing centre, interview transcript, my own translation.

[37]Jenny, head of asylum unit, reception and processing centre, interview transcript, my own translation.

The quote shows that the less time decision-makers have been working at the office, the more often and thoroughly their decisions are checked because superiors believe that new employees have to (and still can) be formed. At the same time, the quote shows that experienced officials' decisions are often not checked. Here Jenny is saying that there is no point in checking them because it is no longer possible to change "old stagers'" ideas and behaviours. However, I argue that there is also another reason why experienced decision-makers' decisions are often not checked: not simply because their practices cannot be changed but also because there is no need for them to be changed because those decision-makers have already been sufficiently formed. As a consequence of this, instead of thoroughly checking experienced decision-makers' practices, superiors simply trust them to do the right thing. Chris, a head of section at one of the RPCs, explains that if experienced decision-makers say a story is credible in a positive decision, there is no need for him to check that against the minutes of the interview:

> If you read a decision and you see from *the Sachverhalt* (the written 'facts' of the case noted in the final decision) that there was persecution and then it is written that the applicant's statements were coherent, realistic and without contradictions, [...] I don't go and check that in the minutes. I must trust my employees.[38]

The following statement made by another head, Nora, that was already quoted at the very beginning of this book, is similar to that of Chris in that she too says that if experienced decision-makers claim that a story is credible, this assessment can be trusted. What is particularly interesting here is how she explains this:

> All these terms [like "plausible", "comprehensible", "logical" and "realistic" for example] are used [for reasoning positive decisions]. For me that is ok. [...] I mean, if someone uses a word like that who only started [working here] three months ago, I might ask: "Hey, what does that mean for you?" But if [the decision] comes from someone whom I consider to be a valuable, serious, good employee, then I'll allow it, because I know, I can imagine what it means for them.[39]

We can see from this that the reason Nora trusts (some of) her experienced employees is because she has known them for a long time and, thus, knows

[38]Chris, head of asylum unit, reception and processing centre, interview transcript, my own translation.

[39]Nora, head of asylum unit, headquarters, interview transcript, my own translation.

how they work. But Nora is saying more than that. "I can imagine what this means for them", she claims. With this statement, Nora is indicating that she shares an understanding with those decision-makers of what it means for an asylum seeker's story to be "realistic", for example. Thus, what makes Nora (and her fellow superiors) trust their employees is that they have been sufficiently socialised by the office, which allows them to think and act in ways which are familiar to the heads and with which they agree. On the other hand, with new decision-makers, the superiors see it as their duty to form them and, thus, to make sure that they acquire an institutional habitus, so that they can eventually also be trusted.

Jonathan Miaz writes that over time decision-makers acquire "institutional capital", meaning that their decisions are less frequently checked, leaving them with more *marge de manoeuvre* or "autonomy" for taking decisions (2017a: 396–397). I agree with Miaz that if "common institutional practice" is challenged (e.g. by granting asylum to an applicant from a country where the recognition rate is nearly zero per cent), then this will generally be done by experienced decision-makers who have acquired institutional capital. However, I would argue that not having their decisions checked, does not, per se, make decision-makers more "autonomous" in the sense that they (can) take decisions more independently from the office. Rather, by the time they have acquired this institutional capital, they will also have acquired an institutional habitus (the latter being the reason for gaining institutional capital in the first place). Hence, this makes their decisions (or choices) less "free" than it might at first seem. What are perceived as possible courses of action will already be pre-shaped by the institutional habitus they have developed (see Wacquant 1992: 19).

Apart from observing that new decision-makers' decisions by tendency fall under closer scrutiny than those of their more experienced colleagues, I noticed two further common patterns. First, I found that, rather unsurprisingly, "unusual" decisions particularly drew superiors' attention. Thus, if, at the time of my research, a decision-maker had issued a removal order for an applicant from Eritrea or had granted asylum to a Nigerian asylum seeker, these decisions would very likely have been prone to close scrutiny.[40] Second, I noticed that negative decisions based on non-credibility are usually less thoroughly checked than those based on non-eligibility to refugee status. When I

[40]At the time of my research, the protection rate (thus, including asylum and subsidiary protection) was 3.1% for Nigerian applicants in 2014 and 2.3% in 2015, while for Eritrean claimants it was 70.3% in 2014 and 83.9% in 2015 (see https://www.sem.admin.ch/sem/de/home/publiservice/statistik/asylstatistik/archiv.html, last accessed 24.2.2020).

asked a superior who the previous day I had observed checking decisions in precisely that way about this, he explained:

> Hmm, that's a good [question]. Article 7 is about credibility and the scope for discretion (*Ermessenspielraum*) is much bigger there. It's more a question of persuasion; it has more to do with [producing] convincing arguments. [...] There are these criteria (*Merkmale*) for non-credibility [listed in Article 7, AsylA; ...], which are quite vague. [But] there I know how my people reason, so I will often be more easily willing to just "wave [the decision] through". Article 3 arguments I tend to look at more closely, to see whether [my people] have really understood [the issue at stake], because [those arguments] must be legally trenchant. Article 7 arguments, on the other hand, depend more on the authors' writing style, their power of persuasion.[41]

The fact that Oliver, the head of an asylum unit, ascribes much bigger interpretative leeway to credibility assessments, yet does not check these decisions more closely, is telling in many ways. On the one hand, I argue that this is linked to superiors themselves also being accountable to those above them in the institutional hierarchy. The heads of the asylum units keep records of their employees' decisions that were quashed by the Federal Administrative Court. The asylum directorate, in turn, keeps statistics of the numbers of decisions quashed for each asylum unit. It is considered bad decision-making to have too many decisions quashed by the court. However, not all quashing is considered equally bad. Hence, at a team meeting I attended in one of the asylum units, the superior informed his employees that the institutional aim was to not receive more than two per cent of "avoidable quashings" from the courts and that every single decision-maker was expected to contribute to achieving this aim (see also Affolter et al. 2019: 270). He cited decisions quashed because of "formal mistakes", such as forgetting to grant the asylum seeker the proper right to be heard (*rechtliches Gehör*) or not sufficiently establishing the "facts of the case" (*Sachverhalt*), as examples of "avoidable quashings". Furthermore, he instructed that decision-makers should avoid their decisions being quashed for not adhering to the practice set by the Federal Administrative Court (unless they had good reasons for challenging the court's practice). In contrast, he considered diverging assessments of credibility to be unavoidable.[42] This has to do with credibility assessment being to some extent seen as something "subjective". Thus, it is regarded as normal that what one person might find believable, another one might not. It is for

[41] Oliver, head of asylum unit, reception and processing centre, interview transcript, my own translation.

[42] Field notes of asylum unit meeting, my own translation.

this reason that it makes sense for superiors to most thoroughly check those decisions that could potentially lead to so-called "avoidable quashings", which credibility decisions are, as I have just shown, not.

On the other hand, another reason why negative Article 7 decisions fall under less scrutiny than Article 3 decisions is that Article 7 argumentations are by tendency more difficult to refute because of the way "facts" are created in credibility determination, as I showed in Chapter 4. Thus, the assessment of credibility depends largely on *how* the "facts" of the 'case' were generated which mainly happens in and through the asylum interview during which superiors are generally not present (see also Liodden 2016: 260). Superiors tend to trust that experienced decision-makers are capable of professionally conducting asylum interviews.

Patterns of how superiors check their employees' decisions have an impact on the shaping of the latter's practices. Over time, decision-makers learn what decisions are easier and which are more difficult to get past their superiors and come to anticipate their heads' reactions. This may mean several different things. It can mean decision-makers taking a decision they think their superiors will probably not approve of but then putting a great deal of effort into the reasoning behind it in order to convince the superior that the decision can be justified (see also Miaz 2017b: 387–389). But it can also mean the opposite: decision-makers knowing that a particular decision and certain argument will most certainly be approved of and, therefore, putting less effort into it. Or it can mean decision-makers wanting to grant temporary protection, for example, but then deciding not to do it because they assume they would never "get it past" their superiors. Hence, knowing that superiors might check their decisions influences not only what decisions the caseworkers take, but also the arguments they use as well as the amount of time they put into taking those decisions. Furthermore, for experienced decision-makers that have gained the trust of their superiors and can, therefore, count on superiors generally not questioning their decisions, it is important to retain this trust. Hence, Claire a decision-maker working at the headquarters once told me that if she had several cases she wanted to decide positively, she would not give them to her superior all at once, but would keep some of them back for when she also had some negative decisions. This was important because she did not want her boss to think she took positive decisions easily and simply waved cases through without checking them properly.[43]

Not having one's decisions returned by the superiors is important in terms of efficiency. As discussed in Chapter 6, decision-makers work under a lot of

[43]Claire, caseworker, headquarters, field notes, my own translation.

pressure to not only produce qualitatively "good decisions", but also adequate quantities. But it is also about more than that. Every year, decision-makers' performance is evaluated by the superiors of the individual asylum units. The evaluation forms are then passed up the institutional hierarchy and can have an effect on decision-makers' salary. Hence, caseworkers' salary can be either raised or remain the same as a consequence of these evaluations (see also Miaz 2017a: 346). Receiving good evaluations is, furthermore, particularly important for new employees working on fixed-term contracts if they want to ensure that their contracts are renewed at the end of the year. Thus, in one of the training modules I attended, the novices were told: "It is important that you work well, so that your contract will then be renewed".[44] From what I observed and was told by SEM officials, contracts normally get renewed, and "it takes a lot to get fired" from the SEM. Nevertheless, the impact of this form of pressure should not be underestimated.

As stated above, decision-makers are not only accountable to their superiors, but are integrated into a chain of accountability that reaches up to the Federal Councillor in charge of the Federal Department of Justice and Police (FDJP). For example, at a division meeting I attended, in which the heads of several asylum units participated, the division head informed the heads of the units that he had randomly checked a few decisions from each unit. In general, he was pleased with the quality of decision-making, but he did instruct the heads of the units to make some changes in order to improve decision-making. In addition, as several authors have pointed out, accountability also reaches beyond the administration (see Jubany 2017: 212; Liodden 2016: 247–250; Miaz 2017a: 357; Poertner 2018: 288). SEM officials are, to some extent, also accountable to the general public. This became clearly apparent during my fieldwork when, in the run-up to the parliamentary elections in 2015, the handling of applicants by Eritreans became one of the major themes of several political parties' election campaign. This led numerous members of parliament to demand a report from the Federal Councillor in charge of the FDJP, and, thus, of the SEM, which explained and justified the SEM's "Eritrea practice". Such requests by politicians are usually passed down the organisational hierarchy to the *Federführungen*[45] who draft a first response, which is then again passed up the hierarchical line with people working in different positions within the office adding to it

[44] Training instructor, A-modules, field notes, my own translation.

[45] *Federführungen* are decision-makers who are in charge of a particular "country of origin". They are involved in setting the institution's decision-making practice for dealing with 'cases' from "their" country and—to some extent—try to monitor other decision-makers' practices regarding 'cases' by applicants from the country they are responsible for (see Chapter 4).

until it is ready to be sent out to the parliament. Furthermore, one SEM official told me that sometimes there were public events in which the practice of dealing with specific asylum applications had to be justified to a public audience. However, he said that such events were above his and even his direct superior's wage group. Hence, it was not up to people holding the *Federführung* for specific countries to go and defend the SEM's practice at such events. That was the responsibility of people further up in the organisation's hierarchy, he explained.[46]

In 2015, the issue of how asylum applications by Eritreans were dealt with and decided on by the SEM also started to draw a lot of media attention. Criticism on the SEM's practice was voiced, which claimed that asylum was granted to Eritrean asylum seekers "too easily", and demanded that inquiries be made into whether, in some cases, removal orders could be issued for Eritrean applicants. This is something I was, unfortunately, unable to follow-up on systematically. However, it is important to note that following this considerable political pressure, at a "country situation assessment meeting" (Poertner 2018: 240), a new institutional practice for dealing with asylum applications by Eritreans was established in 2016. An order was given to decision-makers that from then on, all Eritrean applicants who had either never been drafted into the army or had been released from military service were no longer to be regarded as being eligible to refugee status and could therefore be issued a removal order as long as this was reasonable. Of course, this does not tell us what exactly this meant with regard to everyday decision-making practices; whether and/or why, for example, following this order decision-makers became more suspicious of asylum seekers saying that they had left Eritrea while still in active military service or whether this order had an effect on how, in practice, the decision-makers assessed the reasonableness of return and so on. Also, we do not know what other factors might also have influenced this change in practice. Nevertheless, what this example does point to, is how the SEM's accountability towards politics and the media contributes to the shaping of asylum decision-making practices.

A Brief Summary: Acquiring an Institutional Habitus

In this chapter, I have argued that how organisational socialisation works can only be understood if we take three crucial factors into account and see how

[46] Nick, caseworker, headquarters, interview transcript, my own translation.

they interplay: how decision-makers learn to do their job; how they are made by other actors to take on certain ideas and behaviours; and what belonging to the office means for them. I have shown that decision-makers affiliate themselves to and are affiliated with different communities within the office. They either try hard to fit into these communities or not to be associated with them. Primarily, decision-makers identify themselves with the centre they work in—the headquarters or one of the RPCs—and with the specific asylum unit they belong to. It is important to take this sense of belonging into account because it has an influence on other aspects of socialisation; on what decision-makers learn from their co-workers; on how they are coached to take decisions; on why they are teased; on what it means to fit in; and on how superiors monitor their employees' work. Hence, it influences what decision-makers come to understand as normal and appropriate practices or, to put it differently, it influences the institutional habitus they acquire.

The concept of institutional habitus assumes that the dispositions to understand, act, think and desire in a particular way are shaped by the experiences the holders of the habitus have had on the job. Enquiring into how decision-makers acquire such an institutional habitus on the job is therefore crucial because it allows us to understand how decision-makers come to interpret law in practice—thereby shaping and making it—when fitting it with specific 'cases' or situations. In this book, I argue that we need to pay attention to the shaping and structuring of decision-makers' discretionary practices, since "applying" written law to specific situations requires discretion. However, when decision-makers use discretion to interpret written law and fit it to a 'case', we should not assume that their interpretations of written law are based on "free", "autonomous" choices; on what decision-makers "personally" see as fit. One reason for this—and this is what has come out of this chapter—is that what decision-makers come to "personally" see fit is shaped through the office; through them acquiring an institutional habitus through the socialisation processes I have described.

The chapter has set forth that SEM officials are disciplined, incentivised and at times also compelled to act in certain ways. At the same time, however, caseworkers are also "ideationally conditioned to conduct themselves" in those ways (Gill 2009: 219–220). Thus, in the words of Gill, they come to volitionally align themselves with the office (ibid.: 215). Hence, it is through this that the state officials—who through their daily actions make and shape the state—are governed by the institution (see also Affolter et al. 2019: 264; Gill 2016; Mountz 2010).

References

Affolter, Laura, Jonathan Miaz, and Ephraim Poertner. 2019. "Taking the 'Just' Decision: Caseworkers and Their Communities of Interpretation in the Swiss Asylum Office." In *Asylum Determination in Europe: Ethnographic Perspectives*, edited by Nick Gill, and Anthony Good, 263–284. Cham: Palgrave Macmillan.

Ashford, Sue, and Samir Nurmohamed. 2012. "From Past to Present and Into the Future: A Hitchhiker's Guide to the Socialization Literature." In *The Oxford Handbook of Organizational Socialization*, edited by Connie R. Wanberg, 8–26. New York: Oxford University Press.

Ashforth, Blake E., David M. Sluss, and Spencer H. Harrison. 2007. "Socialization in Organizational Contexts." *International Review of Industrial and Organizational Psychology* 22: 1–70. https://doi.org/10.1002/9780470753378.ch1.

Bourdieu, Pierre, and Loïc J. D. Wacquant. 1992. "The Purpose of Reflexive Sociology (The Chicago Workshop)." In *An Invitation to Reflexive Sociology*, edited by Pierre Bourdieu, and Loïc J. D. Wacquant, 61–215. Cambridge: Polity Press.

Campbell, Colin, and Graham Wilson. 1995. *The End of Whitehall: A Comparative Perspective*. Cambridge: Blackwell.

Chao, Georgia T. 2012. "Organizational Socialization: Background, Basics, and a Blueprint for Adjustment at Work." In *The Oxford Handbook of Organizational Psychology. Vol. 1*, edited by Steve W. J. Kozlowski, 579–614. Oxford: Oxford University Press.

Dahlvik, Julia. 2018. *Inside Asylum Bureaucracy: Organizing Refugee Status Determination in Austria*. IMISCOE Research Series. Cham: Springer.

Gill, Nick. 2009. "Presentational State Power: Temporal and Spacial Influences over Asylum Sector Decisionmakers." *Transactions of the Institute of British Geographers* 34 (2): 215–233. https://doi.org/10.1111/j.1475-5661.2009.00337.x.

Gill, Nick. 2016. *Nothing Personal: Geographies of Governing and Activism in the British Asylum System*. Oxford: Wiley-Blackwell.

Good, Anthony. 2009. "The Taking and Making of Asylum Claims: Credibility Assessment in the British Asylum Courts." http://www.sps.ed.ac.uk/__data/assets/pdf_file/0014/31154/GoodSOAS.pdf, last accessed February 3, 2020.

Good, Anthony. 2011. "Witness Statement and Credibility Assessments in the British Asylum Courts." In *Cultural Expertise and Litigation*, edited by Livia Holden, 94–122. Abingdon, New York: Routledge.

Greuel, Luise, Susanne Offe, Agnes Fabian, Peter Wetzels, Thomas Fabian, Heinz Offe, and Michael Stadler. 1998. *Glaubhaftigkeit der Zeugenaussage: Theorie und Praxis der forensisch-psychologischen Begutachtung*. Weinheim: Beltz.

Heyman, Josiah McC. 1995. "Putting Power in the Anthropology of Bureaucracy: The Immigration and Naturalization Service at the Mexico-United States Border." *Current Anthropology* 36 (2): 261–287. https://doi.org/10.1086/204354.

Jubany, Olga. 2011. "Constructing Truths in a Culture of Disbelief: Understanding Asylum Screening from Within." *International Sociology* 26 (1): 74–94. https://doi.org/10.1177/0268580910380978.
Jubany, Olga. 2017. *Screening Asylum in a Culture of Disbelief: Truths, Denials and Sceptical Borders.* Cham: Palgrave Macmillan.
Kälin, Walter. 1986. "Troubled Communication: Cross-Cultural Misunderstandings in the Asylum-Hearing." *International Migration Review* 20 (2): 230–241. https://doi.org/10.1177/019791838602000206.
Lassman, Peter, and Ronald Speirs, eds. 1994. *Weber: Political Writings.* Cambridge: Cambridge University Press.
Lerner, Jennifer, and Philip Tetlock. 1999. "Accounting for the Effects of Accountability." *Psychological Bulletin* 125 (2): 255–275. https://projects.iq.harvard.edu/lernerlab/files/lerner_tetlock_1999.pdf, last accessed March 2, 2020.
Lewicki, Roy J. 1981. "Organizational Seduction: Building Commitment to Organizations." *Organizational Dynamics* 10 (2): 5–21. https://doi.org/10.1016/0090-2616(81)90029-2.
Liodden, Tone Maia. 2016. "The Burdens of Discretion. Managing Uncertainty in the Asylum Bureaucracy." PhD diss. (unpublished), University of Oslo.
Manning, Peter K., and John E. Van Maanen. 1978. *Policing: A View from the Street.* New York: Random House.
Martinez, Michael. 2009. *Public Administration Ethics for the 21st Century.* Santa Barbara: Praeger.
Miaz, Jonathan. 2017a. "Politique d'asile et sophistication du droit: Pratiques administratives et défense juridique des migrants en Suisse (1981–2015)." PhD diss. (unpublished), University of Lausanne and University of Strasbourg.
Miaz, Jonathan. 2017b. "From the Law to the Decision: The Social and Legal Conditions of Asylum Adjudication in Switzerland." *European Policy Analysis* 3 (2): 372–396. https://doi.org/10.1002/epa2.1018.
Mountz, Alison. 2010. *Seeking Asylum: Human Smuggling and Bureaucracy at the Border.* Minneapolis: University of Minnesota Press.
Oberfield, Zachary W. 2014. *Becoming Bureaucrats: Socialization at the Front Lines of Government Services.* Philadelphia: University of Pennsylvania Press.
Poertner, Ephraim. 2018. "Re-Cording Lives: Governing Asylum in Switzerland and the Need to Resolve." PhD diss. (unpublished), University of Zurich.
Probst, Johanna. 2012. *Instruire la demande d'asile: étude comparative du processus décisionnel au sein de l'administration allemande et française.* Science politique, Université de Strasbourg. https://tel.archives-ouvertes.fr/tel-00985215/document, last accessed February 3, 2020.
Rousseau, Cécile, François Crépeau, Patricia Foxen, and France Houle. 2002. "The Complexity of Determining Refugeehood: A Multidisciplinary Analysis of the

Decision-Making Process of the Canadian Immigration and Refugee Board." *Journal of Refugee Studies* 15 (1): 43–70. https://doi.org/10.1093/jrs/15.1.43.

Schneider, Stephanie. 2019. "Becoming a Decision-Maker, or: 'Don't Turn Your Heart into a Den of Thieves and Murderers'." In *Asylum Determination in Europe. Ethnographic Perspectives*, edited by Nick Gill, and Anthony Good, 285–305. Cham: Palgrave Macmillan.

Schneider, Stephanie, and Kristina Wottrich. 2017. "'Ohne'ne ordentliche Anhörung kann ich keine ordentliche Entscheidung machen …': Zur Organisation von Anhörungen in deutschen und schwedischen Asylbehörden." In *Asyl verwalten: Zur bürokratischen Bearbeitung eines gesellschaftlichen Problems*, edited by Christian Lahusen, and Stephanie Schneider, 81–115. Bielefeld: transcript.

Shuman, Amy, and Carole Bohmer. 2004. "Representing Trauma: Political Asylum Narrative." *The Journal of American Folklore* 117 (466): 394–414. http://doi.org/10.1353/jaf.2004.0100.

Spijkerboer, Thomas. 2000. *Gender and Refugee Status*. Aldershot: Ashgate.

Steller, Max, and Günter Köhnken. 1989. "Criteria-Based Statement Analysis." In *Psychological Methods in Criminal Investigation and Evidence*, edited by David C. Raskin, 217–245. New York: Springer.

Tetlock, Philip. 1985. "Accountability: The Neglected Social Context of Judgement and Choice." *Research in Organizational Behavior* 7: 297–332.

Toren, Christina. 2002. "Socialization." In *Encyclopedia of Social and Cultural Anthropology*, edited by Alan Barnard, and Jonathan Spencer, 512–514. New York: Routledge.

Van Maanen, John E., and Edgar H. Schein. 1979. "Toward a Theory of Organizational Socialization." *Research in Organizational Behavior* 1: 209–264.

Volbert, Renate, and Max Steller. 2009. "Die Begutachtung der Glaubhaftigkeit." In *Psychiatrische Begutachtung: Ein praktisches Handbuch für Ärzte und Juristen*, edited by Klaus Foerster, and Harald Dressing, 817–850. München: Elsevier, Urban & Fischer.

Wacquant, Loïc J. D. 1992. "Toward a Social Praxeology: The Structure and Logic of Bourdieu's Sociology." In *An Invitation to Reflexive Sociology*, edited by Pierre Bourdieu, and Loïc J. D. Wacquant, 1–59. Cambridge: Polity Press.

Wagenaar, Hendrik. 2004. "'Knowing' the Rules: Administrative Work as Practice." *Public Administration Review* 64 (6): 643–656. https://doi.org/10.1111/j.1540-6210.2004.00412.x.

Wanberg, Connie, ed. 2012. *The Oxford Handbook of Organizational Socialization*. Oxford: Oxford University Press.

Weber, Max. 2013 (1978). *Economy and Society*. Edited by Guenther Roth, and Claus Wittich. Berkeley: University of California Press.

Wenger, Etienne. 2003. "Communities of Practice and Social Learning Systems." In *Knowing in Organizations: A Practice-Based Approach*, edited by Davide Nicolini, Silvia Gherardi, and Dvora Yanow, 76–99. Armonk: M.E. Sharp.

6

The Good Decision-Maker or Protecting the System

As I have shown in the previous two chapters, digging deep is the epitome of professional decision-making. Digging deep refers to the practice whereby decision-makers interrogate asylum seekers during asylum interviews in a way that is aimed at "discovering" indicators of so-called non-credibility; most notably inconsistencies. Hence, decision-makers ask as many questions in asylum interviews and/or undertake as many extra investigations until they have enough arguments for rejecting a claim or they are convinced that a story is true "after all". This practice is not only characteristic of the SEM, but of asylum administrations in the Global North in general, as many authors have shown (see Bohmer and Shuman 2008: 136; Johannesson 2017: 12; Jubany 2017: 135–137; Kelly 2012: 765).

Helen's example in Chapter 5 showed that she fears being judged by her co-workers for not digging deep enough and "lightly" granting an applicant asylum on the basis of the principle *in dubio pro refugio* ("when in doubt, for the refugee"), which means that if decision-makers do not know whether an applicant's claims "are" credible or not they should decide in favour of the applicant. Helen does not want to be seen as taking decisions in an unprofessional way. Taking positive decisions is not per se an unprofessional and "bad" thing to do. To the contrary, it is an essential part of why decision-makers do the job—and why they like doing it. However, as the following statement by SEM official Denise further exemplifies, in order to take positive decisions with a "clear conscience", digging deep is a necessity:

> Sometimes you do an additional interview when technically everything indicates that a story could be true but there are two, three contradictions in it. In

L. Affolter, *Asylum Matters*, Palgrave Socio-Legal Studies,
https://doi.org/10.1007/978-3-030-61512-3_6

> such cases it just feels strange to grant asylum when there are still some uncertainties, some open questions. So, then you do [an additional interview] so that if you then get an answer that really satisfies you, you can write a positive decision with a clear conscience.[1]

In theory, the principle of *in dubio pro refugio* would allow Helen and Denise to grant the applicants asylum without digging deep. Yet, they feel uncomfortable doing so. Furthermore, from Denise's statement we can deduce a kind of moral obligation she feels to dig deep. Her professional conscience requires it. But why, and where does this moral "obligation" come from? These are the questions I pose in this chapter.

I argue that the professional values that guide decision-makers' work—and that are, as Helen's and Denise's examples show, incorporated by the caseworkers, forming a "personal" sense of what it means for them to morally do the right thing—are shaped by decision-makers' understanding of what their duty and that of the office as a whole consist of. Bureaucracies operate in ideological environments and they develop their own ideologies (see Downs 1967: 243–244). Hence, as Julia Eckert argues, "ideological projects" always underpin and are "translated and produced in administrative practice" (2020: 9). This chapter explores the ideological environment underlying and being produced by SEM officials' work. It analyses what it means for SEM officials to professionally fulfil their duty, perform their tasks and align themselves with the office (see Eckert 2020; Gill 2009: 215).

In this sense, the distinction Julia Eckert—drawing on Max Weber—makes between ethos and ethics is helpful. According to Eckert,

> [e]thos denotes the assemblage of values that underpin procedures, such as, for example, rule orientation, consistency, efficiency, efficacy, equality before the law and depersonalisation. […] Ethics, on the other hand, concerns orientation towards "the good". In the case of bureaucratic ethics, values and norms associated with the substantive goals of a bureaucratic apparatus are geared towards ideas of a good society, a good life, welfare or justice. (2020: 11–12)

Both ethos and ethics must, therefore, be taken into account if we want to understand how administrative decision-making works. Hence, in this chapter I show not only what the procedural values associated with asylum decision-making are but, more importantly, also how they are shaped by the ethics of the office. I argue that decision-makers' understanding of *what*

[1] Denise, caseworker, headquarters, interview transcript, my own translation.

their role is, shapes their understanding of *how* to carry it out professionally. Furthermore, since what administrative caseworkers think they should do informs their everyday practices, and their everyday practices shape and mediate the policies and laws they are charged with implementing (see, for instance, Silbey 2005: 324; Wedel et al. 2005: 34), we need to explore the ethics and ethos of the office in order to understand how asylum law and policies work.

I start this chapter with an anecdote from the field in which two SEM officials—a supervisor and his employee—discuss the rightfulness of a decision. From it I extract what the officials consider their duties as decision-makers to be, which then forms the basis from which I work out the ethics of the office. Following this, I discuss the different norms of what it means to be professional in the SEM and how these norms are connected to and influenced by the two substantial goals of the office: that of protecting the abstract, "noble" value of asylum and that of protecting Switzerland's "borders", meant here not in a territorial sense, but in terms of access to rights and goods.

Negotiating "the Right" Decision: A Field Anecdote

A decision-maker, Rebecca, and her superior, Alberto, are discussing a decision she has made. As Rebecca's superior, it is Alberto's duty to check and countersign her decisions before they are sent to the applicants. In this case, he does not agree with Rebecca's decision to grant temporary protection to a family from Iraq. I quote this excerpt from my field notes in detail because it brings to light several aspects of what Alberto and Rebecca believe professional decision-making involves.

I am sitting in Alberto's office, watching him go through his employees' decisions and case files. The documents he appraises, decisions that need his signature before they can go out, were left by his employees on a table outside his office. The first decision he picks up is for a family from Iraq. The decision-maker, Rebecca, has rejected the family's asylum claim, but has granted the family temporary protection. For my benefit, Alberto comments on the decision as he reads through it. I learn that the family came to Switzerland a couple of years ago because the husband started work with a human rights organisation. When the husband's contract ended, the family stayed on and filed for asylum.

Alberto tells me that he agrees with the negative decision. He says the family's problems do not qualify them as refugees. Then, looking at the internal application for temporary protection Rebecca has submitted, he says: "Ok, the kids are still quite young and they've been here for quite a while, so they haven't lived in their country of origin for a long time. But someone else might still have decided differently". He feels that it is a very "generous" decision. "I mean", he goes on, "they're an upper-class family. It wouldn't be a problem for them to be socially reintegrated. [...] They're a family, they're together, they can travel. They could go anywhere they want". Alberto is not quite sure what to do about the case, but he feels he cannot just let it pass like that. In the end, he decides to put it aside for two hours and then return to it. Quickly, he goes through the other decisions from the pile on his desk, reading through them, flicking through the case files and then countersigning them. Once he has finished with the other decisions, he turns back to the case of the Iraqi family even though the two hours have not yet passed.

Seemingly out of the blue, and slightly defensively, he says to me: "The question of nation states and whether one thinks nation states are good or not, has nothing to do with what we do here. It cannot be solved by what we do. I'm all for granting protection", he continues, "but we don't have to hand it to them on a plate" (*aber man muss es den Leuten nicht nachschiessen*). He explains to me that seeing so many cases over the past several years has made him stricter and less naïve. What is important to him is that whatever leaves his desk is fair. This, he explains, also means protecting the asylum system from abuse. Saying that, he grabs the Iraqi family's case file and tells me he will take the decision back to the caseworker, Rebecca, to discuss it with her. He says that she will either have to add more reasons for granting the family temporary protection or reconsider her decision. Alberto asks if I would like to join him. Slightly hesitant, but also curious, I follow him to Rebecca's office.

Alberto explains to Rebecca that he thinks this is a very opportunistic, upper-class family that does not need temporary protection. Rebecca says that she can see his point, but she worries that because the children are still quite young, their decision denying the family temporary protection might be quashed if the 'case' is taken on appeal to the Federal Administrative Court. "Also", she argues, "the wife has health problems". But Alberto does not think her problems are severe enough. He also does not think the fact that the young children have not lived in their country of origin would pose a problem in the event of an appeal, and he feels that the risk is worth taking. Together they discuss other possible "obstacles to removal", but Rebecca had already ruled them all out after consulting the *Federführung*.[2] The discussion ends with the following dialogue:

> *Alberto*: "I think the decision is too generous".
> *Rebecca*: "That's my problem. I'm too nice."
> *Alberto*: "I'm also nice."
> *Rebecca*: "Yes, of course".[3]

Alberto and Rebecca agree that she will work on the case again and rethink her original decision. Before leaving to go back to his office Alberto asks Rebecca whether she "can live with" this new decision. Rebecca assures Alberto that she can, and that she will still be able to sleep at night. She promises that it will not take her long to change the decision.

As Alberto and I set off towards his office again, Rebecca holds me back, causing Alberto to come back too. She explains to me that this is just a normal part of the job. Sometimes, though not often, decisions are given back and one has to work on them again. She says that in this case she was probably influenced by the fact that she had interviewed the family herself and that they had come across as being very pleasant. Alberto says that he finds this understandable and that this is something that has really changed for him since he was put in charge of the subdivision and stopped doing asylum interviews himself. "I have become stricter, because I see so many cases", he explains, "but I can also see things more clearly now, from a certain distance, more objectively".[4]

This ethnographic vignette could be analytically explored in several different directions. In this chapter, I limit myself to mapping out both Alberto's and Rebecca's understandings of professional decision-making. Rebecca and Alberto mention several different aspects of what they believe professional decision-making involves. From Alberto we learn that professional decision-making is fair, objective and apolitical. The latter characteristic he expresses by saying that one's personal opinion of nation states (and of the restrictions on freedom of movement and residence associated with

[2] *Federführungen* are SEM officials who hold lead positions for particular countries of origin. They are responsible for (co-)determining and monitoring the institution's decision-making practices in dealing with cases from these countries (see Chapter 4).

[3] I argue that this short dialogue must at least in part be read as an expression of the defensive position decision-makers at times adopted towards me—and outside actors in general (see Chapter 2; see also Eule 2014: 104; Lentz 2014: 197).

[4] Field notes, my own translation.

them) has nothing to do with their job. He also has clear ideas of what constitutes fair and objective decision-making. For him, fair decision-making relates to strictly following the law, and objective decision-making to making decisions "from a distance" and not becoming too personally involved in the case. From Rebecca, we learn that being a good and professional decision-maker means working fast, not becoming too personally involved in one's cases, and making decisions that one can personally endorse. We further infer from this anecdote that being naïve, "too generous" and "too nice" are considered to be features of unprofessional decision-making. Protection should be granted, but not too easily. In Alberto's words: "It shouldn't be handed to [asylum seekers] on a plate". In order to understand why all of this has come to define professionalism for Rebecca and Alberto, I turn to the ethics of the office to demonstrate how it can be derived from what caseworkers understand their duties as decision-makers and state officials to be.

Ethics of the Office: Decision-Makers as Protectors of the System

In "*Modernity and the Holocaust*", Zygmunt Bauman (1989: 159) suggests, as Tone Liodden writes, "that there is a tendency in bureaucracies to shift the sense of moral obligation from those who are affected by decisions, towards colleagues and the demands of the system" (2016: 242). In Bauman's understanding, this makes bureaucracies anethical and amoral (see also Graeber 2015; Herzfeld 1992). This shift of moral obligation that Bauman describes is important and is something I also observed in the SEM. However, I challenge his interpretation that this makes administrations anethical and amoral. Rather, following Julia Eckert (2020), I argue that ethics should be understood not in a normative, but rather in an empirical way (see also Fassin 2012: 4). In this sense, "ethics are intrinsic to bureaucracy" (Eckert 2020: 9). Decision-makers' sense of moral obligation is ethical, whoever or whatever they feel it towards.

In his study of different "asylum sector intermediaries" Nick Gill argues that "states [...] command powers that are capable of engendering the *will* to act in accordance with state objectives, rather than simply generating the necessity or imperative to do so" (2009: 215, 219, emphasis in the original). This "will to act in accordance with state objectives" was something I frequently observed. Many decision-makers I spoke to strongly identified themselves with the office and with what they perceived to be the state's—and, therefore, the office's—objectives (see also Affolter et al. 2019: 273–274).

According to Max Weber's ideal-typical bureaucracy, "loyalty to the office" (*Amtstreue*) is a characteristic of bureaucratic rule (2013 [1978]: 705). Decision-makers in the SEM share this ideal-typical value. Thus, being loyal to the office is regarded as very important, as exemplified by a SEM official who in a conversation with Jonathan Miaz said: "I have to do what the office says, otherwise I will somehow betray the office and I don't want that either" (Affolter et al. 2019: 276). Similarly, Olga Jubany observed amongst immigration officers in the UK that "[i]n their exercise of their professional role, officers' responsibility and accountability is not directed to the asylum seekers but to the immigration service and the organisation. Officers' responsibility is almost invariably related to their feelings of professional duty" (2017: 192). This sense of duty she argues "is inextricably linked to defending the system" (ibid.: 209).

My analysis differs from that of Jubany in that I do not claim that decision-makers feel no responsibility towards asylum seekers. They do, as I will show later on in this chapter. However, I concur with her in that decision-makers often put their responsibility towards "the system" over responsibility towards asylum seekers (see also Poertner 2018: 288). Or, rather, I argue that responsibility towards asylum seekers is aligned with and subsumed under the responsibility to protect the system.

In the field anecdote above, we can see that for Alberto the Iraqi family does not deserve protection because, as an "upper class family", they are not sufficiently vulnerable. They do not fit the image of victims in need of help.[5] "They could go anywhere they want", he claims. From this, we can deduce decision-makers' dual duty. On the one hand, decision-makers must make sure that those "really deserving of protection" receive protection. On the other hand, they must protect the system from being abused by "undeserving" applicants. This dual duty of protecting people—but only deserving people—and filtering out the undeserving in order to protect "the system" becomes apparent in the wording the SEM uses to describe the "[b]asic principles of asylum legislation" on its website:

> It is the duty of asylum proceedings to identify those asylum seekers among the new arrivals who are entitled to protection under the terms [of the Geneva Convention]. Many asylum seekers cannot be classified as refugees or persons

[5] Several authors have shown that asylum (and immigration) politics, law and decision-making produce a very particular "'figure' (Fassin 2007: 512) of the deserving aid recipient, framing him or her as a victim in need of protection" (Cabot 2013: 453; see also Ticktin 2006; Zetter 2007).

> displaced by war. On the basis of their situation, they clearly belong to the group of migrants. They are in search of a better place to live in Switzerland. Knowing that they would hardly obtain an entry or work permit, they cross the border illegally. Many of them invent a dramatic story of persecution for the hearing by the authorities. With such tactics they hope to be granted refugee status. From the viewpoint of the person concerned, this behaviour is understandable, from the perspective of asylum legislation it constitutes abuse of asylum proceedings. The authorities must reject such applications without delay and execute removal systematically, making asylum proceedings unattractive for foreigners seeking employment.[6]

The quote illustrates a common assumption in the SEM that many (or even most) asylum seekers will lie. While deemed understandable ("anyone in that situation would do it", I was often told), it is, nevertheless, the decision-makers' duty to separate the "real" from the "false" refugees, the ones "telling the truth" from the ones "who are lying" (see also Bohmer and Shuman 2018: 160; Fassin and Kobelinsky 2012: 446; Kobelinsky 2015: 67). This is regarded as important because the asylum system is only seen to work if those "not deserving of protection" are denied asylum. The following quote from Jonathan Miaz's fieldwork shows this distinction nicely: "I think that saying 'no' to someone who's not a refugee in the sense of the UNHCR and of the Refugee Convention contributes to the protection of the asylum institution. One has to say 'no' to those who are not refugees in order to be able to say 'yes' to those who are" (Affolter et al. 2019: 273).

Reserving refugee protection for those "truly deserving of it", therefore, becomes a necessity for upholding the value of the asylum system. Thus, as Didier Fassin and Carolina Kobelinsky argue, "[t]he less frequently [asylum] is granted, the more precious refugee status becomes" (2012: 464). This means that in order to maintain the value of asylum, many applications need to be rejected (ibid.: 465).

Under "basic principles of asylum legislation" the SEM states on its website that it is decision-makers' duty to make "asylum proceedings unattractive for foreigners seeking employment". I argue that the ethics—understood in an empirical sense—underlying this is that Switzerland must be protected from so-called "foreigners" or "outsiders" (see Jubany 2017: 212) by making sure that not "too many foreigners" come to and are allowed to reside in Switzerland. Decision-makers thereby become "guardians of a restricted good": in this case, the right to reside in Switzerland (Heyman 2009: 381; see also Lipsky 2010: 4). As a kind of "meta-message" (Jubany 2017), this duty is

[6]https://perma.cc/ZG4B-NN6U, last accessed 26.02.2020.

frequently conveyed in the SEM. This became particularly visible in the induction training, where it was not explicitly taught, but was consistently implied, as the following examples show.

In one of the training courses I attended, the instructor presented us with a graph comparing the number of new asylum applications in Europe and in Switzerland between 1998 and 2014. The graph showed that, in 2014, the percentage of asylum applicants in Switzerland was at its lowest point since 1998, dropping from 8.2 per cent in 2012 to 3.8 per cent in 2014. Drawing attention to this, the instructor commented: "Switzerland must have done something right, since the percentage of applications has gone down like this".[7] The message was quite clear. If Switzerland—through its frontline decision-makers—did its job well, this reduced the number of applications (especially in comparison with other European countries).

The second example comes from a course on how to deal with applications for family reunification. The instructor told the new decision-makers that the institutional practice for dealing with Eritrean applications was to request DNA proof that the applicants were indeed related to the people they intended to bring to Switzerland. The instructor said: "If they do not hand in DNA proof, the case is ready to be decided, namely negatively. I have seen that people have still been granted entry in such cases. Please don't do that. That's the worst signal we could be sending out".[8] With this statement, the instructor urged trainees to make sure their decision-making did not send out the wrong message to avoid creating a "pull-effect". The wrong message would therefore be that Switzerland is a country where family reunification is easy.

The two substantial goals the office is geared towards can be deduced from the examples above. As a Federal institution, the SEM—and, therefore, its staff—are requested to represent "national interests". On the one hand, this means fulfilling Switzerland's duties under international law (particularly the Geneva Convention and the UN Convention on the Rights of the Child) and maintaining its self-ascribed image as a humanitarian country. Upholding the noble value of asylum succeeds by excluding those "undeserving" of it. The scarcer asylum protection becomes, the more precious its value. On the other hand, it also means securing Switzerland's "borders" by restricting non-citizens' access to rights and goods, and by making sure that there are not too many "foreigners" residing in Switzerland. My analysis subsumes both sets of practices within the phrase "protecting the system", which, via two ostensibly

---

[7]Training instructor, A-modules, field notes, my own translation.

[8]Training instructor, C-modules, field notes, my own translation.

opposed logics, comes to mean keeping numbers of asylum applicants low. This is at least partly achieved by keeping acceptance rates low.

My point here is not to say that all decision-makers consciously strive towards keeping numbers low. Many explicitly do not. Furthermore, many decision-makers do not per se share the political view that immigration to Switzerland should be restricted. However, I argue that regardless of decision-makers' personal political views and ideologies, the ethics of the office have an impact on and implicitly shape decision-makers' understanding of what it means to do their job well. This explains how and why "digging deep" becomes subsumed under professional, objective and neutral decision-making, while "easily believing" asylum seekers is associated with lazy, naïve, sometimes even politically motivated, and, thus, unprofessional decision-making.

Ethos of the Office: Professional Norms and Values

What administrative caseworkers "think they should do shapes what they actually do as much as other constraints", Julia Eckert argues (2020: 8). Decision-makers' role perception; what they perceive their duty to consist of; what commonweal or just order they believe they must work towards; and who or what they feel loyal to are crucial in this regard (ibid.). But also, the more procedural norms and the dominant values in the office regarding *how* decision-makers should carry out their duty as protectors of the system and the tasks connected to this duty, shape what decision-makers do. In this part of the chapter I explore such institutional norms and values that prevail in the SEM; many of which were already brought up by Alberto and Rebecca in the field anecdote described above.

The aim is not to paint a coherent picture. Good decision-making in the SEM suggests juggling different norms and values; many of which stand in (potential) conflict to one another. Hence, good decision-makers both do justice to the individual 'case' and strictly adhere to the law and institutional practice. They are emotionally distanced from the applicants but at the same time understanding and compassionate towards them. They are "politically neutral", yet, they have a political "state-duty" to fulfil. They live up to the professional role of the sceptic, but, at the same time, they are not cynical. And they work fast, while still carrying each task out carefully in order not to create more work at a later stage.

Each of these values is now separately explored in more detail. I analyse the meanings ascribed to them; how they structure everyday decision-making and how they are linked to the ethics of the office.

The Efficient, Fast and Economical Decision-Maker

The quality charter given to all caseworkers in the SEM's asylum directorate reflects common characteristics of what is known as New Public Management. It states that

> [w]e decide who is granted protection in our country and who has no such need. We are aware of the fact that our job has major consequences for the lives of affected people. That is why our actions must meet high quality standards. [...] We treat asylum seekers in a fair and correct manner, regardless of what their claim consists of. Asylum applications are treated competently and in consistence with the law and institutional practice [...]. In doing so, we work efficiently, fast and economically. [...] We make quality measurable: we set quality targets, define binding standards and make use of the necessary measuring instruments.[9]

New Public Management reforms were introduced in the SEM and other public administrations in Switzerland "from the early 2000s onwards" (Poertner 2018: 274).[10] Typical of these reforms was, amongst other things, the introduction of explicit performance standards and measurements as well as a strong emphasis on the so-called "output" of public administrations (see Gill 2016: 39; Hood 1991; Rose 1999: 150–151).

In the SEM today, quantitative targets are regularly defined for the whole institution, each division and section as well as for every individual decision-maker. All decision-makers, as well as the sections and divisions themselves, receive monthly statistical charts which show them what they have achieved and whether they have fulfilled their quantitative aims or not. While reaching their targets never posed a problem for a few of the decision-makers I spoke to—some did not even know how many decisions they were supposed to take each month, it was so easy for them—the majority of my interaction partners suffered because of this time pressure and struggled, and often failed, to reach their monthly target. Hence, they work under a lot of pressure to produce

[9] Quality charter, training material for new employees of the SEM's asylum directorate, field documents, my own translation.

[10] Other asylum administrations such as the FAO in Austria (see Dahlvik 2018: 63–72); the OFPRA in France (see Probst 2012: 214–222), the BAMF in Germany (see Probst 2012: 214–222) and the UDI in Norway (see Liodden 2016: 236–242) underwent similar developments.

the quantitative output expected of them (see also Fresia et al. 2013: 54–55; Liodden 2016: 237; Poertner 2018: 275).

The targets for individual decision-makers are set at meetings with their superiors at six monthly intervals. They depend on officials' working hours, their customary productivity and any other tasks they might have. At the time of my research, such targets often consisted of four to five asylum interviews a month and eighteen to twenty decisions or rather, marks on their tally list, every month. What counts as output and what does not, keeps changing. During my fieldwork, both the number of asylum interviews conducted and the number of asylum decisions sent out, counted towards caseworkers' output. However, some types of decisions, like decisions concerning family reunification, for instance, did not. Yet, it was not actually the number of decisions per se that counted, but rather the number of people asylum decisions had been taken for. Thus, if a decision-maker wrote a decision for a five-person family this yielded five marks, while a decision for a single person resulted in one (see also Poertner 2017: 15).

Output pressure is often particularly strongly felt by decision-makers working on fixed-term contracts because they are told that whether or not they will have their contract prolonged depends, amongst other things, on whether they manage to produce the output requested of them. Hence, one decision-maker, whom I have called Sebastian, told me that in the organisational division he worked in they had been told that whoever produced the least marks by the end of the year had to fear their contract not being renewed. He complained that this had led to rivalry between co-workers and to decisions being taken very hurriedly and badly. For people with an open-ended contract this had not been so bad, he explained, but in his unit, there were only a handful of them, the rest all held fixed-term contracts. His output was not very good, he told me, because he was at the time mainly working on 'cases' from single young men from what he called a "complicated country". But he hoped that his superior would be able to see beyond quantity and would also take into account the quality of his employees' decisions.[11]

Quantity and quality must be weighed against each other in everyday decision-making. Producing quantity is important because of the output targets set by the institution, but also because of the large caseloads relative to their time capacity decision-makers must deal with, which, according to Michael Lipsky is a typical characteristic of street-level bureaucracies (2010: 29). This is immediately apparent when one enters a decision-maker's office. Everywhere—in and on top of bookshelves, on the desks and on the little

[11] Sebastian, caseworker, headquarters, field notes, my own translation.

tables which have been added and sometimes even on the floor—there are piles of case files: cases that need to be decided, cases which are still waiting for an answer from further investigations, interviews that need to be conducted, and cases that will "just have to wait" because they are not a priority.

I was often told by superiors that it was their job, for the abovementioned reasons, to make sure that their employees produced enough decisions. However, most of them, like Nora, claimed that they valued quality higher than quantity: "I have to make sure my people write decent (*ordentliche*) and correct decisions. And enough. And exactly in this order. You see, for me quality is more important than quantity".[12] At the same time, they told me—and complained about the fact—that for several of their fellow superiors, the opposite was often the case.

Pressure to produce enough output and to work efficiently is not only attributed to the office itself, but also to "politics" as the following statement by a superior from Jonathan Miaz's fieldwork illustrates: "[W]e [the SEM (officials)] have a responsibility towards the Swiss people and the tax payers to not just take correct decisions but decisions of the 'right quality'. […] And I deliberately speak of 'the right quality' and not of 'optimal quality' because it could always be done better" (Affolter et al. 2019: 271). The "right quality" for this head of an asylum unit thereby means that the quality of the decision matters, but that the effort put into producing qualitatively good decisions "has to be measured against the quantitative demands of the office" (ibid.). This for him constitutes a political demand he is required to fulfil. The statement, therefore, shows how the superior has "internalised a certain accountability toward these imagined, generalised and blurred figures" of the "Swiss people" and "tax payers" (ibid.). Thus, the procedural norms regarding how officials should go about taking decisions are interpreted in the light of what decision-makers understand their duty to be. As my fieldwork has shown, my interaction partners, as state agents, felt that they had to act in the interest of "the state". What this means for them is illustrated by the above-quoted statement. State interests are, at least partially, perceived as what "Swiss people"—in a rather abstract sense—want.

According to the quality charter quoted above, decision-makers are not only expected to work fast, they must also work economically. Amongst other things, working economically implies taking decisions that will not likely be quashed by the Federal Administrative Court, since every decision that is rescinded and obliges decision-makers to revisit the 'case', costs time.

[12]Nora, head of asylum unit, headquarters, interview transcript, my own translation.

As shown in Chapter 5, this fear of having decisions quashed may have an impact on the type of decision taken and the legal reasoning used to justify them. How the procedural norm of working economically shapes officials' everyday work can, for instance, be seen in the example of Theodor who once explained to me

> that his superior had instructed him to stop always looking for material evidence in order to argue for the non-credibility of asylum claims using the criterion "contradiction to facts" (*Tatsachenwidrigkeit*). The superior considered this too time-consuming and had asked him to focus instead on framing his arguments along the lines of "insufficient substance", which could be done on the basis of the asylum interview minutes alone. (Affolter et al. 2019: 271)

Time should, therefore, be spent "wisely". The same also holds true for money. Hence, during induction training, the novices were instructed not to frivolously request that the authenticity of asylum seekers' documents be assessed by specialists, because this would cost the office a lot of money. Rather, the expectation was that this was only to be done if decision-makers were not otherwise able to assess the credibility of asylum claims in the ways described in Chapter 4. Furthermore, for some of my interaction partners—mostly occupying higher hierarchical positions in the SEM—money was even a concern beyond what it meant in terms of procedural costs. Hence, some officials claimed that it was important not to grant asylum and temporary protection "too easily" because if all "those people" then brought their families here that would cost Switzerland a lot of money. Yet, at the same time, as I will show below, other officials did not share and even explicitly criticised this view. Worrying about money in this sense was indicative of politically motivated decision-making which, in their eyes, was unprofessional.

The Neutral, Apolitical Decision-Maker

When Alberto, slightly defensively, brought up "the question of nation states" in the conversation introduced earlier in the chapter, and "whether one thinks nation states are good or not", he was referring to a particular political ideology that questions the fundamental idea of nation states. Even if he was sympathetic towards this idea—Alberto did not really state his opinion and left this possibility open—the message he conveyed is clear: on the job, there is no place for personal political opinions. But not only that. By saying that these problems "cannot be solved by what we do", he insinuated that decision-making is also apolitical. Both of these statements reflect perspectives that are common in the SEM and other public administrations (see Dahlvik 2018: 56; Johannesson 2017: 116–117; Liodden 2016: 207–209).

The apolitical norm fits with the impersonal spirit Weber depicts as an important feature of the bureaucratic ethos. He writes: "'*Sine ira et studio*,' without hatred or passion, and hence without affection or enthusiasm. The dominant norms are concepts of straightforward duty without regard to personal considerations. [...] This is the spirit in which the ideal official conducts his office" (2013 [1978]: 225). In contrast, the "politician's element" is "*ira et studium*" (Weber 1991: 95). Thus, according to Weber, politicians must have passion and fight, whereas bureaucrats should do neither. A similar opinion is widespread in the SEM: there all an official should do is to follow rules and "neutrally apply the law". This is illustrated in the following quote by SEM official Barbara:

> I have a problem with "missionaries". And there are some here in the SEM. We don't have a mission here. We just have to decide upon cases. We don't have to protect Switzerland from foreigners. That is not our role. But some people here feel this way. They think that there are too many asylum seekers here. But that is not my problem. I am paid to take decisions, so I take decisions. On the other hand, there are some who proselytise on behalf of the asylum seekers. They think that everybody should be able to stay here. But that is not the case. We have the law. [...] And then there are the others who say: "If you give a temporary permit to this guy, who is only 20, and then he stays for 30 years, that will cost Switzerland 10 million francs." Again, that is not my problem. If he fulfils the eligibility criteria he can stay. If you're not happy with it, you have to change the law. But then you have to go into politics, you shouldn't be working here.[13]

In her statement, Barbara is tellingly advocating for "political neutrality", which is widely recognised as an important norm within the SEM. She situates this "political neutrality" in the middle between what she identifies as two kinds of political "extremes": wanting to "protect Switzerland from foreigners" and believing that "everybody should be allowed to stay". This view was shared by all my interaction partners. While some tended to be more critical of "hardline" decision-making and others were more disturbed by their colleagues' "lenient" decisions, neutrality was always associated with this middle ground.

[13]Barbara, caseworker, headquarters, interview transcript, my own translation.

Barbara uses the word "missionaries" to describe a role decision-makers should not take on. Missionaries pursue clear goals with their decision-making: they either want to enable everybody to stay, or to make sure that as few people as possible are allowed to remain in Switzerland. In contrast, for Barbara, professional decision-making has no room for ideologies and pursuit of goals other than following the law. She claims that a professional decision-maker's only aim should be to "correctly" and "neutrally" apply the law, which is a common self-understanding and professional value in bureaucratic institutions (see Dubois 2005; Lavanchy 2013: 69; Miaz 2017b: 384).

Barbara claiming that it is not her role "to protect Switzerland from foreigners" could be read as standing in contradiction to her duty as protector of the system and what I have called the ethics of the office. However, I argue that it does not. As stated above, making sure that not "too many foreigners" come and are allowed to stay in Switzerland is only rarely stated—and perceived—by caseworkers as an explicit aim of asylum decision-making. But, at the same time, protecting the system is self-evidently accepted as being a decision-maker's duty and as such is rather unquestioningly adopted and incorporated by the officials. Protecting the system, which builds on the idea that Switzerland must be protected from "outsiders", lies at the heart of professionalism in the SEM, shaping decision-makers' understanding of what it means to do the job well. Yet, protecting the system is not perceived as an ideology, as lying outside the law. Rather, it informs what "correct" and "neutral" rule-following means. In this sense, protecting the system becomes apolitical as do the professional norms and decision-making practices, like "digging deep", that are associated with it (see also Johannesson 2017: 120–121). In the words of Cris Shore and Susan Wright, this is, therefore, how the political becomes masked "under the cloak of neutrality" (1997: 8).

The Objective, Sufficiently Distanced and Emotionally Detached Decision-Maker

Since he has seen so many cases as a superior, he is now able to "see things more clearly, from a certain distance, more objectively", Alberto explains to Rebecca and me. For him distance and objectivity are what it takes to be professional and reach good decisions. He considers Rebecca's decision to be a bad one because it is "too generous". Rebecca thinks that the fact that she was "too nice" and made "too generous" a decision might have been influenced by the family's pleasant appearance when she interviewed them. In other words, she thinks she had liked them too much. In the SEM, emotional attachment and personal involvement are seen as the antithesis of objective decision-making. For a decision to be objective, it should be based solely on the "facts" of the case: on applicants' recorded statements and all the written documents applicants have supplied or decision-makers have acquired. Distance and emotional detachment are considered crucial for achieving this (see also Dahlvik 2018: 56, 77; Liodden 2016: 243–244). In the following, I examine what SEM officials understand by distance and emotional detachment, and what measures are undertaken to create such distance in order to enable objective decision-making.

SEM officials are not allowed to interview asylum seekers they know personally. If they are assigned the case of an applicant they know, they are obliged to give it back or pass it on to a co-worker. Moreover, in a training module dealing with the role of decision-makers in the interviews, trainees were told to maintain appropriate distance—not just towards asylum seekers, but also towards other professionals who participate in asylum interviews. They were informed that whereas it was not forbidden to befriend these professionals outside work, the interview was not a place for informal or personal conversation.[14]

Separate waiting rooms reflect the distance created between different types of actors. At the headquarters, one waiting room is for asylum seekers, and a separate room is shared by interpreters, social aid representatives and other visitors such as myself. The minute-takers have their own keys and move around the buildings freely. At the two reception and processing centres where I conducted my fieldwork, the auxiliary personnel sit in the same common room as the decision-makers themselves, while asylum seekers wait elsewhere. This separation ensures that all personal encounters and interactions between officials and asylum seekers are confined to interviews, where they are entirely "professional". This not only secludes the decision-makers but the interpreters, minute-takers and social aid representatives are also kept apart from the asylum seekers (although they all might go outside to smoke together). Several officials told me that these separate waiting rooms enabled interpreters to keep their distance from asylum seekers because otherwise they might be approached by the latter. An asylum seeker may, for instance, ask them for help in answering questions appropriately or may ask

[14]In practice, this is somewhat different. Several decision-makers maintain friendly ties with minute-takers and interpreters and this was evident during interviews when they initiated personal conversations or took breaks together. However, caseworkers are always careful to maintain a certain distance between themselves and the asylum seekers. Thus, conversations between decision-makers and asylum seekers are usually limited to the interview itself and, at times, to some formal small talk on the way to and from the office and the waiting room.

them to tell them what questions might be asked. I argue that SEM officials are thereby not only preoccupied with keeping interpreters and asylum seekers apart for the sake of the interpreters, but also for the sake of their own decision-making. This has to do with the moments of translation in the asylum interviews simultaneously playing a crucial role in the decision-making process and yet being very difficult for the decision-makers to control since they do not know what is being said between the asylum seekers and the interpreters.

Another feature that promotes professional distance is the seating arrangement during the interviews, which usually take place in an official's personal office. The offices are equipped in a standard manner. The minute-takers sit at a desk with a computer. All the other participants are placed around a larger rectangular table. These small rooms become very cramped during an interview when five participants (including me) are sitting in them. This forces people to sit close together. Although seating arrangements are generally not conscious decisions, but merely copied from other officials, most decision-makers sit at opposite ends of the table from asylum seekers, and so it is they who sit the farthest apart. When I asked an official called Gabriel why they always sat like that he replied: "Well, for me it's important that I can look the applicant in the eye, that I can look at him during our conversation, that I'm opposite him and sometimes I am also grateful for the distance".[15]

Gabriel's quote points not only to the importance of distance, it also illustrates the value decision-makers ascribe to the "proximity" of face-to-face encounters. Face-to-face encounters are valued for a number of reasons. As shown in Chapter 4, they are seen as an important source of professional-practical knowledge. Furthermore, decision-makers believe that by seeing the applicant they can do better justice to the individual case, because they get a better feeling of what is really at stake. Moreover, many decision-makers told me that it was easier to stand by their decisions if they had personally interviewed the asylum seeker. They usually felt more confident that they were making "the right" decision when this was the case (see Chapter 4). Finally, one decision-maker, Lucy, told me that she found doing asylum interviews important, because "you sit opposite these people time and again and you realise that it is not just a number [you are dealing with], but a human being with all his hopes and dreams" (see also Dahlvik 2018: 61).[16] Yet, while close encounters in the interviews are acknowledged as important for the aforementioned reasons, decision-makers also see a danger that, like Rebecca, they will become emotionally attached. Hence, being a good decision-maker requires

[15]Gabriel, caseworker, headquarters, interview transcript, my own translation.

[16]Lucy, caseworker, headquarters, interview transcript, my own translation.

maintaining the right balance between proximity and distance. All my interaction partners told me that, for this reason, they usually put the case file aside for a couple of days after the interview, to (re-)gain some distance, so that their decision would not be influenced by sentiments the interview might have triggered. In this way, they become objective again.

What I have described so far is the meaning given to "distance" as a professional norm by the SEM officials themselves. At the same time, in academic literature, "distance" and "distancing" are used in a more analytical and often critical way to describe bureaucratic work. Tobias Eule, for instance, uses the term to describe how people become cases, numbered files and outputs in and through administrative procedures (2014: 109; see also Fuglerud 2004: 36; Scheffer 2001). This is something I too observed in the SEM and is most clearly expressed in the language decision-makers use when talking about the people they deal with. However, in terms of institutional values, reducing people to numbers and not recognising them as individuals is regarded as doing one's job badly. Thus, in the training sessions, the new decision-makers were frequently reminded that they were dealing with "people and not numbers" or in the words of one instructor: "You decide whether someone has to go back home or not. This isn't just a piece of paper".[17] The common outside critique of reducing people to numbers, cases or files is thereby mirrored in this internal value. Good decision-makers are supposed to care for the people they deal with (see also Watkins-Hayes 2009: 70). Therefore, following Veena Das, I argue that (emotional) detachment should not be equated with cold disinterest (2015: 103–106; see also Candea et al. 2015: 24).

Academics engaging critically with bureaucratic institutions have, furthermore, argued that administrative caseworkers take decisions, which lead to inhumane circumstances and may at times even prove to be lethal, because they are physically and psychologically distanced from the outcomes of their actions. Thus, they do not feel responsible for them (see Arendt 2013; Bauman 1989; Eule 2014: 109; Gill 2016). In the SEM, decision-makers are also to some extent physically and psychologically distanced from the outcomes of their decisions. Hence, on the one hand, they are very rarely present when asylum seekers learn of their decision because, especially at the headquarters, almost all decisions are sent out as letters.[18] On the other hand,

---

[17]Training instructor, A-modules, field notes, my own translation.

[18]Theoretically, there is the possibility of passing judgement verbally. However, this is rarely done at the headquarters and then mostly for positive decisions. At the reception and processing centres it happens a bit more frequently and there mostly with negative decisions.

they are not present when rejected applicants are deported since once a negative decision has been taken and becomes legally binding, the 'case' is passed on to the return division of the SEM and the responsibility for deporting this person is transferred to the canton of residence.

This was different during the three years, between 2007 and 2010, in which Federal Councillor Eveline Widmer-Schlumpf was in charge of the SEM. During this time, the two SEM divisions "asylum" and "return" were merged. This meant that caseworkers had to do everything from interviewing asylum seekers, to taking decisions, to organising so-called "voluntary returns" (see Loher 2020) and deportations, including, at times, being present for the deportations. While some decision-makers said they valued this time for the new perspectives it gave them on their job, most decision-makers said that, in retrospect, they did not enjoy doing their job during those three years. Whether having to carry out all these tasks had an impact on the officials' decision-making and the outcome of their decisions I do not know. However, based on the office gossip I heard, it can be assumed that following decisions through to the end in this way does not necessarily lead to more lenient decision-making. Thus, several decision-makers told me that their colleagues from the return division were much stricter and, if it were up to them "would send everybody back".[19] Working together with them had, therefore, been quite challenging.

In their work, SEM officials are confronted with stories of brutal and traumatising experiences and endured hardships on a daily basis. Furthermore, they are aware of the potential consequences their decisions might have for asylum seekers. Psychological distancing, in this regard, functions as an important coping mechanism. Psychological distancing mainly works through the shifting of responsibility. In Chapter 4, I showed how through rejecting asylum claims on the basis of non-credibility, the responsibility for the outcome of the decisions is shifted to the asylum seekers themselves: it is their fault for not telling the truth. Moreover, responsibility is shifted to "the law" (see also Jubany 2017: 210). Hence, decision-makers often explained to me that they had no choice but to take a certain decision in the 'cases' they were working on because that was what "the law" required. In this regard, one decision-maker told me that when people who had "no reasons for being granted asylum at all" asked him why he would not help them, he sometimes explained it like this: "Look, it's like you've just come into a TV shop and I'm the shop assistant. You come into the shop and ask for a broom, but all I have here are TVs. I have no brooms I could give you. You want a

[19] Kristina, caseworker, headquarters, field notes, my own translation.

broom and I only have TVs".[20] Finally, and in connection with the above, in my conversations with decision-makers the latter occasionally also shifted the responsibility to politicians and the electorate, since, in their view, it was ultimately the politicians and the electorate that make asylum law and politics. They were the ones who had turned asylum law into what it was today.

Nevertheless, despite responsibility being to some extent shifted to others in this way, this does not mean that the caseworkers do not also assume responsibility for their decisions. In fact, this responsibility "of actually making a difference" is one of the things several of the decision-makers said they liked best about their job. Assuming responsibility for the outcome of one's decisions is seen as a virtue and regarded as a necessity for good decision-making. Hence, it is something of a credo in the SEM that, as a decision-maker, one must always be able to stand by one's decisions. Not only this, but also as caseworker Alexandra put it:

> Principally one has to ask oneself: If I took a negative decision, if I decided that this person has to go home again, would I be capable of accompanying this person home. And if you say, phew, I'd have scruples doing that, looking a person in the eye and saying: "You have to go home", then in difficult cases this might "tip the balance" (*das Zünglein an der Waage spielen*).[21]

What Alexandra is referring to here is the granting of temporary admission in the case that asylum has been denied. The question decision-makers must then decide upon is whether the person should be allowed to stay in Switzerland or not, which, in the latter case, might lead to the person being deported. I regularly observed that such decisions are not easy ones for caseworkers to take. Hence, they like it when there are "clear standards" they can measure their 'cases' against: for instance, if the APPAs explicitly define areas that are "safe", meaning that people can be sent back to them, and such that are not; or if they lay out clear criteria applicants from a certain country or region must fulfil in order to be eligible for subsidiary protection. But even so such decisions often remain difficult. The 'case' of the Iraqi family constituted a difficult case for Rebecca—and it had "tipped the balance" for her. For Alberto it had not, which had to do with his understanding of fairness, as I will discuss in more detail below. I do not know what decision Rebecca finally ended up taking because I left her asylum unit soon after the encounter with her and Alberto. Maybe she tried finding "better arguments" in order to convince Alberto that her decision was "the right one" after all. However,

[20] Nick, caseworker, headquarters, interview transcript, my own translation.

[21] Alexandra, caseworker, reception and processing centre, interview transcript, my own translation.

from the conversation I observed, it seemed more likely that Rebecca would re-write the last part of her decision completely, providing justification for why sending the family back to Iraq was both permitted under international law and reasonable in humanitarian terms.[22]

The Sufficiently but Not Overly Suspicious Decision-Maker

A very important professional norm in the SEM is "suspicion" or non-naivety. To be sufficiently suspicious is regarded as "a sign of professionalism" (Alpes and Spire 2014: 269). Conversely, "naively" believing asylum seekers' statements without properly testing their credibility is regarded as a sign of unprofessionalism, as Alberto insinuates in the field anecdote described above (see also Miaz 2017a: 347). The same has also been described for other administrations where people make (rights) claims on the state (Borrelli et al., forthcoming), such as French consulates (Alpes and Spire 2014: 269; Spire 2008), German asylum administrations (Scheffer 2003: 456), Swiss registry offices (Lavanchy 2014) and welfare offices in the USA (Watkins-Hayes 2009: 50–51).

The norm of "suspicion" is linked to decision-makers' self-understanding as protectors of the system. In other words, it is connected to the ethics of the office.

> Many asylum seekers cannot be classified as refugees or persons displaced by war. On the basis of their situation, they clearly belong to the group of migrants. They are in search of a better place to live in Switzerland. [...] Many of them invent a dramatic story of persecution for the hearing by the authorities. With such tactics they hope to be granted refugee status. [...] The authorities must reject such applications without delay and execute removal systematically.[23]

The quote from the SEM website shows that the common assumption is that most asylum seekers are "bogus", that they belong to the so-called group of "economic migrants" and are trying to manipulate the system in order

[22] I would like to remind the reader that the family was not actually from Iraq, so no conclusions should be drawn regarding the SEM's practice in connection to different countries. For reasons of anonymity I have changed several identity markers of 'cases' so that the officials dealing with them remain anonymous and can, to the best of my knowledge, not be identified by their co-workers and superiors.

[23] https://perma.cc/ZG4B-NN6U, last accessed 26.02.2020.

to be able to stay (see also Kelly 2012: 755; Souter 2011: 48). It is therefore the decision-makers' duty to combat "fraud", uncover the "undeserving" and reject their claims as quickly as possible. This understanding of asylum decision-making leads to "a shift from trying to find the truth to searching for untruth, from a concern with proof to a concern with lies" (Kelly 2012: 765). Or, put differently, it calls for suspicion. Hence, the way several caseworkers described their role—particularly in asylum interviews—to me was that of a "sceptic". They see it as their duty to ask as many questions as necessary until they are convinced that the asylum seeker's story is true, or to produce sufficient arguments for writing a negative decision (see Chapters 4 and 5).

Yet, while being sceptical is a sign of professionalism, being overly suspicious is regarded as a vice. Decision-makers who are said to enter asylum interviews with closed minds, always already knowing that everything will be a lie, are criticised by their colleagues for doing their job badly. They are called "cynics" by their critics. This "cynical" attitude to decision-making opposes the professional norm of open-mindedness. Hence, during my research, I was frequently told what is also taught in the training modules; that decision-makers must be open-minded in order to do their job well. They should go into every interview with a *tabula rasa* even if, at the same time, they should already have an idea of what the decision might be in order to conduct the interview efficiently.

Becoming a cynic is perceived as a greater risk for older employees who have already "seen too much". Naivety, in turn, is mostly attributed to new decision-makers. It is seen as something newcomers have to grow out of. They first have to learn to become sceptical enough and dig deep enough in asylum interviews. Accordingly, as a sort of newcomer myself, I was also perceived as being naïve and believing asylum seekers "too readily". Connected to these perceptions is a crucial difference in critique. Whereas naïve decision-making is regularly equated with being *unprofessional*, I have never come across the same criticism for cynical decision-making.[24] New decision-makers who "naïvely believe everything the claimants tell them" appear to lack sufficient understanding of what it means to properly fulfil their duty, and experienced decision-makers who naïvely believe an applicant are often criticised as being lazy—too lazy, one could interpret, to properly fulfil their duties. On the other hand, the term often used to describe an overly suspicious and cynical attitude is *déformation professionelle*, or occupational hazard. Used by SEM officials to describe how the views of decision-makers may become distorted by long service on the job, this term is applied when veracity is disparaged

[24]And neither have Jonathan Miaz and Ephraim Poertner who also conducted research in the SEM (see Affolter et al. 2019: 281).

too much.[25] Thus, critiques of cynical decision-making do not criticise officials for being unprofessional or not protecting the system, but for taking protection too far, and losing sight of those who are "deserving".

Ethos Is Ethics: The Fair Decision-Maker

Alberto tells me that for him it is very important that all the asylum decisions leaving his section are fair. That is why he does not want the Iraqi family to be granted temporary protection. For him, fairness is about reserving protection for those "truly deserving" of it. This view is also expressed by Gabriel, who once explained to me that it was the decision-makers' duty to meticulously examine the credibility of each case—and, thus, to be sufficiently suspicious—because otherwise "everybody could just receive asylum and that would be unfair to those who really deserve asylum, who really need protection".[26]

Fairness is something that comes up a lot in my ethnographic material. As a procedural norm it means treating equal things equally and unequal things unequally. Hence, it stands for legal equality. However, the way this procedural norm is interpreted in the SEM "indicates that more is at stake than concerns about pure procedure" as David Loher has shown for so-called "return migration bureaucrats" in Switzerland (2020: 122). For SEM officials, taking fair decisions means using "the same standards for evaluating each claim".[27] Ideally, they said, it should not matter who decides a particular case, the outcome should always be the same. The way to achieve this is for them is to strictly follow the law as well as the rules set out by institutional practice. Hence, strict rule-following is crucial in this regard.

For SEM officials, strict rule-following or application of the law is understood in this sense: if there are legal arguments for rejecting a case, it must be rejected. One should not grant asylum or temporary protection in such cases just because making a positive decision might be quicker than meticulously arguing a negative decision, because one has become emotionally attached to the applicant, or because of personal political opinions, for example. At the same time, if there are clearly no justifications for rejecting a claim, reasons

[25] In academia, the term *déformation professionelle* can be traced back to the sociologist Daniel Warnotte, who used it to describe how "bureaucrats" become "intellectually and emotionally damaged by their roles" (Maccoby 2007: 62).

[26] Gabriel, caseworker, headquarters, interview transcript, my own translation.

[27] Nora, head of asylum unit, headquarters, field notes, my own translation.

should not be made up out of thin air. That too would be considered unfair. Fairness and strict rule-following, therefore, subsume and build on many other professional values: apolitical-ness, emotional detachment, professional suspicion, objectivity and non-cynicism.

Furthermore, they are connected to the ethics of the office. Or as Julia Eckert by drawing on David Loher (2020) claims, in this case, because fairness is equated with strict rule-following which, in turn, is understood in the above-discussed way, "ethos is ethics" (2020: 21). Fittingly, in the SEM, good decision-makers are those who in the name of fairness properly fulfil their duty of digging deep in every 'case' in order to make sure that there are "truly no reasons" for rejection. Consequently, decision-makers who take justice into their own hands by trying to help someone who is "undeserving" are portrayed as behaving in an unfair and unprofessional manner. Thus, one caseworker, Lucy, once explained to me that trying to help an "undeserving" applicant—even someone who had suffered great injustice, for example, by being "so poor he could not feed his five kids"—would be unfair to others because:

> This can rapidly lead to one marching to a different drum. And in my opinion, then you are not being *fair* anymore, even though you want to be. Because your decisions don't conform with our asylum practice, you're not maintaining a *unité de doctrine*. [...] It is not up to us to decide what is *just* or not. [...]. Really, it's the politician who should ask himself that question.[28]

As we see, Lucy fears that by "over-generously" helping one person she might end up being "unfair" towards other (more "deserving") asylum seekers. This view was shared by many of my interaction partners. The world is an unjust place, several of them offered in explanation, but it was not up to them to change that. Justice, they felt, was the responsibility of politics and politicians (see also Liodden 2016: 208).[29] Their duty, in turn, is to protect the system. That is what fairness means.

---

[28]Lucy, caseworker, headquarters, interview transcript, my own translation.

[29]This fits with what Veena Das argues when she writes that "detachment is done by an explicit distancing from the political process, taking it as a given for the particular outcomes to be produced" (2015: 104).

Conclusion

This chapter has dealt with what decision-makers think they should do. This is important because, as Julia Eckert (2020) has argued, what administrative caseworkers think they should do shapes what they do. What decision-makers do again leads to the creation of certain (legal) truths. Hence, for instance, if a decision-maker in-line with the professional norm of suspicion—and in the name of fairness—digs deep, thereby creating the contradictions needed to reason a negative decision on the basis of non-credibility, a particular figure of the "false refugee" is created. And once asylum seekers have been classified as "false refugees" by assigning them to the legal category of "non-refugee", their existence becomes a fact, leading to and reinforcing the perception that, indeed, there "are" many false refugees which, in turn, strengthens the office's and individual decision-makers' endeavours to identify and exclude them from asylum (see also Zimmermann 2011: 337). At the same time, if after digging deep the decision-maker reaches the conclusion that there are no (or not enough) reasons for disbelieving an applicant, a certain image of the "genuine refugee"—of a person "deserving of protection"—is (re-)produced.

What decision-makers do is structured not only by procedural norms—the ethos of the office—but also by the broader ideological environment the administration is embedded in. The ideological environment is expressed through the ethics of the office. It is not, however, without contradictions. Decision-makers in the SEM embody the role of protectors of the system. It is their duty to "help people" (in the name of Switzerland, so to say). At the same time, they must make sure Switzerland fulfils its humanitarian duty. They must protect the abstract, noble value of asylum and they must protect the asylum system from being abused. Sometimes these duties were reflexively made explicit by decision-makers when explaining their job to me. But more often they came out of decision-makers retrospectively justifying their actions, and out of their assessments of co-workers' practices. Furthermore, decision-makers' role as protectors of the system can be discerned from what they do in practice. Therefore, I argue that this role constitutes part of officials' implicit professional identity. In this way, it shapes what decision-makers do, generating certain "truths" and thereby (re-)producing the norms and values at the heart of their everyday work.

Much concern in street-level bureaucracy literature is with the dilemma caseworkers experience between caring for people, wanting to help them and becoming personally involved in their 'cases', on the one hand, and their duty to follow the rules, on the other (see Lipsky 2010). Other authors working on bureaucratic administrations are less concerned with this dilemma but rather argue that caseworkers' concern and compassion for the people they deal with is overridden by other concerns: most notably instrumental-rational rule-following (Gill 2016: 136; see also Arendt 2013; Bauman 1988, 1989; Herzfeld 1992). My take on this, which derives from this chapter, is a different one. I do not wish to claim that SEM officials never struggle with the dilemma between "compassion and flexibility on the one hand, and impartiality and rigid rule-application on the other hand" (Lipsky 2010: 15–16). Nor do I argue that decision-makers never act indifferently towards asylum seekers. However, an observation I made was that mostly, decision-makers care about the people they deal with. Yet, this compassion for people is not necessarily perceived as the opposite pole of strict rule-following. For decision-makers, it is the morally and ethically right thing to reserve protection for those "truly in need and deserving" of it—and to limit it to them. In this sense, compassion and strict rule-following are brought together in the name of fairness. For understanding what administrative caseworkers do we should, therefore, not only pay attention to the dilemmas they experience, but also to how they overcome such dilemmas and why they might not experience certain dilemmas we—from the outside—expect them to.

References

Affolter, Laura, Jonathan Miaz, and Ephraim Poertner. 2019. "Taking the 'Just' Decision: Caseworkers and Their Communities of Interpretation in the Swiss Asylum Office." In *Asylum Determination in Europe: Ethnographic Perspectives*, edited by Nick Gill, and Anthony Good, 263–284. Cham: Palgrave Macmillan.

Alpes, Maybritt Jill, and Alexis Spire. 2014. "Dealing with Law in Migration Control: The Powers of Street-Level Bureaucrats at French Consulates." *Social & Legal Studies* 23 (2): 261–274. https://journals.sagepub.com/doi/10.1177/0964663913510927.

Arendt, Hannah. 2013. *Eichmann in Jerusalem: Ein Bericht von der Banalität des Bösen*. München: Piper.

Bauman, Zygmunt. 1988. "Sociology after the Holocaust." *The British Journal of Sociology* 39 (4): 469–497. https://doi.org/10.2307/590497.

Bauman, Zygmunt. 1989. *Modernity and the Holocaust*. Cambridge: Polity Press.

Bohmer, Carol, and Amy Shuman. 2008. *Rejecting Refugees: Political Asylum in the 21st Century*. London: Routledge.

Bohmer, Carol, and Amy Shuman. 2018. *Political Asylum Deceptions: The Culture of Suspicion*. Cham: Palgrave Macmillan.

Borrelli, Lisa Marie, Annika Lindberg, and Anna Wyss. Forthcoming. "States of Suspicion: How Institutionalised Disbelief Shapes Migration Control Regimes." *Geopolitics*.

Cabot, Heath. 2013. "The Social Aesthetics of Eligibility: NGO Aid and Indeterminacy in the Greek Asylum Process." *American Ethnologist* 40 (3): 452–466. https://doi.org/10.1111/amet.12032.

Candea, Matei, Joanna Cook, Catherine Trundle, and Thomas Yarrow. 2015. "Introduction: Reconsidering Detachment." In *Detachment: Essays on the Limits of Relational Thinking*, edited by Matei Candea, Joanna Cook, Catherine Trundle, and Thomas Yarrow, 1–25. Manchester: Manchester University Press.

Dahlvik, Julia. 2018. *Inside Asylum Bureaucracy: Organizing Refugee Status Determination in Austria.* IMISCOE Research Series. Cham: Springer.

Das, Veena. 2015. "Professionalism and Expertise: Comment." In *Detachment: Essays on the Limits of Relational Thinking*, edited by Matei Candea, Joanna Cook, Catherine Trundle, and Thomas Yarrow, 102–111. Manchester: Manchester University Press.

Downs, Anthony. 1967. *Inside Bureaucracy*. Boston: Little, Brown and Company.

Dubois, Vicent. 2005. "L'insécurité juridique des contrôleurs des CAF: Une perspective sociologique." *Informations sociales* 126: 46–57.

Eckert, Julia. 2020. "The Office: Ethos and Ethics in Migration Bureaucracies." In *The Bureaucratic Production of Difference*, edited by Julia Eckert, 7–26. Bielefeld: transcript.

Eule, Tobias G. 2014. *Inside Immigration Law: Migration Management and Policy Application in Germany*. Farnham: Ashgate.

Fassin, Didier. 2007. "Humanitarianism as a Politics of Life." *Public Culture* 19 (3): 499–520. https://doi.org/10.1215/08992363-2007-007.

Fassin, Didier. 2012. *Humanitarian Reason: A Moral History of the Present.* Berkeley: University of California Press.

Fassin, Didier, and Carolina Kobelinsky. 2012. "How Asylum Claims Are Adjudicated: The Institution as a Moral Agent." *Revue française de sociologie* 53 (4): 444–472. https://doi.org/10.3917/rfs.534.0657.

Fresia, Marion, David Bozzini, and Alice Sala. 2013. "Les rouages de l'asile en Suisse: Regards ethnographiques sur une procédure administrative." Etudes du SFM 62. Neuchâtel: SFM.

Fuglerud, Oivind. 2004. "Constructing Exclusion: The Micro-Sociology of an Immigration Department." *Social Anthropology* 12 (1): 25–40. https://doi.org/10.1111/j.1469-8676.2004.tb00088.x.

Gill, Nick. 2009. "Presentational State Power: Temporal and Spacial Influences over Asylum Sector Decisionmakers." *Transactions of the Institute of British Geographers* 34 (2): 215–233. https://doi.org/10.1111/j.1475-5661.2009.00337.x.

Gill, Nick. 2016. *Nothing Personal: Geographies of Governing and Activism in the British Asylum System.* Oxford: Wiley-Blackwell.

Graeber, David. 2015. *The Utopia of Rules: On Technology, Stupidity, and the Secret Joys of Bureaucracy*. Brooklyn and London: Melville House.

Herzfeld, Michael. 1992. *The Social Production of Indifference: Exploring the Symbolic Roots of Western Bureaucracy*. New York: Berg.

Heyman, Josiah McC. 2009. "Trust, Privilege, and Discretion in the Governance of US Borderlands with Mexico." *Canadian Journal of Law and Society* 24 (3): 367–390. https://doi.org/10.1017/S0829320100010085.

Hood, Christopher. 1991. "A Public Management for All Seasons?" *Public Administration* 69 (1): 3–19. https://doi.org/10.1111/j.1467-9299.1991.tb00779.x.

Johannesson, Livia. 2017. *In Courts We Trust: Administrative Justice in Swedish Migration Courts*. Stockholm University. http://www.diva-portal.org/smash/get/diva2:1072557/FULLTEXT01.pdf, last accessed February 3, 2020.

Jubany, Olga. 2017. *Screening Asylum in a Culture of Disbelief: Truths, Denials and Sceptical Borders*. Cham: Palgrave Macmillan.

Kelly, Tobias. 2012. "Sympathy and Suspicion: Torture, Asylum, and Humanity." *Journal of the Royal Anthropological Institute* 18 (4): 753–768. https://doi.org/10.1111/j.1467-9655.2012.01790.x.

Kobelinsky, Carolina. 2015. "In Search of Truth: How Asylum Applications Are Adjudicated." In *At the Heart of the State: The Moral World of Institutions*, edited by Didier Fassin, 67–92. London: Pluto Press.

Lavanchy, Anne. 2013. "L'amour aux services de l'état civil: régulations institutionnelles de l'intimité et fabrique de la ressemblance nationale en Suisse." *Migrations Société* 150: 61–77.

Lavanchy, Anne. 2014. "Die Gefühlswelt des Gesetzes. Die kritische Umsetzung von eherechtlichen Vorschriften im Zivistandsamt." *FAMPRA* 1: 92–117.

Lentz, Carola. 2014. "'I Take an Oath to the State, Not the Government': Career Trajectories and Professional Ethics of Ghanaian Public Servants." In *States at Work: Dynamics of African Bureaucracies*, edited by Thomas Bierschenk, and Jean-Pierre Olivier de Sardan, 175–204. Leiden and Boston: Brill.

Liodden, Tone Maia. 2016. "The Burdens of Discretion: Managing Uncertainty in the Asylum Bureaucracy." PhD diss. (unpublished), University of Oslo.

Lipsky, Michael. 2010. *Street-Level Bureaucracy, 30th Anniversary Edition: Dilemmas of the Individual in Public Service*. New York: Russell Sage Foundation.

Loher, David. 2020. "Governing the Boundaries of the Commonwealth: The Case of So-Called Assisted Voluntary Return Migration." In *The Bureaucratic Production of Difference*, edited by Julia Eckert, 113–134. Bielefeld: transcript.

Maccoby, Michael. 2007. *The Leaders We Need: And What Makes Us Follow*. Boston: Harvard Business School Press.

Miaz, Jonathan. 2017a. "Politique d'asile et sophistication du droit: Pratiques administratives et défense juridique des migrants en Suisse (1981–2015)." PhD diss. (unpublished), University of Lausanne and University of Strasbourg.

Miaz, Jonathan. 2017b. "From the Law to the Decision: The Social and Legal Conditions of Asylum Adjudication in Switzerland." *European Policy Analysis* 3 (2): 372–396. https://doi.org/10.1002/epa2.1018.

Poertner, Ephraim. 2017. "Governing Asylum through Configurations of Productivity and Deterrence: Effects on the Spatiotemporal Trajectories of Cases in Switzerland." *Geoforum* 78: 12–21. https://doi.org/10.1016/j.geoforum.2016.11.004.

Poertner, Ephraim. 2018. "Re-Cording Lives: Governing Asylum in Switzerland and the Need to Resolve." PhD diss. (unpublished), University of Zurich.

Probst, Johanna. 2012. *Instruire la demande d'asile: étude comparative du processus décisionnel au sein de l'administration allemande et française.* Science politique, Université de Strasbourg. https://tel.archives-ouvertes.fr/tel-00985215/document, last accessed February 3, 2020.

Rose, Nikolas. 1999. *Powers of Freedom: Reframing Political Thought*. Cambridge: Cambridge University Press.

Scheffer, Thomas. 2001. *Asylgewährung: Eine ethnographische Analyse des deutschen Asylverfahrens.* Stuttgart: Lucius & Lucius.

Scheffer, Thomas. 2003. "Kritik der Urteilskraft: Wie die Asylprüfung Unentscheidbares in Entscheidbares überführt." In *Migration steuern und verwalten: Deutschland vom späten 19. Jahrhundert bis zur Gegenwart*, edited by Jochen Oltmer, 423–458. Göttingen: Vandenhoeck & Ruprecht.

Shore, Cris, and Susan Wright. 1997. "Introduction: Policy: A New Field of Anthropology." In *Anthropology of Policy: Critical Perspectives on Governance and Power*, edited by Cris Shore, and Susan Wright, 3–30. London and New York: Routledge.

Silbey, Susan S. 2005. "After Legal Consciousness." *Annual Review of Law and Social Science* 1: 323–368. https://doi.org/10.1146/annurev.lawsocsci.1.041604.115938.

Souter, James. 2011. "A Culture of Disbelief or Denial? Critiquing Refugee Status Determination in the United Kingdom." *Oxford Monitor of Forced Migration* 1 (1): 48–59.

Spire, Alexis. 2008. *Accueillir ou reconduire: enquête sur les guichets de l'immigration.* Paris: Raisons d'agir.

Ticktin, Miriam. 2006. "Where Ethics and Politics Meet: The Violence of Humanitarianism in France." *American Ethnologist* 33 (1): 33–49. https://doi.org/10.1525/ae.2006.33.1.33.

Watkins-Hayes, Celeste. 2009. *The New Welfare Bureaucrats: Entanglements of Race, Class, and Policy Reform.* Chicago: University of Chicago Press.

Weber, Max. 1991 (1948). *From Max Weber: Essays in Sociology*. Translated, edited and with an introduction by Hans H. Gerth, and C. Wright Mills. London and New York: Routledge and Kegan Paul.

Weber, Max. 2013 (1978). *Economy and Society*. Edited by Guenther Roth, and Claus Wittich. Berkeley: University of California Press.

Wedel, Janine R., Cris Shore, Gregory Feldman, and Stacey Lathrop. 2005. "Toward an Anthropology of Public Policy." *Annals of the American Academy of Political and Social Science* 600 (1): 30–51. https://doi.org/10.1177/0002716205276734.

Zetter, Roger. 2007. "More Labels, Fewer Refugees: Remaking the Refugee Label in an Era of Globalization." *Journal of Refugee Studies* 20 (2): 172–192. https://doi.org/10.1093/jrs/fem011.

Zimmermann, Susan E. 2011. "Reconsidering the Problem of 'Bogus' Refugees with 'Socio-economic Motivations' for Seeking Asylum." *Mobilities* 6: 335–352. https://doi.org/10.1080/17450101.2011.590034.

7

The Normalisation of Disbelief

I started this book with a quote from Nora, a superior in the SEM. She was confident that she knew what words like credible, persuasive, plausible and logical meant to established employees. They shared a common understanding; she could imagine what the words meant to them and therefore did not question their decisions. My focus in this book has been to investigate this shared understanding, to focus on the regularities of administrative practice rather than the divergences or deviances.

I do not deny that divergences exist. It has been shown by several authors that the outcomes of asylum decisions sometimes differ depending on which asylum administration or court, which unit within these administrations and courts and which individual decision-maker takes the decisions (see Anker 1991; Eule 2014; Fassin and Kobelinsky 2012; Hamlin 2014; Johannesson 2017; Miaz 2017; Ramji-Nogales et al. 2009; Rehaag 2012; Spirig 2018). Furthermore, decision-makers may at times consciously decide to deviate from a certain rule or norm. And indeed, the ways in which caseworkers interpret rules and norms, of course, will vary.

However, my point is that we cannot fully understand bureaucratic processes without considering how routine practices are generated and reproduced within administrations. Studying the regularities is as important as studying divergences for a comprehensive understanding of how institutions function, and how the laws and policies they are in charge of "applying" work. I argue that by overtly focusing on the divergences and inconsistencies in asylum determination, we run the risk of reproducing the common criticism that asylum and credibility determination are done in an "arbitrary" and "subjective" way (see Anker 1991; Crawley and Lester 2004; Einhorn

L. Affolter, *Asylum Matters*, Palgrave Socio-Legal Studies,
https://doi.org/10.1007/978-3-030-61512-3_7

2009; Goodwin-Gill 1996; Kagan 2003; Macklin 1998; Ramji-Nogales et al. 2009; Thomas 2009). I find this criticism problematic because of the implicit assumption that, as Tobias Kelly writes, "so long as the right reforms are put in place, the correct training initiated and the most suitable technical fixes rolled out, everything will be, if not perfect, then at least considerably fairer and more just" (2011: 184). The problem of discrepancies is either attributed to the individual decision-makers and their "subjective views" or to the law for leaving a loophole for such "subjective views" to be able to play a role in the first place. However, I argue that a critical understanding of asylum decision-making practices—and administrative practice in general—must go beyond this.

"Subjective views" always play a role in the "application" of law and policies. People's interpretations of law or, in other words, their discretionary practices constitute a necessary part of what law itself is. Thus, law does not sometimes leave a loophole and sometimes not leave a loophole for discretionary practices. When "applying" laws and policies to specific situations or cases they must always be interpreted by the people "applying" them, as this book has shown (see Eule et al. 2019: 101; Hawkins 1992: 11; Heyman 2004: 493; Poertner 2018: 10–11; Wagenaar 2004: 651). Through these interpretative practices, law and policies are continuously "(co-)produced" in practice (Poertner 2018: 10; see also von Benda-Beckmann 1991; Brodkin 2011: 253–254; Eckert, Behrens, et al. 2012; Eule 2014; Shore and Wright 2011; Wedel et al. 2005: 34). However, while it is individual caseworkers who must interpret the law and policies, this is not done in an individualistic way. What is rather at stake here is "socialised subjectivity" (Bourdieu and Wacquant 1992: 126), as has been brought to light by this book.

The criticism that asylum decisions and particularly credibility assessments are based on subjective views and are arbitrary seems to be partially ascribed to what is commonly referred to as "gut feeling". The importance of "gut feeling" for asylum, and administrative decision-making in general, has been stressed by numerous authors (see Dahlvik 2018; Dubois 2010; Fassin 2013; Fassin and Kobelinsky 2012; Johannesson 2017; Jubany 2011, 2017; Kelly 2012; Lavanchy 2014; Liodden 2016; Macklin 1998; Miaz 2017; Thomas 2009). "Gut feeling" may give the impression of being highly individual, which seems to be at the core of the criticism of credibility assessment as being "subjective"—a view that was sometimes also conveyed by SEM officials themselves. However, in this book I have shown that "gut feeling", which forms part of SEM officials' "professional-practical knowledge", is shaped by the office. Decision-makers acquire it through their socialisation on the job, through belonging to and becoming a member of the office, and through carrying out their daily tasks.

That "gut feeling" plays such an important role in asylum decision-making and credibility determination is not exceptional. As Andreas Reckwitz (2003) argues, (professional-)practical knowledge forms part of practice itself. This practical sense of self-understanding underlies all our actions: including administrative ones (see Dahlvik 2018: 57–62; Reckwitz 2003: 289–294; Wagenaar 2004: 651). Understanding practice, therefore, demands that "gut feeling" should be taken seriously rather than criticising its existence. We must pay attention to "the almost unthinking actions, tacit knowledge, fleeting interactions, practical judgements, self-evident understanding and background knowledge, shared meanings, and personal feelings that constitute the core of administrative work" as Hendrik Wagenaar writes (2004: 643).

Practical judgements are at the core of this book, since they lie at the heart of asylum decision-making. Asylum decision-making—just like any administrative-legal procedure—requires clear-cut classifications into "categories of inclusion and exclusion" (Handelman 1995: 280; see also Kelly 2015: 188). This is what SEM caseworkers are tasked to do; a responsibility which requires them to sufficiently overcome the uncertainties inherent in asylum decision-making to be able to reach "final" decisions, clearly classifying asylum seekers into one of four legal categories: refugee with asylum, refugee with temporary admission, non-refugee with temporary admission and non-refugee without temporary admission.

Shared meanings, self-evident understandings, professional-practical knowledge and routine behaviours play an important role. I have shown how for Teresa (in Chapter 5), for instance, it is self-evident that the applicant not asking his father about the letters the latter had asked him to deliver constitutes a clear marker for non-credibility and that for Gabriel (in Chapter 6) it is self-evident that he always seats himself and the asylum seeker at the opposite ends of the rectangle table which are furthest apart from each other. These are things decision-makers "simply" do or know, just like the many times decision-makers told me that they "simply knew" from experience whether an asylum seeker's narrative was authentic or not. However, when questioned, they mostly found it very hard to articulate how they knew this. Nevertheless, this type of know-how is an integral and critical part of the essence of practice. In a similar way, decision-makers come to know with experience what questions to ask in asylum interviews and rather routinely go about digging deep. Such "shared repertoires of knowledge" (Affolter et al. 2019: 265; see Wenger 2003) exist for the office as a whole, but also for different organisational units. And they depend on other "communities of interpretation" (Affolter et al. 2019) that the officials align themselves with or are affiliated with by others, for instance, in connection with their educational background, institutional age or the hierarchical position they occupy. These forms of belonging, combined with their "shared repertoire of knowledge", often emerge from office banter; through how decision-makers distinguish themselves—and their units, for example—from others. However, officials' badmouthing of others as being too lenient, too strict, cynical, naïve or behaving in a political way not only sheds light on the fissures and fractures that run through the administration, it also points to commonly shared meanings; the unquestioned middle ground, so to say.

"Allowing everybody to stay" is considered bad decision-making and so is "wanting to keep everybody out". Naively and readily believing the asylum seeker is considered another quality of unprofessional decision-making, but so is its counterpart of being overly suspicious and not believing every applicant. Good decision-makers are perceived as those who reserve refugee protection for those "truly deserving", are sufficiently suspicious and dig deep in asylum interviews. These are the shared—and for the most part unquestioned—values and practices of professional decision-making. As such, they are crucial for understanding how asylum decision-making works.

By dealing with everyday practices of asylum determination, this book has highlighted the "everyday production of stateness" (Eckert, Biner, et al. 2012; see also Beek 2016; Bierschenk and Olivier de Sardan 2014; Fassin 2015). I thereby followed Didier Fassin who argues that such practices of state-making should not be treated as happening in a vacuum since state "agents are confronted with explicit and implicit expectations formulated in discourses, laws and rules while keeping sizable space to manoeuvre in the concrete management of situations and individuals" (2015: 4). By analysing everyday practices and by showing how decision-makers acquire an institutional habitus on the job which shapes how they think, feel, know and act, I addressed how decision-makers go about concretely managing situations and individuals and how they deal with the space to manoeuvre, as described by Fassin. At the same time, the book also shed light on the ideological, normative and regulatory environments in which SEM officials work; how these are constitutive of the institutional habitus, but are also constituted by the institutional habitus through the everyday practices the latter generates.

Didier Fassin and Carolina Kobelinsky put forward the thesis that "the institution is the product of both policies and practices, but also that it contributes in turn to fashioning the former and determining the latter" (2012: 448). In bringing together the discussions of the different chapters of this book, I conclude by showing how this happens: how normative, structural and regulatory constraints as well as the institutional habitus constitute each other and how practices generate the institution and are also determined by the latter.

A majority of asylum applications in the different countries of the Global North are rejected, mostly on the grounds of non-credibility (see Fassin 2013: 47; Kelly 2012: 759; Probst 2012). This was the puzzle I initially set out to study: How could this pattern be explained? There seem to be two common opposing answers to this from the view of the different actors involved in or dealing with refugee status determination. On the one hand, the reasons for the majority of asylum seekers being refused refugee status is seen to arise from the "fact" that the majority of applicants "are" so-called "economic migrants" and are thought to lie in the asylum interviews in order to try and receive a residence permit. By doing so they are perceived as abusing the system. As I showed in Chapter 4, this view is, for instance, clearly stated in the SEM's online manual on asylum and return. On the other hand, it is often argued by NGOs, legal advisors and activists that the recognition rate for the granting of asylum remains consistently low because the SEM (or possibly even the Federal Council) set quotas as to how many people may receive asylum. Both views are challenged in this book. Hence, the in-depth study of everyday practices in the SEM allows us to look beyond (and challenge) both the tautological explanation proposed by the SEM, on the one hand, and the political instrumentalism (implicitly) proposed by activists, on the other. What I hereby propose is, thus, a different critique—or critical understanding—of asylum decision-making and policies.

My point is not to say that asylum seekers do not lie, or feel forced to lie. Nor do I want to suggest that I am more accurately able to assess "the truth" of asylum seekers' narratives. What I have rather shown in this book is that so-called "lies", "liars" and elements of non-credibility are produced through the questioning techniques used in asylum interviews themselves (see also Crawley 1999: 52; Sbriccoli and Jacoviello 2011: 184–185; Scheffer 2001, 2003). At the same time, I heard no evidence of recognition quotas during my fieldwork. This is not to say that there is no political influence on asylum decision-making. However, I argue that it mostly does not play out in this top-down instrumental way. Many different factors concur to produce restrictive asylum policies and outcomes of asylum decisions, and they mutually influence and reproduce each other.

One structural condition is posed by the "individual protection regime" (Poertner 2018: 5) of countries in the Global North itself (see also Fassin

2016a: 66–67; Fassin and Kobelinsky 2012: 448). Asylum or refugee protection is not a right people who have fled from other places per se have or are entitled to. Rather, their entitlement to the right of asylum is assessed on an individual basis through extensive administrative procedures. These procedures resemble other administrative procedures in which people make (individual) rights claims on the state or apply for "goods" or "benefits". A common trait in these administrations is that caseworkers assume and are ascribed the role of "gate-keepers" (see Lipsky 2010: 4). They become "guardians of a restricted good" (Heyman 2009: 381) which in the case of decision-making in the SEM is the right to reside in Switzerland. This is what protecting the system is about. Yet, protecting the system also goes beyond this.

Asylum decision-makers in the SEM are state agents, which rather self-evidently is taken to mean that they must act in the interest of the state. Two commonly shared interpretations of what this means emerged from my data. One the one hand, it means upholding Switzerland's "humanitarian tradition" and the value of the asylum system, which, as Didier Fassin and Carolina Kobelinsky argue, paradoxically leads to restrictive decision-making. They write that "[t]he less frequently [asylum] is granted, the more precious refugee status becomes" (2012: 464). On the other hand, acting in the interest of the state for decision-makers means that they must "fight abuse" and thereby again reserve asylum for those "truly deserving" of it. The underlying assumption behind this is that not everybody should be allowed to stay; that the state has an interest in ensuring that "too many foreigners" are not allowed to reside in Switzerland. This is linked to the "politics of deterrence" (Poertner 2017) which has a direct impact on practices of decision-making, but is also the outcome of decision-making practices. As Ephraim Poertner shows, the politics of deterrence translates into and manifests itself in the different priority categories in the SEM (2017: 19). Certain asylum claims are decided on very quickly, while others are deliberately held back in order to avoid creating a so-called "pull-effect", thus intending to make Switzerland an unappealing country in which to apply for asylum.

The politics of deterrence are linked to broader political discourses. Asylum seekers, as well as migrants in general, are today in political discourse often portrayed as a "problem" and as a "threat" to national security and a country's economy, culture and identity (see Boswell 2007: 589; Dahlvik 2018: 9; Gill and Good 2019: 5–6; Huysmans 2000; Jubany 2017; Miaz 2017: 11–14). These discourses have figured as the drive behind and as a legitimation for the numerous restrictive changes made to Swiss asylum legislation since the introduction of the Asylum Act in Switzerland in 1981. Several of these changes were initiated by, as well as the consequences of, political referenda. The media, political discourses and parliamentary inquiries into decision-making practices in the SEM have an impact on those practices. Political pressure is felt by the SEM officials, especially by those occupying higher hierarchical positions who are, thus, more directly accountable to the Federal Councillor in charge of the SEM. As a consequence of this, quite drastic changes to practice doctrine are occasionally made, but more often, political pressure seems to more subtly shape decision-making practices, leading to gradual shifts in collective patterns of decision-making. Yet, this does not happen in a unilateral way. Hence, political discourse is also influenced by decision-making practices and the outcomes these produce. And, of course, political discourses do not stand alone, but are embedded in broader social contexts. This can be seen in the historical accounts of asylum and migration politics which argue that the shift towards ever more restrictive asylum politics in the 1980s was linked to the economic crisis and to the fact that the people requesting refugee protection at that time had not all fled from communist countries and, thus, did not so clearly fit into the East/West divide anymore (see Däpp 1984; Fassin 2016b; Fassin and Kobelinsky 2012; Jubany 2017: 44–46; Kobelinsky 2015; Piguet 2006).

Asylum law as it exists today sets its own structural constraints and limits. Decision-makers are required to take clear-cut either/or decisions which have drastic effects on asylum seekers' lives; a fact that decision-makers are well aware of. These decisions must be reasoned in writing, although it is only the reasoning for negative decisions that is then sent out to asylum seekers (and their legal advisors). As I showed in Chapter 4, such decisions must be taken and reasoned in a context of several "known unknowns" (Kelly 2012). Material evidence corroborating asylum seekers' stories often does not exist. Hence, decision-makers mostly rely on other "facts" which are created through the asylum procedure—or, rather, which the decision-makers themselves create in the course of the proceedings. I have argued that creating such "facts" for reasoning negative asylum decision is easier with regard to "non-credibility" than it is for "non-eligibility to refugee status". This is reflected in the fact that reasoning negative asylum decisions on the basis of non-credibility whenever possible (and appropriate) is a widespread policy in the SEM.

The way "facts" are, and necessarily must be created due to structural constraints, shapes how asylum interviews are carried out. Research on asylum procedures in different countries has shown that asylum interviews are mainly about "searching for untruths" (Kelly 2012: 765) and checking asylum narratives for inconsistencies and discrepancies (see Bohmer and Shuman

2008: 136; Johannesson 2017: 12; Jubany 2017: 135–137). The absence of such discrepancies and inconsistencies (and of other markers of non-credibility known to decision-makers) speaks for the "truth" of an account, while their presence indicates the opposite. This fits with Article 7 of the Swiss Asylum Act which also defines "credibility" in a negative sense. Thus, it is the criteria which characterise "non-credibility" that are listed in Article 7 AsylA rather than criteria which would characterise a credible account.

My research has shown that it is easier to produce "facts" for reasoning negative asylum decisions on the basis of non-credibility rather than on non-eligibility to refugee status; this is also an institutional policy since such decisions are mostly more difficult to refute on appeal. Additionally—and equally importantly—my research has shown that reasoning negative decisions with non-credibility is also an important coping strategy for decision-makers. By rejecting asylum claims on the basis of non-credibility, the responsibility for the outcome of the decision is shifted to the asylum seeker: it is the latter's fault for not telling the truth.

Generating facts for positive decisions is also not necessarily difficult, particularly since such decisions must only be reasoned internally. However, as I have shown, granting asylum is, nevertheless, not something decision-makers do "easily", for other reasons. The book has brought to light how digging deep becomes the neutral, ethical and apolitical thing for decision-makers to do. Digging deep represents what it means to act in the name—and in the interest—of the state. As a practice, digging deep is important because of the way "facts" have to be created for reasoning clear-cut either/or decisions, but it is also linked to the professional norm of suspicion. The professional norm of suspicion plays out and is reaffirmed through shared stories amongst co-workers, peer pressure, organisational socialisation including the way novices are coached by their co-workers and controlled by their superiors as well as decision-makers' need to fit into the office and its different "communities of interpretation". Furthermore, it is continuously reproduced by the outcomes digging deep produces. Digging deep actively generates the "liars" and "false refugees" it sets out to "uncover", thereby reinforcing the perception that, indeed, there "are" many false refugees which, again, strengthens the office's and individual decision-makers' endeavours to identify and exclude them from asylum, reaffirming decision-makers' role as protectors of the system. Disbelief becomes normal.

While the empirical focus of this book has been on asylum decision-making, its discussions contribute to a broader understanding of state administrations. Understanding state administrations requires studying the everyday practices of state agents. But, as Didier Fassin argues, such practices do not take place in a vacuum (Fassin 2015: 4). We must pay attention to the ideological environments in which caseworkers carry out their work; to the norms and values underlying their practices. These are not just explicit norms and values, but also feelings and desires which are incorporated into caseworkers' institutional habitus. They are expressed through practice, which is at the same time constituted by and constitutive of the institutional habitus.

Rules matter, setting the possibilities and limits of decision-making. But rules and laws only acquire meaning through people's grasp of them (see Wagenaar 2004: 65). This grasp is structured by the dispositions decision-makers acquire on the job and, thus, by their institutional habitus. The regulatory frameworks and ideological environments I describe in this book, to a greater or lesser extent, also apply to other migration administrations (see Borrelli et al., forthcoming; Eckert 2020). Beyond the field of migration, it is particularly the structural constraints arising from administrative-legal decision-making and the important role of professional-practical knowledge, which I identified in this book, that appear relevant for other bureaucratic administrations.

It has been argued that what the state is, how it works and how it is produced, can only be understood by examining state agents' everyday practices. I argue that this means studying what caseworkers do, what they say they do, why they say they do what they do, and what they think they should do. Furthermore, I have highlighted the crucial role of professional-practical knowledge in everyday decision-making. Knowledge is practice. Understanding administrations and understanding the "everyday production of stateness" (Eckert, Biner, et al. 2012: 5), therefore, means paying attention to what state agents know; paying attention to what constitutes this knowledge, how it is acquired, how it is (re-)produced in and through everyday practice and paying attention to how what administrative caseworkers know, produces the patterns of administrative-legal decisions we can observe from the outside. It is these regularities that matter.

References

Affolter, Laura, Jonathan Miaz, and Ephraim Poertner. 2019. "Taking the 'Just' Decision: Caseworkers and Their Communities of Interpretation in the Swiss Asylum Office." In *Asylum Determination in Europe: Ethnographic Perspectives*, edited by Nick Gill, and Anthony Good, 263–284. Cham: Palgrave Macmillan.

Anker, Deborah. 1991. "Determining Asylum Claims in the United States: An Empirical Case Study." http://repository.forcedmigration.org/show_metadata.jsp?pid=fmo:709, last accessed February 3, 2020.

Beek, Jan. 2016. *Producing Stateness: Police Work in Ghana.* Boston: Brill.

Bierschenk, Thomas, and Jean-Pierre Olivier de Sardan. 2014. "Studying the Dynamics of African Bureaucracies: An Introduction to States at Work." In *States at Work: Dynamics of African Bureaucracies,* edited by Thomas Bierschenk, and Jean-Pierre Olivier de Sardan, 1–33. Leiden and Boston: Brill.

Bohmer, Carol, and Amy Shuman. 2008. *Rejecting Refugees: Political Asylum in the 21st Century.* London: Routledge.

Borrelli, Lisa Marie, Annika Lindberg, and Anna Wyss. forthcoming. "States of Suspicion: How Institutionalised Disbelief Shapes Migration Control Regimes." *Geopolitics.*

Boswell, Christina. 2007. "Migration Control in Europe after 9/11: Explaining the Absence of Securitization." *Journal of Common Market Studies* 45 (3): 589–610. https://doi.org/10.1111/j.1468-5965.2007.00722.x.

Bourdieu, Pierre, and Loïc J. D. Wacquant. 1992. "The Purpose of Reflexive Sociology (The Chicago Workshop)." In *An Invitation to Reflexive Sociology,* edited by Pierre Bourdieu, and Loïc J. D. Wacquant, 61–215. Cambridge: Polity Press.

Brodkin, Evelyn Z. 2011. "Policy Work: Street-Level Organizations under New Managerialism." *Journal of Public Administration Research and Theory* 21 (Suppl. 2): 253–277. https://doi.org/10.1093/jopart/muq093.

Crawley, Heaven. 1999. *Breaking Down the Barriers: A Report on the Conduct of Asylum Interviews at Ports.* London: Immigration Law Practitioners' Association (ILPA).

Crawley, Heaven, and Trine Lester. 2004. *Comparative Analysis of Gender-Related Persecution in National Asylum Legislation and Practice in Europe.* Geneva: UNHCR.

Däpp, Heinz. 1984. "Bankrott einer staatspolitischen Maxime." In *Asylpolitik gegen Flüchtlinge,* edited by Heinz Däpp, and Rudolf Karlen, 211–226. Basel: Lenos.

Dahlvik, Julia. 2018. *Inside Asylum Bureaucracy: Organizing Refugee Status Determination in Austria.* IMISCOE Research Series. Cham: Springer.

Dubois, Vincent. 2010. *The Bureaucrat and the Poor: Encounters in French Welfare Offices.* Translated by Jean-Yves Bart. Farnham: Ashgate.

Eckert, Julia. 2020. "The Office: Ethos and Ethics in Migration Bureaucracies." In *The Bureaucratic Production of Difference,* edited by Julia Eckert, 7–26. Bielefeld: transcript.

Eckert, Julia, Andrea Behrends, and Andreas Dafinger. 2012. "Governance—And the State: An Anthropological Approach." *Ethnoscripts* 14 (1): 14–34.

Eckert, Julia, Zerrin Özlem Biner, Brian Donahoe, and Christian Strümpell. 2012. "Introduction: Law's Travels and Transformations." In *Law against the State: Ethnographic Forays into Law's Transformations,* edited by Julia Eckert, Brian Donahoe, Christian Strümpell, and Zerrin Özlem Biner, 1–22. Cambridge: Cambridge University Press.

Einhorn, Bruce J. 2009. "Consistency, Credibility, and Culture." In *Refugee Roulette: Disparities in Asylum Adjudication and Proposals for Return*, edited by Jaya Ramji-Nogales, Andrew I. Schoenholtz, and Philip G. Schrag, 187–201. New York: New York University Press.

Eule, Tobias G. 2014. *Inside Immigration Law: Migration Management and Policy Application in Germany*. Farnham: Ashgate.

Eule, Tobias G., Lisa Marie Borrelli, Annika Lindberg, and Anna Wyss. 2019. *Migrants before the Law: Contested Migration Control in Europe*. Cham: Palgrave Macmillan.

Fassin, Didier. 2013. "The Precarious Truth of Asylum." *Public Culture* 25 (1): 39–63. https://doi.org/10.1215/08992363-1890459.

Fassin, Didier. 2015. "Introduction: Governing Precarity." In *At the Heart of the State: The Moral World of Institutions*, edited by Didier Fassin, 1–11. London: Pluto Press.

Fassin, Didier. 2016a. "Vom Rechtsanspruch zum Gunsterweis. Zur moralischen Ökonomie der Asylvergabepraxis im heutigen Europa." Translated by Frank Jakubzik. *Mittelweg 36* 1: 62–78.

Fassin, Didier. 2016b. "From Right to Favor: The Refugee Question as Moral Crisis." *The Nation*. https://www.thenation.com/article/from-right-to-favor/, last accessed February 11, 2020.

Fassin, Didier, and Carolina Kobelinsky. 2012. "How Asylum Claims Are Adjudicated: The Institution as a Moral Agent." *Revue française de sociologie* 53 (4): 444–472. https://doi.org/10.3917/rfs.534.0657.

Gill, Nick, and Anthony Good. 2019. "Introduction." In *Asylum Determination in Europe: Ethnographic Perspectives*, edited by Nick Gill, and Anthony Good, 1–26. Cham: Palgrave Macmillan.

Goodwin-Gill, Guy S. 1996. *The Refugee in International Law*. 2nd ed. Oxford: Clarendon Press.

Hamlin, Rebecca. 2014. *Let Me Be a Refugee: Administrative Justice and the Politics of Asylum in the United States, Canada, and Australia*. Oxford: Oxford University Press.

Handelman, Don. 1995. "Comments on 'Putting Power in the Anthropology of Bureaucracy: The Immigrations and Naturalization Service at the Mexico–United States Border' by Josiah McC. Heyman." *Current Anthropology* 36 (2): 280–281. https://doi.org/10.1086/204354.

Hawkins, Keith, ed. 1992. *The Uses of Discretion*. Oxford: Clarendon Press.

Heyman, Josiah McC. 2004. "The Anthropology of Power-Wielding Bureaucracies." *Human Organization* 63 (4): 487–500. https://doi.org/10.17730/humo.63.4.m9phulu49a1l2dep.

Heyman, Josiah McC. 2009. "Trust, Privilege, and Discretion in the Governance of US Borderlands with Mexico." *Canadian Journal of Law and Society* 24 (3): 367–390. https://doi.org/10.1017/S0829320100010085.

Huysmans, Jef. 2000. "The European Union and the Securitization of Migration." *Journal of Common Marked Studies* 38 (5): 751–777. https://doi.org/10.1111/1468-5965.00263.

Johannesson, Livia. 2017. *In Courts We Trust: Administrative Justice in Swedish Migration Courts*. Stockholm: Stockholm University. http://www.diva-portal.org/smash/get/diva2:1072557/FULLTEXT01.pdf, last accessed February 3, 2020.

Jubany, Olga. 2011. "Constructing Truths in a Culture of Disbelief: Understanding Asylum Screening from Within." *International Sociology* 26 (1): 74–94. https://doi.org/10.1177/0268580910380978.

Jubany, Olga. 2017. *Screening Asylum in a Culture of Disbelief: Truths, Denials and Sceptical Borders*. Cham: Palgrave Macmillan.

Kagan, Michael. 2003. "Is Truth in the Eye of the Beholder? Objective Credibility Assessment in Refugee Status Determination." *Georgetown Immigration Law Journal* 17 (3): 367–415. https://scholars.law.unlv.edu/facpub/633, last accessed February 3, 2020.

Kelly, Tobias. 2011. "The Legalization of Human Rights and the Protection of Torture Survivors: Asylum, Evidence and Disbelief." In *Are Human Rights for Migrants? Critical Reflections on the Status of Irregular Migrants in Europe and the United States*, edited by Marie-Bénédicte Dembour, and Tobias Kelly, 1–22. New York: Routledge.

Kelly, Tobias. 2012. "Sympathy and Suspicion: Torture, Asylum, and Humanity." *Journal of the Royal Anthropological Institute* 18 (4): 753–768. https://doi.org/10.1111/j.1467-9655.2012.01790.x.

Kelly, Tobias. 2015. "Afterword." In *Of Doubt and Proof: Ritual and Legal Practices of Judgement*, edited by Daniela Berti, Anthony Good, and Gilles Tarabout, 183–192. Farnham: Ashgate.

Kobelinsky, Carolina. 2015. "In Search of Truth: How Asylum Applications Are Adjudicated." In *At the Heart of the State: The Moral World of Institutions*, edited by Didier Fassin, 67–92. London: Pluto Press.

Lavanchy, Anne. 2014. "Die Gefühlswelt des Gesetzes. Die kritische Umsetzung von eherechtlichen Vorschriften im Zivistandsamt." *FAMPRA* 1: 92–117.

Liodden, Tone Maia. 2016. "The Burdens of Discretion: Managing Uncertainty in the Asylum Bureaucracy." PhD diss. (unpublished), University of Oslo.

Lipsky, Michael. 2010. *Street-Level Bureaucracy, 30th Anniversary Edition: Dilemmas of the Individual in Public Service*. New York: Russell Sage Foundation.

Macklin, Audrey. 1998. "Truth and Consequences: Credibility Determination in the Refugee Context." Conference Paper. Ottawa: International Association of Refugee Law Judges. http://refugeestudies.org/UNHCR/97%20-%20Truth%20and%20Consequences.%20Credibility%20Determination%20in%20Refugee%20Context.%20by%20Audrey%20Macklin.pdf, last accessed February 3, 2020.

Miaz, Jonathan. 2017. "Politique d'asile et sophistication du droit: Pratiques administratives et défense juridique des migrants en Suisse (1981–2015)." PhD diss. (unpublished), University of Lausanne and University of Strasbourg.

Piguet, Etienne. 2006. *Einwanderungsland Schweiz: Fünf Jahrzehnte halb geöffnete Grenzen*. Bern: Haupt.

Poertner, Ephraim. 2017. "Governing Asylum through Configurations of Productivity and Deterrence: Effects on the Spatiotemporal Trajectories of Cases in Switzerland." *Geoforum* 78: 12–21. https://doi.org/10.1016/j.geoforum.2016.11.004.

Poertner, Ephraim. 2018. "Re-Cording Lives: Governing Asylum in Switzerland and the Need to Resolve." PhD diss. (unpublished), University of Zurich.

Probst, Johanna. 2012. *Instruire la demande d'asile: étude comparative du processus décisionnel au sein de l'administration allemande et française*. Science politique, Université de Strasbourg. https://tel.archives-ouvertes.fr/tel-00985215/document, last accessed February 3, 2020.

Ramji-Nogales, Jaya, Andrew I. Schoenholtz, and Philip G. Schrag, eds. 2009. *Refugee Roulette: Disparities in Asylum Adjudication and Proposals for Reform*. New York: New York University Press.

Reckwitz, Andreas. 2003. "Grundelemente einer Theorie sozialer Praktiken: Eine sozialtheoretische Perspektive." *Zeitschrift für Soziologie* 32 (4): 282–301.

Rehaag, Sean. 2012. "Judicial Review of Refugee Determinations: The Luck of the Draw?" *Queen's Law Journal* 38 (1): 1–58. https://dx.doi.org/10.2139/ssrn.2027517.

Sbriccoli, Tommaso, and Stefano Jacoviello. 2011. "The Case of S: Elaborating the 'Right' Narrative to Fit Normative/Political Expectations in Asylum Procedure in Italy." In *Cultural Expertise and Litigation*, edited by Livia Holden, 172–194. Abingdon and New York: Routledge.

Scheffer, Thomas. 2001. *Asylgewährung: Eine ethnographische Analyse des deutschen Asylverfahrens*. Stuttgart: Lucius & Lucius.

Scheffer, Thomas. 2003. "Kritik der Urteilskraft: Wie die Asylprüfung Unentscheidbares in Entscheidbares überführt." In *Migration steuern und verwalten: Deutschland vom späten 19. Jahrhundert bis zur Gegenwart*, edited by Jochen Oltmer, 423–458. Göttingen: Vandenhoeck & Ruprecht.

Shore, Cris, and Susan Wright. 2011. "Conceptualising Policy: Technologies of Governance and the Politics of Visibility." In *Policy Worlds: Anthropology and the Analysis of Contemporary Power*, edited by Cris Shore, Susan Wright, and Davide Però, 1–25. New York: Berghahn Books.

Spirig, Judith. 2018. *Like Cases Alike or Asylum Lottery? Judicial Decision Making at the Swiss Administrative Court*. Zürich: University of Zurich. https://doi.org/10.5167/uzh-157718.

Thomas, Robert. 2009. "Refugee Roulette: A UK Perspective." In *Refugee Roulette: Disparities in Asylum Adjudication and Proposals for Return*, edited by Jaya Ramji-Nogales, Andrew I. Schoenholtz, and Philip G. Schrag, 164–186. New York: New York University Press.

von Benda-Beckmann, Franz. 1991. "Pak Dusa's Law: Thoughts on Legal Knowledge and Power." In *Ethnologie im Widerstreit*, edited by Eberhard Berg, Jutta Lauth, and Andreas Wimmer, 215–227. München: Trickster.

Wagenaar, Hendrik. 2004. "'Knowing' the Rules: Administrative Work as Practice." *Public Administration Review* 64 (6): 643–656. https://doi.org/10.1111/j.1540-6210.2004.00412.x.

Wedel, Janine R., Cris Shore, Gregory Feldman, and Stacey Lathrop. 2005. "Toward an Anthropology of Public Policy." *Annals of the American Academy of Political and Social Science* 600 (1): 30–51. https://doi.org/10.1177/0002716205276734.

Wenger, Etienne. 2003. "Communities of Practice and Social Learning Systems." *In Knowing in Organizations: A Practice-Based Approach*, edited by Davide Nicolini, Silvia Gherardi, and Dvora Yanow, 76–99. Armonk: M.E. Sharpe.

Index

L. Affolter, *Asylum Matters*, Palgrave Socio-Legal Studies,
https://doi.org/10.1007/978-3-030-61512-3

The manufacturer's authorised representative in the EU is Springer Nature Customer Service Centre GmbH, Europaplatz 3, 69115 Heidelberg, Germany. If you have any concerns regarding our products, please contact ProductSafety@springernature.com

Printed and bound by CPI Group (UK) Ltd, Croydon, CR0 4YY
30/09/2026
02225286-0017